EYE RHYMES

EYE RHYMES

SYLVIA PLATH'S
ART OF THE VISUAL

Edited by
Kathleen Connors and Sally Bayley

OXFORD
UNIVERSITY PRESS

OXFORD
UNIVERSITY PRESS

Great Clarendon Street, Oxford OX2 6DP

Oxford University Press is a department of the University of Oxford.
It furthers the University's objective of excellence in research, scholarship,
and education by publishing worldwide in

Oxford New York

Auckland Cape Town Dar es Salaam Hong Kong Karachi
Kuala Lumpur Madrid Melbourne Mexico City Nairobi
New Delhi Shanghai Taipei Toronto

With offices in

Argentina Austria Brazil Chile Czech Republic France Greece
Guatemala Hungary Italy Japan Poland Portugal Singapore
South Korea Switzerland Thailand Turkey Ukraine Vietnam

Oxford is a registered trade mark of Oxford University Press
in the UK and in certain other countries

Published in the United States
by Oxford University Press Inc., New York

British Library Cataloguing in Publication Data
Data available

Library of Congress Cataloging in Publication Data
Data available

Typeset by SPI Publisher Services, Pondicherry, India
Printed and bound in Italy by
Rotolito Lombarda SpA

978–0–19–923387–8

1 3 5 7 9 10 8 6 4 2

To readers of Sylvia Plath

I catch up: each night, now, I must capture one taste, one touch, one vision from the ruck of the day's garbage. How all this life would vanish, evaporate, if I didn't clutch at it, cling to it, while I still remember some twinge or glory. Books & lessons surround me: hours of work. Who am I? A freshman in college cramming history & feeling no identity, no rest? I shall ruminate like a cow: only that life end not before I am born: the windows jerk & sound in their frames. I shiver, chilled, the grave-chill against the simple heat of my flesh: how did I get to be this big, complete self, with the long-boned span of arm & leg, the scarred imperfect skin? I remember thick mal-shaped adolescence & the colors of my remembering return with a vivid outline: high school, junior high, elementary school, camps & the fern-huts with Betsy: hanging Joanne: I must recall, recall, out of the stuff is writing made, out of the recollected stuff of life.

9 February, 1958

[From The Unabridged Journals of Sylvia Plath page 328]

CONTENTS

LIST OF ILLUSTRATIONS

In-text illustrations

Colour plates

LIST OF ABBREVIATIONS

BL   Ted Hughes, *Birthday Letters* (New York: Farrar, Straus and Giroux, 1998)

CP   Sylvia Plath, *The Collected Poems*, ed. Ted Hughes (New York: Harper and Row, 1981)

CSM   *Christian Science Monitor*

JP   Sylvia Plath, *Johnny Panic and the Bible of Dreams,* and other prose writings (London: Faber, 1977)

LH   Sylvia Plath, *Letters Home: Correspondence 1950–1963*, ed. Aurelia Schober Plath (New York: Harper and Row, 1975)

PM II/III   Plath Mss II/III, Lilly Library, Indiana University, Bloomington, IN

TBJ   Sylvia Plath, *The Bell Jar* (London: Heinemann, 1963)

UJ   *The Unabridged Journals of Sylvia Plath*, ed. Karen V. Kukil (New York: Anchor Books, 2000)

NOTE TO THE READER

In Connors's essay, the term 'diary' refers to notes Plath made from childhood through high school, and 'journal' is used for writing she started at Smith College in 1950 at age 17. The term 'juvenilia' also refers to art and manuscripts she made before college.

Titles of works in quotes indicate Sylvia Plath's or Aurelia Plath's name, or references Sylvia Plath made in texts, while the majority of others were named for the 2002 exhibition of her arts and manuscripts at Indiana University.

Introduction

On the 75th birthday anniversary of Sylvia Plath, we are pleased to present an in-depth look at this influential writer as the multidimensional artist she viewed herself to be. Drawing from the collections at Lilly Library and Mortimer Rare Book Room, this volume brings to light a wide range of Plath's paintings, drawings, manuscripts, and memorabilia from childhood on—works so richly varied and interconnected, they suggest a wider lens is needed to gauge their resonances. Joining us in this endeavor, and to the great fortune of this volume, essayists Diane Middlebrook, Langdon Hammer, Christina Britzolakis, and Fan Jinghua offer new facets of Plath's life in art, with a final word on the topic given by Susan Gubar.

Eye Rhymes: Sylvia Plath's Art of the Visual follows the entire trajectory of Plath's creative genius, from her first signs of artistry on the seashores of New England, to the final culmination of her craft as poet, essayist, and novelist, and mother of two children in London. In an attempt to answer the question, How did Plath arrive at *Ariel?*, we look closely at juvenilia made during her adolescent years, when she developed a strong identity as a professional artist, evidenced by unpublished teen diaries, visual art, and school papers made years before her famous 'I am I' diary notes of age 17, when critical examination of her writing usually begins. Plath's college years at Smith and Cambridge are also central to this volume, as are her last two years in America before returning to England, when she transited from authoring her second batch of modernist-inspired 'art poems' of 1958, to her Yaddo writing that marked a turning point in the development of her *Ariel* voice.

Since Sylvia Plath was continually fascinated by her own imaginative expressions, and struggled all her life to master their forms, her comments of these issues are highlighted. Indeed, the abundance of material she left behind allows us to follow her handprints as she tracks her entire journey as an artist and student, from the world of fairies, myths, and magic flights found in children's books, to the reaches of her own psyche and scrutiny of mid-century culture that informed her late poetry and prose. The fact that Plath kept her goals in sight, when women seeking careers faced serious obstacles, makes her story as a writer especially compelling. As she admits in a draft letter to *Vogue* while seeking the 'golden apple' of their Prix de Paris: 'I like riding up glass hills.' And for those interested in the ride, she made these processes unusually transparent in her astounding *oeuvre*. *The Bell Jar, Ariel*, and the *Journals* in particular offer a boon to literature and feminist studies that changed the way readers—particularly women—experience the unique power of poetry and the written word in relation to personal being.

Yet Plath's impact as a cultural icon is a phenomenon that goes beyond literature or any so-called myth, cult, or 'scare' of Sylvia Plath. Whether portrayed as the poster child for 1950s American women struggling for agency and identity, a feminist heroine of Greek-like tragedy, or a 'dangerous influence' on the young, Plath's influence is now international, cross-cultural, and interdisciplinary in scope, and continues to expand in surprising ways. She has motivated a huge cultural production, where her readers share a force of inspiration, if no common perspective. Musicians and writers, visual artists, dancers, and filmmakers have all made creations based on Plath's art and life, largely undocumented and noncollaborative. What Plath called her kaleidoscopic writing, with its layered colors, patterns, and meanings, is at times seen to blur lines between author and audience, evoking her intrigue with the 'magic mirror' that reflects many possibilities of selfhood. For some, the experience is frightening and repugnant; for others, it is thrilling and positively life changing, perhaps all at once. The relationship between Plath and her audience might even be characterized as a spectacle of quantum mechanics, another mid-century *wonderbox*: as they indulge their gaze on Plath, she looks back at them and interacts, while denying them any objective truths in the process—a quandary that literary critics and biographers have commented upon for decades. It is indeed this sense of intimacy, revelation, and even prophesy that Plath elicits in her works that seems to speak directly to her 'followers', some of whom are dismissed as worshippers at the 'altar of Plath'. But the boundaries between Plath literary critics, biographers, and devotees are also unclear, as approaches to her life and works are negotiated in what has been called the Sylvia Plath legend and 'industry' of productions.

Because Plath is generally read as a confessional writer, there is a tendency to interpret her body of works in terms of her 'family romance', her pathology and suicide, and the controversial voice exhibited in many mature poems. While the allure or relevance of these elements is undeniable, we feel her works deserve broader contexts. Considering Plath's excellent liberal arts education and the encouragement she received from family, friends, and mentors throughout her schooling, these may include the research of arts advocates and cognitive development specialists who affirm the positive impact of visual learning and cross-disciplinary arts education for young people, specifically on self-identity and the life-long learning process. We hope that making these works available to the public will shed new light on Sylvia Plath as artist, critic, and intellectual, and the creative processes she employed throughout her life.

1

Living Color
The Interactive Arts of Sylvia Plath

KATHLEEN CONNORS

Child Artist

FAMILY GIFTS

Sylvia Plath's extraordinary dedication to writing is central to the many stories told of her life and work. What is not commonly known about Plath is her serious devotion to the visual arts from a very early age. She moved between art-making and writing constantly, often recreating the colorful world of children's books that inspired her to become an artist and storyteller. As a child she considered a poem she had written or transcribed to be complete when illustrated by a picture, whether copied, cut out of magazines, or formed from her imagination. As a young teen she recorded her 'technicolor' dreams that told complete stories, and drew figures that either evoked her story characters or were based upon them. She worked in most forms of media, using a wide range of styles, an experimental approach to the arts also reflected in her writing genres. Her diaries are full of doodles and self-portraits, as are many of her school notebooks and letters.

From the time Plath had her first poem published at age 8, and her first drawing at age 9, she saw herself as a serious artist, and was determined to find a job that utilized her creative talents. And until her junior year at Smith College, she considered her two favorite disciplines as offering equally promising careers. At age 20, however, when her considerable prizes and income from her poetry and prose were not being matched by her artwork—judged to be merely 'good' and even worse by teachers and critics—she finally accepted writing as the more practical option. So she declared a major in honors English, and discontinued formal art studios.

But Plath continued to look back. After a dozen years of intensive art activities and praise for her work, she was not willing to abandon her interests or her investments in the field. Intricate drawings of England, France, and Spain that she made during her student years at Cambridge were published in essays such as 'Leaves from a Cambridge Notebook', 'American in Paris', 'Sketchbook of a Spanish Summer', and 'Mosaics—An Afternoon of Discovery', some of which were written, in fact, to accommodate her best illustrations. By then she had switched her study of visual art to museums, galleries, and libraries, where she incorporated the work of modernists, or as she would call her favorites, 'the primitives', into her poetry and essays. After returning to the classroom to audit a course on these artists at age twenty-five, Plath created her second collection of 'art poems' in a spell of inspiration she characterized in a letter home as flying all day and night 'on great wings in clear blue air through brightly colored magic and weird worlds', and in her journal as having 'deep visions of queer and terrible and exotic worlds'.[1]

These 1958 poems based on the works of Rousseau, Gauguin, Klee, and de Chirico would not, as she predicted, make her famous. Yet the brilliant and intriguing spheres these artists portrayed, in conjunction with her return to psychiatric counseling, brought Plath to a new focus in poetry. She began unraveling the puzzle of the psyche, memory, and the unconscious, most notably, as inspired by de Chirico's 'hour of the enigma', which he characterized as the 'fancied song, the revelatory song of the last, morning dream of the prophet'—perhaps an apt metaphor for *Ariel*.[2] The following year she described her next poetry sequence, 'Poem for a Birthday', as 'a dwelling on madhouse, nature: meanings of tools, greenhouses, florist shops, tunnels, vivid and disjointed. An adventure. Never over.'[3] Instigated by a drawing she made of the greenhouse, it is in this seven-part poem that critics locate Plath's emerging *Ariel* voice.

Whatever the source of inspiration, Plath was very conscious that it came in fleeting moments, and that it couldn't be forced. She thus returned to her former works at regular intervals to mine them for new art, look into her past, and assess her creative progress, all of which was recorded in diaries, journals, and letters.

Delighting in all the arts, she treated her daily activities as creative and often competitive enterprises that warranted careful documentation and critique. Though prone to a methodical ordering of her works, she continually expanded, reshuffled, or cut them to best fit into her immense portfolio. And when she found an interesting topic or image, she would often interrupt whatever she was doing to record it. She recreated significant themes or events for artwork, letters, poems, essays, and fiction—in many cases, simultaneously—which were frequently carried through from childhood, when they were made for her first audience: her family. The resulting opus is an interactive weave of artifacts and meta-narratives, often toppling or tumbling under the weight of other art and memorabilia. The life and mind of Sylvia Plath, after all, was her favorite subject.

At age 7, while her mother tended to her ailing father and brother, Sylvia Plath stayed temporarily with her grandparents at their ocean front home in Winthrop, Massachusetts. She often corresponded by mail, and two letters and a valentine she sent to her parents reveal her early self-awareness and seriousness as a writer, artist, and evaluator.[4] Both letters comment on their short length, and provide amusing anecdotes and descriptions of other letters she sent to family members, noting their preferences for her use of color. After duplicating the drawing she referred to in the letter to her mother, she discussed her color restrictions, possibly referring to the rainbow spectrum of a prism, while the letter to her father addresses the colors of her script (see Pl. 1):

February 20, 1940

Dear Mother
I liked your letter.
The waves were up to our
front steps they were as high
as the window!
And I wrote a letter to
Aunt Dot.

The letter said how
Dlightful it is to fly!
And showed a picture
of aunt dot flying
with a wand (which
grandpa said was an ice-cream
cone, or a flower.) (Ha Ha)

(My letter is short)
The only colors I may use
are, yellow, purple, orange red blue.
the light that is glass
is rainbow colors! bye now.
From Sylvia
With Love

Feb 19, 1940

Dear Father
I am coming home soon.
Are you glad as I am?
Over in Frank's work room
I got some ink on my fingers which never comes of!
I had to rub them with a stone.
And the stone took it of.
I wrote a letter to Mother and Warren to.
If you want to you may ask
them to read it to you.
My letter is not very
long.

Warren likes me to wright
in orange.
Mummy likes me to wright in red.
But nearly everybody likes me to wright in blue or black.
As I told you my letter
is not very long.
'So good by now. I'll be home soon.

With love, from Sylvia

The enclosed valentine reads as follows:

Dear Father,
I hope you are better.
Over grandma's there were
many ice-cakes and
on every one sat a
Seagull! Isn't that
funny (HaHa)[5]

Sylvia Plath's involvement with the arts and literature was broad-based and pervasive from early childhood on, largely due to her mother Aurelia's efforts. As Aurelia Plath stated, Otto Plath was proud of his daughter's precociousness, but she 'did nothing with Daddy'.[6] It was up to Mrs. Plath to support the creative abilities of Sylvia and her younger brother, Warren. She covered their playroom with colorful art prints and equipped it with a record player and records, ranging from children's songs to classical music, a blackboard and easel, long-handled paint brushes and paints, modeling clay, blocks, newsprint—all the creative materials she could gather. The siblings made up rhymes and stories patterned on those read to them, and considered illustration an integral part of their letters, poems, and cards. The family listened to music and dramatic serials on the radio, and Sylvia recalled her mother singing German folk songs at the piano and starting her on piano lessons at age 7. The children spent much of their free time exploring the seashore, which she called their 'main entertainment',[7] and the family took special outings to Boston's museums, theaters, and gardens.

Sylvia Plath grew up with a Depression-era awareness of money, its budgeting, and its privileges. She made careful lists of money she had raised and items she had purchased, yet Christmas gifts and packages sent to summer camp noted in her diary indicate that the children's needs and wishes were accommodated. Whatever she requested in terms of art, dance or music lessons, art and writing supplies, or simple treats such as fresh fruit while at camp, seemed to have been provided by Aurelia and her parents, 'Grampy' and 'Grammy', Aurelia and Frank Schober. Sylvia, in particular, was indulged. Since Sylvia was already reading simple sentences and stories by age 4, and felt unchallenged by her kindergarten, Mrs. Plath gave in to her wish to join the children at the small, private 'Sunshine School' for first grade.

Aurelia Plath's love of books, and poetry in particular, was shared with her children. She read them works of poets Eugene Field, Emily Dickinson, Robert Louis Stevenson, and A. A. Milne. Among Sylvia's favorite books were those of Dr. Seuss, *The Wind in the Willows*, *Mary Poppins*, and Tolkien's *The Hobbit*—a story she would find superior to Homer's *Ulysses*. Aurelia also read books with her children that tackled contemporary issues on human nature and sexuality, including Huxley's *Brave New World*, Ibsen's *The Dollhouse*, Millay's *Renaisance,* and works of Havelock Ellis, the sexologist who wrote about lesbians. They also read from *A Case for Chastity* and the writing of Margaret Sanger in the context of discussions on birth control, venereal disease, and abortion. Aurelia talked to them of 'the unfairness of the double standard and the forces that lay behind it', including the gendered division of labor—a condition she knew well as a daughter and wife of men who promoted what she called *paterfamilias*.[8] After finishing her Masters thesis on the medieval physicist and alchemist Paracelsus, taken from English and German sources, Aurelia had accepted her father's wish that she take practical instruction at a business college instead of pursuing her interests in creative writing and literature. She met Otto Plath, a respected professor of biology at Boston University, as his student of German, and he took the advice of a colleague to wait until she graduated to pursue his personal interests in her. After they married, he was able to fully benefit from her excellent writing, editing, and organizational skills when writing his definitive book on the topic of bumblebees.

Following Otto Plath's death in 1940 after a four-year illness, when Sylvia was 8, the Plath and Schober households were combined for economy and convenience. Aurelia Plath went to work, initially teaching German and Spanish, and the children were often cared for by their beloved grandparents, as well as Aunt Dorothy and Uncle Frank Schober, who lived nearby. While she would remain in education, teaching secretarial and administrative skills, what she called her own adventure in life-long learning would be advanced by Sylvia's sharing of her extraordinary educational experiences—just as she had done with her own mother. And everything generated along the way, from her daughter's theatre stubs and children's art to college essays and published poems, was kept by Aurelia Plath. Admitting to pack-rat habits, she would collect what is surely one of the most complete records of a great artist's life ever assembled.

Sylvia Plath was a brilliant, enthusiastic student who garnered the respect of her teachers and top grades all of her life. She was also strong-minded and opinionated, and her personal views were often incorporated into her school assignments and artistic works. Mrs. Plath supplemented the siblings' school lessons by instruction in writing and drawing from an early age, and Sylvia demonstrated a special talent for visual art. In a letter written to her daughter at age 6, Aurelia encouraged her to 'write as nicely as you color' and to try using longhand instead of print.[9] She also gave the young Sylvia an art lesson that suggested how the painter Whistler showed love for his mother, a cue Sylvia would take in trying to please her own mother:

In grandmother's living room is a black and white picture of an old lady sitting in a chair. She was the mother of the man who made the picture. He made such wonderful picture that he was called an <u>artist</u>. He loved his mother so much, that he made this picture of her. Can you find curved lines in this picture?

Plath's frequent gifts to her family were her art: items made in arts, crafts, and sewing classes at school and camp, illustrated letters and postcards, and colorful birthday and greeting cards with humorous drawings and ditties. Warren worked hard to keep up with his sister's level of creative and academic drive, and they sometimes collaborated on art projects. She drew various versions of 'Plath & Plath' and 'Plath Mark' logos onto the back of greeting cards, imitating the style of professionals. Even as an adult she continued to make these special cards for her family that closely resembled those she made as a child.

At age 9, when Plath learned to type, she began the habit of transcribing her latest poetry in letters home, some of which she copied onto separate sheets and decorated with drawings. Her diaries are also full of original poems, as well as details about her own artistic preferences and works in progress. She enjoyed drawing intricacies and elaborate features, as seen in the richly designed cloak worn by the goddess 'Pallas Athene', a picture she made in a draft and final version at age 12. She derived most of her early artwork, however, from popular images of fairies and Mother Goose figures that she copied from all forms of publications, at a time when the Victorian aesthetic of flower bouquets and bluebirds, rosy-cheeked children, and cherubic angels dominated commercial and popular art forms. Plath was ambitious in trying to capture multifaceted perspectives such as those found in building complexes and landscapes, an early indication of her life-long attraction to jumbled assortments of objects that present varying patterns of line, texture, and color. In one brightly colored crayon drawing of a waterfall made at age 10 or 11, she used a wide range of hues to capture the greenery in front of houses layered into a hillside, an image likely taken from a photograph[10] (see Pl. 2). But even while learning to draw by copying from concrete images, as seen in this colorful scene, she used abstract shapes to represent intricate objects, in this case, the spiral-shaped flowers that pepper the field. Along with magazines, illustrated books were a major source for her drawing subjects, and numerous heavily lined pencil drawings suggest she also traced pictures while learning to draw.[11] Her diary notes, for example, mention she was 'copying' a Normal Rockwell picture, as well as two drawings of 'Resi' that she traced at age 11 from the book *An Ear for Uncle Emil*:

Pallas Athene

Sylvia Plath

1. 'Pallas Athene', 1945, pencil

Resi

By Sylvia
July 19, 1944
Copied

19 JULY: After lunch I started to copy one of the etchings. It featured a little Swiss girl sitting in the midst of some flowers playing an accordion. . . . when we started home I finished the picture. I think it is the best I have ever drawn.

Postcards Plath sent from camp as a child often include cartoon-like illustrations, including pictograms, where she substituted words with pictures to relay daily events. Many of these cards reflect the patriotic themes prevalent during World War II, though Plath made infrequent references to the war as a child. She also drew portraits of her friends as gifts—in one summer, for just about the entire camp— where she became known as particularly talented in drawing from models.

'WHEN I WAS YOUNG'

Sylvia Plath began to record much of her childhood experiences in her mid-teens, and after she left home for college she expressed nostalgia for her youth, a period she associated with the ocean at Winthrop. Her enthrallment with the sea provided important imagery and familial associations that would impact her writing through-out her life. As an adult she would describe the seaside at Winthrop as her poetic heritage and central metaphor for her childhood. In the final sentence of her 1962 essay on the topic, 'Ocean 1212-W', she talked of her early years as having 'sealed themselves off like a ship in a bottle—beautiful, inaccessible, obsolete, a fine white, flying myth', and her belief in mermaids—not Santa or God.[12] This essay also recalls her often-quoted epiphany that occurred as a child, when her mother read aloud a poem by Matthew Arnold called 'The Forsaken Merman':

I saw the gooseflesh on my skin. I did not know what made it. I was not cold. Had a ghost passed over? No, it was the poetry. A spark flew off Arnold and shook me, like a chill. I wanted to cry; I felt very odd. I had fallen into a new way of being happy.

Poetry, happiness, and fulfillment in reading and literature was a common theme in Plath's youthful writing, where she connected common equations of the sea, lakes, rivers, and pools—as well as the moon that rules the tides—to the unconscious mind, memory, and the imagination, and its potential sources of artistic inspiration. For one of Plath's drawings, identified by her mother as the sort she made 'happily' while in grade school, she likely traced an illustration from another source, though she made her own renditions of mermaids, the ocean, and lake scenarios in numerous works. This particular picture, however, must have intrigued her, for she also mentioned it in

2. 'Resi' with accordion, 1944, pencil

Dear Mother,   ⑩   July 15,

Today was our patriotic day [flag]. I wore a red [drawing], red [drawing], white [drawing], blue [drawing] (borrowed). Our TenT (4) won inspection This week as well as last. In inspection for no papers our [drawing] in Neyati won !! All the [drawing] Tables were decorated, Neyatis were like This,

[drawings of sailboats]   white

ved   blue paper

water. All of The units had To sing a song. Neyati was said To be by The judges "A jump ahead of The others". Are we proud [scribble]

                    Love [drawing]
                    Sylvia

3. Illustrated postcard with patriotic theme, 1944, pencil

her diary at age 12, describing it as her 'original sketch of a mermaid reclining on a rock in the River Rhine and waving to someone in the towers of an old German castle on the bank of the river'[13] (see Chapter 5, p. 202; Afterword, pp. 226–7). But Plath went on to create a truly original scenario using her own version of this figure, as well as her double. In the center of her colored pencil sketch sits a more child-like twin mermaid, facing forward and seated on a small island. Taking the same pose as the mermaid under the moon, another mermaid waves into the distance, joining a circle of three ducks and two sea gulls who look to the upper left cliff at a fantastical cross between owl and parrot that seems to be holding court (see Pl. 7). While the rest of the picture is colored in pale blues and greens, this plumed bird has brighter red and orange feathers and an otherwise magical appearance.[14] The privileged position of this creature, in fact, seems to anticipate Plath's treatment of the grouse or heather-bird of the moors as a sort of personal totem, a symbol of original thought, myth, and the imagination she would develop in her 1952 story 'Initiation'.

Although Plath enjoyed all forms of creative activities, she always took the process of writing seriously. In a BBC interview given in 1962, she recalled her first published work, titled 'Poem' (which she described in a note to the editor as 'what I see and hear on a hot summer night'), stating, 'From then on, I suppose, I've become a bit of a professional'.[15] A journal entry she wrote at age 18 mentions another poem she composed the same year,[16] when she was already looking to her challenges as an adult writer trying to recall her past:

> I remember that as I was writing a poem on 'Snow' when I was eight, I said aloud, 'I wish I could have the ability to write down the feelings I have now when I am little, because when I grow up I will know <u>how</u> to write, but I will have forgotten what being little feels like.'

The world of fantasy and fairy-tale wonders provided Plath with subjects for writing and artwork well into her teens. In another undated journal entry written at age 18, she expressed regret for the passing of her magical youth, now lost to the 'grown-up' reality of late adolescence:[17]

> the lovely never-never land of magic, of fairy queens and virginal maidens, of little princes and their rose bushes, or poignant bears and Eyore-ish donkeys, of life personalized, as the pagans loved it, of the magic wand, and the faultless illustrations—the beautiful dark-haired child (who was you) winging through the midnight sky on a star-path in her mother's box of reels,—of Griselda in her feather cloak, walking barefoot

with the Cucktoo in the lantern-lit world of nodding Mandarins,—of Delight in her flower garden with the slim-limbed flower sprites,—of the Hobbit and the dwarfs, gold-belted with blue and purple hoods, drinking ale and singing of dragons in the caverns of the valley—all this I knew, and felt, and believed. All this was my life when I was young.

In a letter to new pen pal Eddie Cohen written at age 17,[18] Plath again recalled her childhood beliefs, dominated by the sea and the world of books: 'If I tried to describe my personality I'd start to gush about living by the ocean half my life and being brought up on Alice in Wonderland and believing in magic for years and years.'

Plath would continue to associate these 'star-path' flights and magic realms with the creative imagination and the unfettered mind of a child, though she would later position these 'never-never' lands of childhood as just that—they never were—just as Alice's adventures were only a dream. The 'mother's box of reels', however, would be put aside along with the 'fine, white flying myth' to be used as fuel for her art. Plath's extraordinary memory and her extensive diaries allowed her to examine events and creative works from her past, and the importance of self-reflection and reminiscence in her life was expressed in many of her texts. In 1947, the last year that Plath made daily diary entries, she mentioned her purchase of a coveted red scrapbook where she would record her life story, the first pages of which were dedicated to her childhood in Winthrop:[19]

> 1 FEBRUARY: Grammy drove mother and me down to the Book Stall, where I purchased a much-longed-for scrapbook (it's 12″ × 14″ and has a soft red cover), a bottle of India ink, and two rolls of cellophane to mount my pastels with. I mounted them on cardboard as soon as I got home. (The total price was $2.40!) Then I printed 'Scrapbook—Sylvia Plath—1947' (in old English letters) in Indian ink on the first page of my new book, and began taking snapshots of me as a child, and all my friends, filling every space with a more or less running account of my life history and descriptions of my experiences! How I love my new red scrapbook!

Visual Expression

'LIVING COLOR' AND ARTWORK AT SCHOOL

Schoolwork provided an excellent outlet for Plath's habit of illustrating texts, whether or not her subject warranted their inclusion. For example, she added multicolored maps to reports that dealt with history or international issues, or

4. Mermaid and moon, 1945, pencil

spring

Here are Warren and I in our back yard in Winthrop. The flowers are in bloom, and you can see all the lovely petunias. Warren holds his beloved teddy, Trixie, and I have my own Nancy-doll in my arms.

Winter

1938

Winter in Winthrop
This is quite a change from the opposite picture. It is February, 1939, now, and Warren and I are "coasting" together on our small sled. Mother later got us a much larger one which we still have now. This is down on the beach by the bayside. The snow is melting, and the Hamsteins' house is the big one on the right.

Fall

This is Warren in our back yard towards fall. It is quite bare, because flowers do not soften the angular fence with their leaves and blooms any more; the Wood's house is shown over the fence, and you can even see Mrs. Woods closing the window upstairs.

Summer

This was taken by the white sand dunes on the shores of the Ipswich waters. We were driven down there by Grammy to spend a day and have a picnic. I will never forget the clear blue ripply water and the tiny shells along the beach.

Here I am just when I started to grow braids!

WINTHROP

This is the best picture taken of Warren and me together. I am wearing my favorite sunsuit, and Warren holds the huge fish that Frankie caught. We are standing on Frankie's sailboat that he made, and it is drawn up on the shores of the sea that I love so much. The big footprint in the sand is not mine, but Frankie's.

Warren and I are admiring the cat. This is not Mowgli, but his mother, Mitzi. We are in front of our house in Winthrop. Mitzi is willingly posing in my dollie's bonnet, her paws patting my chin. This picture was taken the summer after I had my crucial sinus attack, so I don't look too healthy. The picture is in here to show off Mitzi, anyway!

a picture of Ruth as a little girl still bears quite a semblance to. You can see in the picture on the opposite page taken when she was 12 years old.

magazine photographs to accommodate her school assignments. In fact, the handful of surviving history reports of about 30 she made while in the eighth grade largely consist of watercolor and ink paintings, maps, well-known poems (such as 'In Flanders Fields'), and cartoons. Since she was outspoken about the pacifism her family adopted, these hand-made booklets of 1946 include illustrated slogans that promote her personal politics, many of which are modeled after war relief and propaganda posters (see Chapter 2, pp. 150–1).

Sylvia Plath was fascinated—and perhaps obsessed—with the symbolic and literal uses of color in her written compositions and artworks, as well as in the clothes she wore. Many of her diary entries have 2- to 3-in. self-portraits in full color, made to display her newest outfits or to present the highlights of her day in interesting settings. In one colorful self-portrait she made at age 12, titled 'The Happy Camper',[20] she portrayed herself as a hiker amidst an idyllic nature scene, with a backdrop of mountains that is near literal interpretation of lines from 'America the Beautiful', the national hymn that rivaled the official 'Star-Spangled Banner' anthem in popularity: 'For purple mountains majesties | Above the fruited plain!' Plath would use the song's next line—'America! America!'—as the title of an essay she wrote in 1962, where she gave a critical view of her upbringing[21] (see Pl. 3). Many other diary entries present beautiful outdoor scenes, often carefully composed and colored, that were positioned among detailed notes on outings, as seen in one June 1947 entry about a day of swimming, boating, and meals cooked outdoors with friends[22] (see Pl. 8).

Plath's art assignments in junior high school were broad ranging, and included architecture studies and interior design, subjects that continued to captivate her interest as an adult. As seen in her first letters home at age 7, she was even concerned about which color of ink to use for her writing, a topic she would comment on in diaries, journals, and letters to friends and family. In her early 1947 diary notes she switched from turquoise to green ink to copy her *Hiawatha*-style poem on a 'woodland stranger' named Sylvia who sought to become a 'great scribe' for an Indian tribe, an outdoor theme that formed the center of her carefully prepared (yet unsuccessful) campaign for secretary of student council.[23] A photo of the Hiawatha speech presentation shows one of her campaign assistants being dragged across the stage in a box boat, holding a banner with a promotional slogan topped by a tiny red flag for effect:

5. 'Winthrop' page, 'Scrapbook—1947', mixed medium

10 JANUARY: Gee! Today was just some big day. All through orchestra I was waitin' in wild anticipation for the assembly to begin. Finally I heard the passing bell ring, and I went up to sit on the stage with the fourteen other sufferers. As if in a dream, I saw the hall fill with people, and finally I heard my name called. The sea of orange, blurred faces swam before me as I started with the opening lines of my speech. Gradually the auditorium grew clearer, and I could hear my voice filling the hall:

'Mr. Thistle, Faculty, Friends. For my campaign speech I have chosen to represent the different sections of Wellesley as different Indian tribes. For example, Wellesley Hills becomes the Tribe of Maugus. These tribes feel it is necessary for them all to be represented at the council table of their great chief Maugus. Into the picture comes a humble candidate for the position of secretary, she—well, just listen to my Indian legend.'

In her next diary notes, written again in light blue ink, she described her preparation for a school dance, which had kept her from a sound sleep the previous night:

17 JANUARY: Today is supposed to be exciting, because of the assembly, but to my amazement, I calmly walked to the library with mum, took out 'Vanity Fair' and, upon reaching home, read it until the last minute. I wore my yellow dress with the black velvet bows, and also my white furry evening jacket.

After a month of experimenting with pastel and navy inks, Plath switched to black ink to write about the assembly, perhaps associating the color with the formality of published words, or even hidden secrets that she reserved for her diary, now being referred to as 'you'. She started one entry with a note in parentheses: '(I have decided not to use colored ink anymore for "writing" in someone so confidential as you are)'.[24] A comment on colors so delightfully bright they hurt the eyes appears in a 1947 diary entry that records a class presentation by a visiting speaker. The lecture combined science, current events, and patriotism in a film on the atomic bomb and radar that was accompanied by a demonstration of what Plath called 'a special ray of black light' that illuminated 'the most beautiful phosphorous stones'.[25] Her comment on saluting the flag confirms her color-driven sensibilities:

7 MAY: Each one had a separate color glow—they were really living colors. Then he showed us tapestries, each part of which had been chemically treated with colors from those stones. Held away from the light, they were dead floral patterns, but held before the light—ahh! each color lived—shining for all it was worth! What reds and golds and blues there were. Everyone just groaned because they were so beautiful it just hurt to

look. Then he showed us the American flag that he had had made. It was superb. Now, if only when we salute the flag each morning, we could have the living one fluttering in the breeze, I'm sure we would understand it better.

While this science lesson involving living color was a topic Plath could relate to, other entries during this period reflect her difficulty with science, and her prefer-ence for art, literature, and creative fantasy as more familiar and rewarding pursuits. In a January diary entry she wryly commented on a school film about electricity: 'It must have been very interesting, only I didn't understand it,'[26] and two months later she wrote another humorous note on a disappointing science lesson from her grandfather. This diary entry includes a drawing of a rocket shooting off into space, illustrating her lofty artistic ambitions as well as her soaring imagination:

> 23 MARCH: Grampy told me a great deal about soil, fertilizers, and composts, which was quite interesting, only I don't enjoy the down to earth type of science—only the fantastic theories that would take me soaring to the Moon or Mars with David in one of his spaceships. Well, I can dream, can't I? Didn't you know I'm going to be the greatest most entertaining author and artist in the world? Well, don't feel badly, I didn't either!

As seen in letters home and journal notes, Sylvia's relative weakness in the sciences would later cause her extreme anxiety when facing her 'World of Atoms' physical science requirement at Smith College. She successfully petitioned to change it from a graded to an audited course, though a freshman botany class complemented her life-long love of flower gardens, warranting no written complaints. Her science and history class notebooks in particular are full of drawings not related to the topic. She would continue the habit of drawing on her school papers, where nearby classmates and glamorous women, a favorite doodle since her early teens, are prominent. The act of seeing and the eye itself would also be a common image in many texts Plath created throughout her life, including her *Ariel* poems. She often depicted the traditional tools of writing, particularly ink pens and ink pots, in her diaries and school notebooks. Because she usually drew objects found in her environment, her own hands, sometimes in the act of writing or drawing, made a convenient model. Of the many drawings made of her own hands during high school, she recreated one in a more formal format, using a rare black background.[27]

Always active in extracurricular activities, Plath created many pictures based on school activities, some of which were intended for publication. In 1948 she made a

6. Two hands, *c*. 1948–50, ink

drawing for the local paper's article on high school graduation ceremonies (see Ill. 15 below), and for her senior year book of 1950 she contributed a cartoon-like white-on-black drawing, possibly made with scraped wax, of kids working on a car in an outdoor setting, where a sign gives the direction for finding 'spark plugs'.[28] Perhaps due to the new medium Plath was using, she applied an unusual technique in this picture. The perspective on the horizon is formed by a series of dots, and the trees largely consist of stylized and repetitive leaf patterns. Notes published in the yearbook next to her photo indicate her reputation as a multidimensional artist: 'Bumble boogie piano special . . . clever with chalk and paints . . . those rejection slips from *Seventeen* . . . future writer'.[29]

THE COMPETITIVE EDGE

Like many of her friends with artistic interests, Sylvia Plath was eager to compete for the numerous art prizes awarded by the schools, magazines, newspapers, and various arts organizations, at a time when drawing lessons were still considered a major component of a child's—and especially a girl's—classical education. At age 12 she wrote in her diary, 'I have sent into <u>so</u> many contests that I wish I could win something!'[30] Her first prize for artwork was likely at age 9, when her entry of a stout woman wearing a goofy hat was published with three others in the local newspaper's 'Funny Faces' drawing contest. Postcards she sent home from camp detail her competitive efforts, such as a costume design contest, and comparisons of her artwork with those of others. One 1946 camp diary note states she was thrilled with the purchase of her first set of oil paints and canvases, and a letter to mother sent from camp that summer (almost identical to one she sent to her grandparents) recounts a discussion with her arts and crafts teacher that likely caused her mother to arrange private art lessons the following fall.[31] The drawing of the little house nestled in trees was one of a series she made on the scenery:[32]

> 7 JULY: Yesterday, 'Frenchie', our arts and crafts teacher took eight girls from different units on a two-hour sketch trip. . . . we hiked along the dusty road until we came to the quaintest little house nestled in the trees. We sat down across the road and began to draw. I used broad pencils, and they were swell. I was eager to see the work of the others, and was surprised to see that it was not at all much better than mine. In fact, only one came up to mine. When the girl next to me showed my drawing to Frenchie, she asked me if I was taking art lessons. When I said no, she snapped, 'Why not! You should lap up all the instruction you can get.' I do think that I will take viola with Mrs. Bates next year, and try to save up toward art (preferably sketching) lessons, for I love it so. . . . Art is wonderful, there are so many grand things to do.

Sylvia Plath started senior high school in fall 1947 with her typically breakneck schedule. She took advanced painting courses, worked on the yearbook's arts and activities committee, made decorations for school events, wrote the 'High School Highlights' column for the local paper, and published a number of poems (mostly anonymously, she noted) in the high school paper. She also continued with piano lessons, played viola in the high school orchestra, performed in a class play for the first time, attended numerous plays and concerts, and traveled with the girl's basketball team to games at nearby schools. Her Art Club met four times a week, and her mother arranged for drawing lessons with Miss Hazelton, an elderly artist who lived across the street from the family. She began making still life drawings at these weekly sessions, mostly done in pastels. Her two 'Gold Key' awards allowed her to compete in the Carnegie Institute's annual National High School Art

Exhibition, and in her high school scrapbook, she evaluated progress she had made during her year of private lessons:[33]

> I wish I had some really good samples of my art work in the 9th grade—I took from Miss Hazelton all this year, and really began to improve. I had remained pretty much the same after 6th grade. But in the 9th grade I eventually won a place in Carnegie.

In her 1947 diary, however, she mimicked the breathless style of popular fiction to recreate the setting for receiving the good news:

> 13 MAY: Today was a lucky day for me, all right! In Algebra, Miss Martin got a telephone call from the office and she said that Mr. Thistle wanted to see me. With much curiosity, I hurried over. Jimmy led me into his private office with not a little ceremony, and took from his desk two big certificates, each splashed with a huge, gold seal. 'I', he said, and paused effectively, 'I am happy to tell you that one of your two pictures sent to Carnegie won a place in the exhibition. Also I have a certificate that you received an honorable mention in the national poetry contest.' (I gasped appreciably between the pauses in this little speech). 'In fact, counting the three prizewinners, you have been named eighth in this particular contest!' After delivering this bombshell he heartily congratulated me, pumped my hand up and down, and ushered me out of the office. Well! I was so happy I practically flew on home to tell Mother the wonderful news.

As a junior in high school Plath won two more of these coveted awards for her watercolors titled 'Thanksgiving' and 'Halloween', and expressed hopes of winning a prize for a close-up photograph of a winter scene.[34] She placed the photo in her high school scrapbook and commented on its merit:

> When I enthusiastically shot this picture, I was sure it would be a prize winner of some sort. Now that a year has passed, it seems to have lost its artistic significance for me, and I can only hopefully point out the rhythmic design of white snow on black wire—nothing more.

Plath's extensive efforts in visual art while in junior and senior high school were made with the assumption that she might become a professional artist, and that her works were superior to most of her classmates. She experimented with a wide range of styles and subjects, trying at least one venture with each arts and crafts medium. During junior high she indulged subjects of her childhood in artwork, such as figures from fairy tales and the Mother Goose rhymes 'Mary, Mary, Quite Contrary' and 'Little Miss Muffet'—two of a series of four carefully designed tempera

7. Kids fixing car, *The Wellesleyan* high school year book, 1950

S.Plath

paintings that include Little Red Riding Hood and Snow White[35] (see Pl. 6). She received straight A grades in art classes throughout her school years, and much praise for arts and crafts she made at camp. In a letter home written during the summer of 1948, when Plath was fifteen, she discussed being more knowledgeable than anyone else in camp after being assigned to take over the duties of the arts teacher who had become ill. At summer camp on Star Island the following year, she had watercolor lessons with a woman who took students to nearby towns for painting trips, where Plath made quick scenes of fellow campers, people in a market, and houses on the sea coast[36] (see Pls. 17 and 18).

Artwork Plath made for her high school classes were often signed and hand-framed but rarely dated, yet her competitive efforts can be confirmed by paintings with contest entry forms on the back, and the coveted awards she mentioned in her diaries. She identified many of her portrait subjects by name, nearly always utilizing the profile. With her habit of copying the work of masters, a number of her more serious works are reminiscent of famous painters. For one 1946 tempera she placed in a contest, titled 'Backstage', she mimicked the famous series of ballet dancers painted by Degas in subject matter and setting, yet the color scheme, like many of her early paintings, resembled that of the Fauvres and German Expressionists.[37] One pastel portrait of a man in a hand-made frame, upon which Plath's Gold Key was pasted, has modeled features in blues and grays that approximate works from Picasso's 'Blue Period',[38] as does her largest contest entry, a tempera of three figures in dark tones befitting the somber and near-identical expressions of what appears to be a Christ-like father, a child or mother, and an infant[39] (see Pls. 13 and 16). This work is similar in theme to another high-school tempera, a cubist-like rendering of a Nativity scene that Plath chose to portray with mixed shades of golds, blues, and browns, with the Madonna figure positioned slightly above that of Joseph[40] (see Pl. 14). The 1948–9 tempera of a street scene with a woman seated in the foreground, submitted to a competition the same year, places contrasting dark and light colors in an obtuse layout of intersecting streets and passers-by.[41] Under the effect of a golden light, these shadowed figures, placed at various places along the streets, converge at the central figure, whose features resemble that of Gauguin's Breton women (see Pl. 11). This evocative piece exhibits Plath's attempt at creating mood and perspective, also suggesting influences from Edward Hopper or Giorgio de Chirico in their depiction of human isolation within public settings. The

8. Little house in trees, 1946, pencil

9. Plath's photo of snow on wire, 'Scrapbook—1947', *c.*1946–7

female figure in front and center is similar to many pictures Plath made in high school that feature women sitting at chairs and tables. Her placement of the figure also recalls short stories she wrote during this period that portray older women, often lonely within their dreary apartments, who look at life from their second-story windows. She made numerous loosely formed temperas of women that were likely based on the paintings of Picasso, including one with folded arms and hands placed in the lap[42] (see Pl. 19). Whether quickly sketched or heavily labored, most of her high school artwork is figurative. And while Plath would work within restricted color themes to express mood or fulfill assignment requirements, she generally favored the full color palette and bright rainbow hues she associated with the vitality of life itself. Plath made one particularly colorful tempera painting of a city and seascape that evokes the vibrant lifestyle associated with port towns such as New York or Boston, meccas of learning that Plath visited frequently to take in art and cultural offerings.[43] Seen from above, the many-windowed skyscrapers seem to dance and sway with energy as they stretch in all directions, mimicking the movement of ocean waves, and presenting a world of new adventures (see Pl. 12).

THE 'GEOMETRIC TENSION OF COLOR AND FORM'

Following her own tendency, and as taught in her visual art and writing courses, Plath used colors to symbolize emotional and physical states, or to develop symbolic meaning around objects in her writing and her environment. In a 1951 letter to her artist friend Ann Davidow,[44] she joked about the placement of the desk in her room at Smith's Haven House:

> Do you realize why I have my desk facing the window? (I just figured out why this moment). Hopkins House is yellow. Yellow is a 'morale-building' color (or so the higher-ups say in Art 13.) And there you have it.

The position Plath took here of writing while looking out the window, however, was a habit from childhood. She described her view of Hopkins House in an undated journal entry written during her first year at Smith, underscoring her use of journals for writing exercises that could also incorporate her philosophic musings. She discussed the dorm's appearance in terms of the artist's vision and the transforming power of the human mind, and how she would treat it as a painting subject.[45] Her appreciation of its ugliness confirmed her aesthetic attraction to 'lovely desolation' or the less-lovely grotesque that she would continue to explore in her literary *oeuvre*:

> Hopkins House is ugly. I see it when I get up every morning to shut the window, and whenever I write at my desk. It is all awkward corners, all gawky red chimneys, gables, blue tile roofs, red tile roofs worn to a purple, and yellow walls with white and blackened green woodwork. It is smeared with the year's grime, paint peeling, soiled window frames, and naked shrubs scrounging against the basement windows. I can almost hear their brittle bony branches squeaking hideously as the wind stirs them against the scabby wood of the house. Yet I love Hopkins House. Such is the resiliency of man that he can become fascinated by ugliness which surrounds him everywhere and wish to transform it by his art into something clinging and haunting its lovely desolation. I would paint the geometric shutters patterned against the oblongs of yellow wood, the trapezoids and slouching angles of the roof, the angled jutting of the drain pipes—I would paint in a bleak and geometric tension of color and form—what I see across the street . . . the ugliness which by man's sense of wishful thinking becomes a beauty touching us all.

Although there is no evidence of such a painting, Plath drew a loose colored-ink sketch of Hopkins House onto the back of her 'Den of Lions' story draft, which manages to capture the geometric tension she suggested for a painting on the subject[46] (see Pl. 26). Based on the many works that she made on the verso of other manuscripts, one gets the impression of Plath reaching for the most convenient piece of paper and tools to record the image before her, in this case the last page of her short story. She often referred to having a sudden inspiration and interrupting one activity to start another so as not to lose her thought.

During Plath's first two years at Smith she continued to vacillate on whether to pursue visual arts or writing as a major and a profession. Her favorite classes were literature and art studios, where she studied design the first year in Art 13, described as a 'basic course in understanding the usual properties of color, light, form, space, line, texture', and Art 210: 'Principles and Techniques of Expressive Pictorial Organization' the following year. She devoted many evenings to finishing art projects during the two years of intensive studio courses, and also taught art to children one afternoon a week at The People's Institute in Northampton. Segments from letters home she wrote in fall 1950, the beginning of her freshman year, express excitement in gaining more skills in her design course, and in managing the flow of her creative efforts into quality product. In the first painting Plath made for this course, a watercolor of a Chapel Meeting at Green Auditorium, the excitement she felt in doing the assigment is also reflected in the work itself:[47] (see Pl. 25)[48]

19 OCTOBER: Today I have experienced the pin-point arranging of time. I painted my first art assignment...I did it hurriedly—a splashed color impression of Chapel Meeting, but I got a thrill out of thinking how much I may improve.

31 OCTOBER: Now I will plunge into those darn critical English themes with renewed vigor and go through my art exercises with that 'means-to-an-end' gleam in my eye. If only I can meet all the opportunities![49]

5 NOVEMBER: If only I can wield the now—where I'm living so hard I have no energy to produce—into art and writing later on! It's like animals storing up fat and then, in hibernation or relaxation, using it up.[50]

Excerpts from letters home written during the spring semester of 1951 show continued uncertainty with what route to take in her studies and her career, and how to shore up her artistic skills:

8 FEBRUARY: A girl came up to me from another art section and said, 'Oh, Sylvia, they showed your work in class today as an example of a promising Freshman'. (I never believe anything good about myself.) But I do feel that those loving hours I spend in the studio may help. Keep your fingers crossed.[51]

18 APRIL: I must take a practical art and a creative writing course, but as I am still undecided as to my major, I should also take both an English lit. and a history of art course in case I choose one or the other...or should I major in English and art and have a 'free-lance' career—IF I can ever catch a man who can put up with the idea of having a wife who loves to be alone, and working artistically now and then. I would like to start thinking about where I'll put my emphasis for the rest of my brief life.[52]

15 APRIL: If I got battered and discouraged in my creative course next year, I don't care. Olive Higgins Prouty said I 'had something'. Mr. Mantzi, my art teacher, spent an hour telling me how he liked what I was turning out in art...I have joined the Studio Club (art) and plan to sacrifice the best part of my life next week painting decorations for a dance.[53]

Paintings Plath made during her freshman year, however, brought a negative review at year's end, which she discussed in another letter to Davidow written in May or June 1951:

I just finished my art assignments for the year and got one of life's little blows. I took my first painting together with my last one up to be criticized by Mr. Swinton. (the last was a re-doing of the first, using all the 'skills' we'd learned this year.) Mr. Swinton's comment was hideously encouraging—thought the first was much better, more naive and free—that the last was artificial and gaudy as bad wallpaper. Made me feel I'd really accomplished something! (Now Sylvia, don't be bitter!)[54]

The earlier work that Mr. Swinton called 'more naive and free' may resemble the less rigid forms she employed in high school while studying the modernists, or what she had called her hurried 'splashed color' impressionist-style watercolor of her first Art 13 assignment. Works that may warrant the 'bad wallpaper' critique include a series of giraffe-like animals set in rows with different color combinations[55] (see Pl. 27). Bitter or not about negative reviews, Plath was resilient. She could not give up hope for bringing her visual art skills to professional levels. Her life-long identity as an accomplished visual artist, top grades and encouragement from art teachers, and the numerous Gold Key awards in high school had kept her hopes high for greater achievements. The following year as a sophomore she went on to take Art 210 with no hesitation.

Immersed in the study of modern art, and while teaching art at the local People's Institute, she revised a story in February 1952 for her sophomore writing course called 'Through Dynasties Pass'.[56] The plot features a young woman on a train who has a discussion with a Korean War veteran seated next to her. After he asks her about the book on contemporary art she is reading, stating, 'I could never catch on to that modern art stuff,' she tells him she purchased it at the Museum of Modern Art and explains the topic in simple terms he could understand (ellipses Plath's):

> Well, take apples just for instance. You could draw apples just the way everybody sees them, round and red and shiny. But these guys, they don't want to paint apples the same old way, so that's why they use all these little blocks of color...to make people get excited and see things fresh and all...

Continuing a habit in place as a teenager, and as seen in the works of classical and modern art she studied, pictures Plath made at Smith focus primarily on representations of women. She generally used strong color schemes and dark/light contrasts as well as hard contours to define the subjects of her large-format temperas in particular. Yet these works exhibit a uniformity of palette and tightness of form that may have contributed to other discouraging comments from artist friend Phil McCurdy, who admitted to teasing Plath about her difficulty with 'freedom, color placement and balance' in painting.[57] And while Plath was good at drawing faces, she struggled with painting the human anatomy, most obvious in a tempera 'Two Women at Window', where one is standing and the other sits at a table[58] (see Pl. 30). Her positioning of the figures, however, with the standing woman leaning forward to comfort the other, gives the work an emotional charge lacking in similar assignments. With their faces hidden, their arms seem to extend into each other, creating a sense of tension, despair, and connectedness—perhaps indicative of some of the feelings she was experiencing at the time, and the sympathy she received and extended to her own female friends. The color scheme balances primary colors associated with moods, where the distraught brunette stands out in a red upper garment while the sympathetic blonde wears the cooler colors of white and blue. The bourgeois 'comfortable chair' setting she used in many artworks is here inverted, where the chairs are hard and the interior space dark, while the nature scene outside the window is breezy and light (see Chapter 5, pp. 186–7).

Another tempera painting, 'Yellow House', positions a large home set within trees, surrounded by a circular drive that resembles a cul-de-sac or 'dead end' that creates a sense of this home as a self-contained unit not connected to the neighboring house[59] (see Pl. 28). Likely a result of her Art 13 study of Cape Cod architecture, this supposedly idyllic setting—the dream of the beautiful home in the suburbs—may therefore be a place of isolation (see Chapter 5, p. 190). The earlier painting Plath made of a city by the sea with swaying buildings of many colors reflects the more dynamic life styles available to the urban dweller, as well as career opportunities for women, taken from a higher perspective where the view is expansive and potentially uplifting.

One of Plath's most abstract and compelling works, 'Nine Female Figures', is a tempera of line-drawn women set in bright-colored and multipatterned squares, one of many large-format temperas made in Art 13, most likely the final assignments of her freshman studio[60] (see Pl. 34). With a backdrop that resembles the architectural layering of urban buildings found in earlier works, the painting's nearly indistinguishable women are seated naked, enclosed in static, tight-spaced boxes that prevent them from breaking out, highlighting their unseeing eyes and sexual function. They have no mouths to speak, leaving the viewer with the senses of gaze and touch only, while those figures with arms and hands use them to cover their pubic area. The sense of numbing serenity and subtle torture or dismemberment sets up a nuanced dichotomy. The work gives clear visual expression to the troubling mid-century cultural conditions Plath had been addressing in all forms of texts, including her 1949 story, 'Among the Shadows Throng', where the protagonist states: 'I never wanted to be trapped in one personality'—the seeming fate of the nine females with identical expressions. The double standards for men and women's sexuality, the conformist roles and restrictions placed on the traditional 1950s housewife, and the frustrations of inhabiting a woman's body are also some of Plath's more notable complaints of her teens, the kind of commentary that has caused many feminists to place her within their camp (see Chapter 6, p. 221).

Plath also represented these cultural conditions in compositions she wrote during the same period of spring 1951. In a long journal entry she questioned whether marriage and children might 'sap my creative energy' or provide 'a fuller expression in art'.[61] She then noted the 'blind box houses' she passed before stopping instinctively, 'like the rat in the maze', to enter her own and lock her door to 'the disturbing wasteland of sleeping streets and fenceless acres of night'. Plath's short essay 'Suburban Nocturne', apparently based on this same walk home, recreates the image of these disinterested dwellers viewed through constricting squares of light and menacing shadows cast upon the 'faces' of their homes:[62]

> I can see into squares of warm yellow light where little people revolve inside their brightly colored boxes . . . in all these blind boxes there is no one to listen to me or hear my feet clicking on the pavement . . . But the houses have strange leaf shadows on their faces . . . I think I could be strangled by these shadows.

These menacing shadows may also fall on Plath's own family home, as seen in the essay's final paragraph: 'Going out, I meet myself eternally coming in . . . My umbilical cord has never been cut completely.' Yet the 1950s post-war suburban sprawl of America cannot be separated from the Cold War scare. Plath's poem 'Geography Lesson', written one year after 'Suburban Nocturne', describes the 'million million microscopic towns'—' Bright shine the little houses | Straight go the little Main Streets'.[63] In this poem Plath used children's book cadence and rhyme schemes as well as the layout of colored maps to express her anti-war sentiments. The narrator takes the position of looking down at the map from high above, placing conformist American suburban culture within the war-mongering mentality of the Cold War era. The first four stanzas feature the yellow, orange, green, and red-brown parts of the map, where a million microscopic men, cars, trees, and towns are depicted, while the final stanza presents the violence of bloodshed:

> On the lavendar part of the map
> On the light lavendar part of the map
> Are a million microscopic cannons
> A million million microscopic cannons.
>   Shrill squeak the little bullets,
>   Sharp bark the little shotguns,

> And now a river
> A bright red river
> Stains the lavendar part of the map.

Plath recreated this tension between the idealized suburban yet 'unseeing' lifestyle promoted by mid-century culture and the tools of mass destruction in her political art masterpiece, a 1960 collage composed of black, white, and red photographic images taken from magazines that juxtapose Eisenhower-era politics with American advertising prowess and the sexual thrill of war—one of her most sophisticated depictions of the new age of nuclear fallout shelters, and the latest artwork in the archives.[64] In this picture Vice President Nixon is perched behind President Eisenhower's left shoulder as he sits at a desk, where a label on his lapel reads 'sleep'. The main female figure, wearing a bathing suit and lying in a provocative pose, has a jet fighter pointing towards her; its tip reaches her lower abdomen. Her eyes are closed, and the sleeping couple placed above her wear blindfolds (see Pl. 37). In a 1961 letter home, Plath described the dangers of 'the forces of the John Birch Society' and the American military where 'generals who, on retirement, become board heads of missile plants'.[65] By this time Plath had already highlighted the Cold War Communist scare in her novel, *The Bell Jar*, which opens with the protagonist's empathetic experience of the Rosenberg executions as spies, and recreates a conversation with other guest editors of *Mademoiselle* that reflects some of the facile, anti-Communist rhetoric of the time.

Many of Plath's high school artwork and Smith studio paintings offer possible alternatives to these dark visions, most commonly, figures of women at their leisure, often reading or in the company of friends. Two large format temperas she made at Smith may be seen as foils for her paintings of boxed-in or sorrowful women. Both 'Two Women Reading'[66] and 'Woman with Halo'[67] present similar subjects using the Expressionist palette of blues, greens, yellows, and oranges, though none of the constrictions of mid-century womanhood and rigid conformity are present. In the painting of two women reading, the planes of the buildings do not meet; they seem to float upon a patch-quilt of colored scenery, airy and unenclosed. Freed from the demands of the homemaker, the readers pursue their own interests, relaxing under a tree, drinking a glass of wine. The composition of this tempera may also be seen as an unconventional conflation of cubism and linear perspective, techniques Plath had been studying for years.[68] While cubism tends to flatten geometrical objects into multidimensional fields of monochromatic colors, often presenting multiple viewpoints simultaneously, this painting places vibrant, multicolored forms of shifting dimensions within a prominent two-point perspective. The scene is positioned from the viewpoint of one woman with outstretched legs, whose gaze is aligned with the viewer of the painting, bringing the seeing eye of the artist in line with her audience (see Pl. 33). And in a clear example of recycled imagery, Plath sketched the same design in her history class notebook during her last year of high school (see Chapter 5, p. 191; Chapter 6, p. 208).

The other large-format tempera that departs from the theme of entrapment and sexual stereotyping found in 'Nine Female Figures' is a colorful picture of a woman with a halo sitting on a stool, set within a hilly, spring-like landscape with farmhouses in the distance. With eyes closed, as if indulging an inner vision, she leans forward toward a church (where the steeple's shadow points to her solar plexus), holding her left elbow forward. Perhaps appropriate for a saintly figure, her clothes are dowdy and her shoes comfortable. Yet while the upper portion of her body is poised in air and dressed in white, associated with clouds, purity, and the heavens, her legs look as if they could be in motion,[69] and her skirt is a bright red, hinting at passion or involvement in earthly activity (see Pl. 32). Plath considered herself a non-Christian, yet her study of religion and the lives of saints as a senior in high school and her first year at Smith may have contributed to the spiritual overtones of this tempera. Its basic composition, in fact, can also be found in another pencil sketch she made in high school. Placed amongst her senior year biology notes, this small drawing presents a more fashionable-looking woman sitting outdoors, grounded on a stool, with buildings and hills in the distance. Her arm is extended in the same manner, yet she is holding the scales of justice, in a modernized version of Lady Justice, who traditionally is depicted wearing a blindfold with a set of weighing scales suspended from her left hand. These artworks offer two major yet often conflated personas of Plath, that of society's high judge engaged in her world while pointing out its crippling ills—the position she described in her 1949 diary notes—and the mystic or contemplative who distances herself from the mundane affairs.

If the painting of female entrapment represents the future that Plath fears will overtake her, the two woman reading, the woman with a halo, and its secular prototype might be seen as a future she would choose for herself, with thoughts focused on a just and peaceful society, the beauty of nature, the realm of knowledge, as well as the interior spaces of divine thought. These paintings give a sense of where her famous literary themes may have found shape if she had pursued her ambitions in visual art. Like much of the art Plath created at Smith, her single extant oil painting from the collections (a rare attempt to master the difficult medium), a still life, is an exercise in composition with no emotional value[70] (see Pl. 29). Work from Plath's art scrapbooks, however, full of collages made from cuttings of magazine advertisements and construction paper, reflect Plath's interest in commercial culture, world politics, and women in contemporary society.

In the summer of 1951 following her freshman year at Smith, while working as an au pair in charge of three children, Plath was still enthusiastic about improving her artwork. She created many pictures of these children and the people around her, as well as one unusually evocative self-portrait, likely instigated by her purchase of a new box of pastels.[71] Her journal entry records her pleasure in the artistic process, as well as the techniques she used in creating this piece, perhaps one of the first 'traditional' portraits she had made since starting her Art 13 coursework (see Chapter 6, p. 209; Afterword, p. 229–33):

> 17 AUGUST: I am really enjoying myself, especially since I got those wonderful pastels. Already, I've done a big, full-size self-portrait which came out sort of yellowish and sulky, but the face isn't bad at all. Quite traditional. Thought that when I get home, I could cut it down. I love the hard pastels—much more precise than the soft and cleaner cut. Only thing I've got to get over is the 'rubbing' habit. I liken it to putting too much pedal on a sloppily played piano piece—it only serves to blur mistakes.

What Plath identified as a sulky expression here actually presents a mood that is more complex. The large-format pastel appears to exhibit what has been called dueling or 'two faced' personalities Plath exhibited in her texts—notably, the upbeat 'Sivvy' voice of *Letters Home* presented to her mother versus many of her more candid narratives found in journals.[72] Her face in this self-portrait may be divided down the middle into a left portion, which presents a curious, bright-eyed, and somewhat clear or open expression, and the narrower right portion that reveals a stressed, aged, and sullen personality that signals the potential for depression.[73] The two halves contribute to the potentially ominous tension of the overall portraiture (see Pl. 24). One abstract tempera, 'Triple face portrait', is a Smith classroom exercise in overlapping silhouettes, pattern and color, which presents the concept of the double in two profiles, in a reverse Janus-face layout, that form a third, front-facing portrait[74] (see Pl. 35). The gender of the profiled faces appears to be masculine, yet the combined portrait is a more feminine face, whose pure black eyes look forward in a suggestion of hidden depths behind what resembles a bright colored mask—a topic related to the theatre, multiple identities, and self-analysis that fascinated Plath, and a form of duplicity that many critics address in analysing her life and writing. These carefully designed works are among her final attempts to manage large-scale, full-color figures, for she would soon after transfer her challenges in color patterning and visual play to the written word.

Word Crafts

THE DIARIES BEGIN

Sylvia Plath's love affair with language and self-expression was formally initiated when she started keeping diaries at the age of 10. From then on she would write in them regularly into her sophomore year in high school, where they took on the persona of an intimate confidante and daily companion. In the small diaries of 1944 and 1945, she recorded the many activities that made up her days at home and at school: hiking and picnicking, sailing and swimming, skating, going to museums, movies, and plays, helping with house cleaning and doing homework, cooking recipes in her Home Economics class, making decorations for school events, collecting and trading stamps, tending her flower garden, making outfits for her dolls, taking lessons in piano, viola and dance, listening to the radio (frequently 'The Lone Ranger' and 'Henry Aldrich'), reading, embroidering and sewing clothes, writing poems and stories, copying pictures, and playing with cut-out dolls. School activities in particular were recorded, where she confirmed her love of art, litera-ture, and social studies. Plath often started these early entries with a record of her art projects at school, while the Sunday entries typically began with the color and type of flowers displayed at church, with an occasional reference to the subject of sermons or church events. Her 1944 entries contain few drawings, while activities at summer camp, written up in all forms of texts, are usually accompanied by illustrations. Plath shared her best efforts with her family, friends, and guests, and she regularly described her entire range of activities in her 1944 diary:

9 MARCH: Betsy and I are doing some more costumes. I am lucky because after my work is done we can talk for a few minutes about our drawing only instead sometimes we talk about something else . . . after she had gone I copied two Brownie cards and colored them with my pencil crayons. I love to draw.

10 MARCH: Marcia and I got our stories printed in The Townsman.

26 MARCH: I also sent in for the drawing contest on the Good Sport Page. My drawing is called 'It's Spring'. . . . I drew some cards that had subjects I made up.

11 APRIL: In the evening I cut out a shirt for Cynthia out of a dress up dress of green silk. It will look nice on her because she is blonde.

18 APRIL: Then I went down to the library and copied a pretty picture on one of the magazines for mother's birthday. I copied it over carefully when I got home. It is a beautiful picture.

19 APRIL: Grammy. . . brought 17 of Esther's old books so now I have 100 books in all. I am in a reverie of happiness for I love books.

14 DECEMBER: I wile away the hours searching for a picture that illustrated my subject.[75]

23 DECEMBER: I played the Tarantella and Warren and I sang while I played carols. I showed our guests my best drawings. Marcia and I hung up our stockings. After a hearty supper Warren and I heard carolers and so went out and sat in the apple tree and looked up at the moon, covered now and then by passing clouds.

Plath's early 1945 diary entries, made at age 12, mark her growing awareness of herself as an art student and critic. She began working on a small scrapbook for her poems, drawings, and stories, the first of many books she made to contain a full range of works.[76] Along with having more detailed notes and drawings, these entries become increasingly lyrical and dramatic, often expressing a hunger to gain life experience that her ordinary routine did not offer. Instead of recording daily events with little elaboration, she began to add experiments in descriptive or emotive language, where she employed highly animated commentary of more important topics. Plath's early fascination with design, color, and texture, and her careful study of magazines and books, is revealed in the vocabulary she used to describe character, mood, and plot development. Her familiarity with popular prose is evident in her use of clichéd phrases, often clustered into a few sentences, as seen in this description of her early theater experience:

20 JANUARY: Dear Diary, Today is the biggest day of my life. I had a dreamless sleep and woke as fresh as dew on spring butter cups. All day I was in another world, far better than this. I took the bus to Boston with Mother and Warren to see Shakespeare's 'The Tempest' at the Colonial Theatre. It was too perfect for words.

In another January entry, Plath recorded the first two stanzas of a new poem she wrote in a 'flash of poetic inspiration' that started with the question: 'Is there a face where wisdom and beauty dwell?'[77] But she omitted the third verse as 'pretty weak', adding: 'The poem is meant for Miss Chadwick, but it doesn't do her lovely face and spirit justice.' She also wrote of how her pleasure in creating art was linked to inspiration, and her struggle with visual expression: 'So far my thoughts are not coming out so well in the form of pictures.'[78] While she showed increased sophistication in drawing subjects during these adolescent years, her talents in language had started to excel at a faster pace.

RECORDING THE 'BIG MOMENTS'—INCLUDING DREAMS

For Christmas 1945 Plath asked her mother for an undated diary that would give her space to record what she called 'the big moments', also needed for the drawings that were cropping up with increased frequency. At age 13 she began to write about her dreams, the first clear indication of her interest in the unconscious mind and its uses for art. Her high school essay titled 'Childhood Fears' reveals an incident that may have motivated her to begin her own Dream Book as a young teen:[79]

> . . . a friend and I began to search for small risks which would make our lives more excitingly uncertain . . . We cultivated our list of unreal fears with the loving touch of an orchard grower . . . One dull, rainy day, while we were leafing through an ancient dream book in Ruth's attic, we discovered some impressive fears which we had not yet investigated. We decided to diagnose our dreams and, fascinated, we read the lengthy list of fears that caused these nightly visions.

Plath's 1946 diary discussed her wonderful 'technicolor' dreams that told complete stories, during a period when she was seeing a wide range of films on a regular basis. In one case she assigned them names and numbers, reflecting her habit of organizing material into lists:

19 FEBRUARY: This morning I began to write a Dream Book. Last night I had five dreams. Two of which I thought superior enough to record. The titles are (1) 'Rocketship to

Mars' and (2) 'The Sled that Coasted Around the World.' I could have never thought of the plots unless I had not dreamed them. They had very satisfactory endings because the pictures conveniently faded into each other.

A year later Plath began composing a 'planet story' called 'Mission to Mars' that she discussed in her diary, stating: 'Maybe I will have a wonderful dream and then I will tell it to you alone!' Her hopes were realized:

> 1 FEBRUARY: Last night mother and I talked for ever so long before falling asleep. I did have a nice dream. Warren, Margot and I were climbing up a huge, steep mountain—just hanging onto the edge. It was so high that it must have reached up to heaven. The sky was a sharp, dazzling blue. All around me was just blue, blue—intense blue—so intense that it hurt to look at it. The wind glowed and roared a wild song, and it got colder and colder. Finally we reached the top. All of a sudden Margot and I were standing barefoot in bathing suits on some hard ground in the yard in front of an ordinary brown house. The roots of a maple tree were making hard bumps under our feet, and the leaves made dappled shadows on the rough ground. We were looking down on a fishing village, where Warren was playing on the mud flat. We could see the slender masts and the rigging of the sloops tied up by the weathered old board house. Then the sun went behind a dark cloud, and Margot remarked softly, 'It's raining!' Sure enough, we held out our hands, on which mittens appeared and we could see some of the raindrops which were—odd as it may seem—turquoise-blue sulfa-gum! Then as the pellets began to pile up around us, the scene faded into a misty haze, and soon I completely woke up.

As an adult Plath commented on the active and colorful dream life of her youth, and the inability to have imaginative dreams would show up as the central conflict for the female protagonist of 'Johnny Panic and the Bible of Dreams'. She wrote this short story while working as a secretary for a psychiatric division of Massachusetts General Hospital (the same facility that administered her faulty shock treatments in 1953), where she had access to records of patients' dreams. Plath would continue to report some of her own vivid dreams—including nightmares—in journals.

Sylvia Plath's first 1947 diary, now a larger size and named 'My Memory Book', starts by habit with a description of her Christmas holiday activities and gifts she received, and continues with almost daily entries that run from one paragraph to a few pages, many of which are illustrated. She used dramatic styles that approximate some of the stories she read in magazines such as *Vanity Fair*, *Seventeen*, and *Ladies Home Journal*, usually in describing the affairs of women. In one January entry Plath detailed her progress in Miss Hazelton's drawing lessons with an eye toward character portrayal. She included commentary on what she felt was appropriate reporting as her gaze moved from the apple Miss Hazelton discussed to Miss Hazelton herself, one teacher, she noted, who offered no praise. Plath continued to engage her diary as an entity in its own right, a confidante who was alone promised her secret thoughts—although a future audience could not be ruled out. After reading the memoirs of the children's book illustrator Wanda Hazel Gág, which alternately inspired and bored her, Plath imagined that readers could be interested in her personal life, and twice admitted the possibility that her own diary might some day be in print:[80]

> 31 JANUARY: After school I went across the street to my art lesson with Barbar[a] Adams. I at last finished the pastel of the pitcher and the fruit. I have noticed that Miss Hazelton never praises. She just bustles and rustles around, asking us if we see this shadow, or that curve in the apple. She is a tiny wizened old lady. Her skin is like wrinkled yellow parchment, but her eyes have a keen, twinkling gaze, and her voice, though sounding like staccato, bird-ish chirps, has a ring of sincerity and the tone of one who sees the big, beautiful world as it really is—not dimmed by hazes of prejudice, hate, or anything else. Even though I found a great deal of fault with my finished picture I took it home to mother who was very pleased. (Please I didn't mean to go off on a sermon while I described Miss Hazelton!) I took the picture of my campaigning stunt and my Christmas poster on the bulletin board that Alfred took with his flash camera, my pencil crayons, my handy little calendar, and my big book of Wanda Hazel Gág's Diary and drawings to bed with me. Her diary is such an inspiration. I actually stopped reading because I felt I would rather catch up here, first, for who knows—someday you might be in print. Once I start to write, it is so hard to stop. There are so many things that I feel deeply about and want to get written down before it is to[o] late and they have slipped away. I hear suspicious sounds of Mother stirring downstairs, so I must say 'Good-night' and go to sleep.

In most of these diary entries, Plath featured herself as the major actor, center stage, using a voice that combined humor, satire, and high drama, where the act of recording and the pages she wrote on became part of her performance. While she would eventually discontinue diary reports of artworks-in-progress, dreams, and school activities in favor of comments on social activities during her early high school years, in 'My Memory Book' of early 1947, she was still making regular comments on her creative works, as well as her lack of life experience and attempts to manage the terrific outpouring of her imagination:

20 FEBRUARY: I am all in the mood for Thundery poetry now. I wish I had the experience to write about it. It's so sad to ache to write wonderful poems and not have the things to do it with!

15 MAY: When I came home I was so joyous about getting that stopper out of my wellspring of happy feelings and I was so happy it was such a glorious day that I sat down and wrote the following poem in our cozy back yard: 'May.'

Plath copied down another May poem, 'New England Library', after noting that she had been 'subconsciously putting away thoughts about it and at last they ripened into a poem. Here it is.'[81] In the first of six stanzas, the poem positions the building within a dusty street scene of cars passing, where in the last stanza, lucky browsers are able to explore the wonders hidden in books:

> Each shelf will offer shining spheres—
> New worlds to see with ease,
> Between the cover of each book
> Unveiled to only these.

At this point Plath decided she had enough works to form her first poetry collection, accompanied by illustrations, a new step she recorded with enthusiasm:

15 MAY: It poured buckets all afternoon but little did I care! I am making a book of all my 'bestest' poems and selecting an appropriate picture in lovely color to go on every other page. I am titling it 'Sylvia's Scrapbook' . . . so far I have 24 poems. I made up the 24th just this afternoon to go with a magical color photo of some purple cliffs in Bulgaria. It's titled 'Steely Blue Crags,' and I think it's one of my very best! I certainly have been in the poetry mood this month, having written the following in the past few weeks—April, Steely-Blue Crags, New England Library, May and 'The Earth Had Wilted in the Heart.'

'Steely Blue Crags' evokes the fairy lands, colorful nature scenes, and some of the Gothic and mysterious settings Plath had been writing into prose and poetry. It also addresses the need to hold onto beauty and 'making something permanent' to survive into the future world that is built upon human dust, a theme she would later explore in studying Virginia Woolf:

> Steely-blue cliffs,
> Whence did you come?
> Eeire and strange,
> Stony and glum.

Oh, did some giant, long ago,
Then use you for his castle walls?
Did fairy masons carve your heights
With lacy turrets—high arched halls?

Steely-blue cliffs,
Where do you hold
Learning and lore
Centuries old?

Oh, do your feathered evergreens
Hide treasures from the mortal eye?
And, in their purpled shadows veil
The secrets of years gone by?

Steely-blue cliffs,
Where do you hold
Learning and lore
Centuries old?

Oh, do your feathered evergreens
Hide treasures from the mortal eye?
And, in their purpled shadows veil
The secrets of years gone by?

Steely-blue cliffs,
Will you still reign
After we're gone?
Will you remain?

Oh, tell me that your rough-hewn crags
Will long endure. They must! They must!
And say that you will yet stand here
Long after we have turned to dust.

Plath superimposed light sketches over some of her 1946 and 1947 diary script, indicating she later returned to decorate her notes. These illustrations often feature landscapes with people, and seasonal iconography such as spring flowers, pumpkins on Halloween, a cake with candles on her birthday, and the American flag on the Fourth of July. What she called her 'bathing beauties' are spread throughout, often having no relation to her text, though they themselves are topics of discussion. Figures Plath drew also evoked personalities she felt were suitable for fiction, as seen in one 1946 diary note: 'Drew various girls in various poses. They amounted to four quite extraordinary characters.'[82] Another 1946 diary entry is dominated by two glamorous women ready for action: one standing up, wearing long black gloves and evening dress, and one lying down, in high heels and bodice, showing off two shapely legs that lean up the side of the page. The text above this sexy woman states: 'As usual, I take more time filling up space with crazy drawings'.

LESSONS IN COMPOSITION

Before copying a poem or story idea into her diary during adolescence, Plath would sometimes note the source of the piece, her analysis of it, or her excitement around the process of writing, as well as her willingness to read a book or passage repeatedly when it provided valuable writing techniques. She read extensively for pleasure outside of her school requirements, but it is clear that she was methodically reading to learn the trade. She followed the advice offered by professional writers: read extensively and widely, with an eye toward creating narratives that appeal to a public audience. Her reading included the classics and popular works, a range of magazines and scholarly publications, adventure stories, and biographies, all of which she examined and enjoyed without discrimination to genre. Plath was seriously contemplating her skills in relation to her own career, and looked to models provided by women professionals who were writing about their experiences. At age 13 she wrote about reading accounts of 'exceptionally intelligent' women who discussed their jobs, where it is evident that she placed herself in the category of those who would not dedicate their lives solely to a husband and family. Always eager to publish, she wrote of her beginner-status as a writer and her developing technique in her 1946 diary, again referring to the imagined reading audience or the diary itself as 'you':

> 29 APRIL: Sent in some of my original 'picturesque speech and patter' to the Reader's Digest. I'd be overwhelming happy if I'd get any published. Perhaps my most picturesque on[e] is 'a milkweed parachute hitchhiked on a passing breeze.' It may sound amateurish to you later, but to me it sounded pretty good.

Setbacks as well as progress in her creative work were, of course, noteworthy topics. The day after transcribing her description of the milkweed parachute, she expressed outrage and despair about losing her fancy pen in an equally self-conscious writing style:

Dear Diary~ today I paid a sad farewell to my good old pal Betsy Pawley. I sat on her front steps and talked over all the good times. After our re-hearsal in orchestra afterschool grammy drove me over to Margot's house in Tamacia Plain, I met mum there. The house was cold, and we two spent hours getting home by poor transportation in the dark cold windy night.

Dear Diary~ I(every time it happens) cannot remember what happen ed today except that columbus discovered America, which is a sad state of affairs. As usual I take more time filling up space with craz-y drawings. oh, yes, things are getting clearer now! I have a cold and I am in bad too bad ole kid!

30 APRIL: Today has been about the worst in my life so far. My ten-dollar fountain pen was stolen! . . . I feel as bitter as gall and as awful as salt tears. My world has turned grey and black.

When Plath's subject warranted a plain-spoken narrative style, she would adjust her prose accordingly. One 1946 diary page she placed into a letter home from camp shows her shifting from her unsatisfactory drawings to a writing passage she was proud of, where she recreated the mood evoked by a forgotten family graveyard:

11 JULY: Last night we went on another short sketching trip. I hobbled along as best I could, but was so tired that I did not draw well at all. We went to a very interesting family graveyard that we passed coming up. I was so interested in the names and dates on the old stones, that I felt quite subdued and rather filled with the tragedy that pervaded the air. There were three stones together. A man between two wives, one wife died at the age of 40, the other did die a year after the man—72 years. Another tiny stone was for a little girl that died at the age of two years. The saddest stone was so small that it was overgrown by witch grass. It was for such a little child it only had room for Lovell on it. There were several rather showy and decorative stones, with lovely designs on them.

Plath continued to express her craving for experience that might provide exciting subject matter for her art, yet she accepted the likelihood that serious adventure might have to wait until her career was on track. In the meantime, she made use of summer camp and home life as subjects for drawing and writing while indulging her 'escape' into fantasy worlds. In 'Thought Patterns on Paper', a handwritten school assignment of 1946, she described the ideal setting for making 'word pictures' and provided a brief sample of her 'hobby'.[83] The red-haired, eloquent protagonist of *Ann of Green Gables,* which Plath had noted reading, may have provided a model for her self-narrative as the imaginative, adolescent girl immersed in nature:

The requirements for my hobby are few. All I need are the following: a few soft cushions, a pencil and pad of paper, and a gnarled old apple tree. The weather may be clear or cloudy as the spirit demands.

Snuggled up in a comfortable apple tree seat, made by three joining branches, it is truly easy to find 'scope for imagination'. All the lovely thoughts that have been stored up in my mind for weeks come tumbling out to be jotted down in word pictures. Inevitably, a story or poem develops.

10. 1946 Diary, 11–12 Oct. entry

Rarely do I feel the urge to write coming on when I want it most—for it can't be forced. But up there, a little above the rather gray, everyday world, the air seems to be clearer—the deep blue sky and wispy clouds a little nearer. Just looking off in the distance to the woods and seeing the sunlight dancing on the green leaves and making dappled shadows here and there is enough to make myriads of magical thoughts weave gay patterns in my mind's eye. Why! My pencil can hardly fly fast enough!

The feeling of putting down word pictures on paper and making other people see them as you saw them is wonderful. Even if you capture only an essence of the piney scent of the woods at Christmas or a speck of the roaring majesty of a turbulent ocean, it is worthwhile to keep writing for your own enjoyment, if not for that of others. It is hard to express here the love I have for my hobby, but I feel it every time I see a bit of nature's beauty or find an inspiration hidden in my heart. Writing is not only my favorite hobby but a means by which I can escape to another world—a world of lovely fantasy.

While reading murder mysteries and writing tales of intrigue and horror, Plath was also planning 'a beautiful long fairy tale' that would be developed during the summer of 1946 and completed a year later. In the middle of writing this 26-page 'Stardust' story, she reviewed her work-in-progress in a diary entry that displays a sophisticated understanding of story development and narrative voice, where her evocation of waking to the sounds of the neighborhood at the story's opening are carefully crafted:[84]

2 FEBRUARY: I looked over the first chapter to my fairy story, and decided that I should either make the happenings seem natural, or marvel on the impossibility of them. I decided on the first, and made a few important changes. I've decided not to make it all goody-ish, preachy, or morally, unless sometimes I make an action, seemingly innocent, take on a deeper meaning. This is quite impossible since I am not that experienced (yet!)

'Stardust' Chapter 1

Nancy awoke with the pleasant sensation that a whole, unbroken stretch of summer vacation lay ahead of her—no more tutors, no more lessons for ever and ever so long. She turned over and yawned luxuriously.

A soft breeze blew the lazy, white curtains away from the screened windows. Sunbeams made their way through the blinds and gave the room a warm, golden, glow. Outside a lawnmower clacked monotonously. A milk truck stopped, and Nancy heard the clinking of the bottles as the milkman carried them to the doorstep. The truck started up again. Brrrooomm, it went, and caught its breath.

Brrrrrrroomm—and it was gone. The rasping drone of a locust predicted a hot day, and the sparrows and robins were having a gay conversation in the apple orchard.

Nancy was debating to herself whether she should tiptoe out into the fresh dawn of early morning or stay drowsing in the bed until breakfast, when her thoughts were interrupted by a tiny voice at her elbow.

"Hello, Nancy," it said.

Nancy stopped right in the middle of deciding that she would take a jam sandwich with her when she went out, and the voice repeated a little louder, "Hello, Nancy."

This time it came from right next to Nancy's ear. Cautiously she opened one eye. What she saw made both of her blue eyes fly open wide.

Standing on her pillow was a tiny little fairy!

After entering high school in fall 1947 Sylvia Plath began a three-year course of honors English studies with Wilbury Crockett, an innovative and inspiring teacher who would make a major impact on her understanding of literature and criticism, writing technique, and the socialist politics he embraced. As part of his group of students called the 'Crocketeers', Sylvia was required to participate in writing and producing class plays, provide articles for the school newspaper, get involved with some level of community service, and donate a few dollars she had earned to charity. Crockett was pivotal in forming Plath's professional identity as a writer, and he encouraged her to push her talents to the limit. Her enthusiasm for his class is recorded in an illustrated letter she wrote to her mother while in hospital, where she provided updates on school subjects as well as gossip on a fellow student.[85] As often seen in letters home or diary entries, Plath mentioned when her writing was singled out as the best in class. But she also made an unusual admittance as to how her work was egged on by her mother, always ambitious for her children's success, before adding a final note about competing with Shakespeare:

9 September: English 21 Here is the class I just love. I could sit and listen to Mr. Crockett all day. We finished reading our paraphrases and after we were through, Mr. Crockett said 'Now, after we've gone through the whole bunch, whose paper do you think was the best?' John Pollard raised his hand immediately and said, 'Sylvia's,' whereupon dear old Davy (Mr. Crockett) replied, 'I decidedly think so'. He also praised about 5 others, not Perry either! Well! Our combination (your suggestion and my effort, of course) worked nicely in this case, didn't it? In Art We worked in using masses of mixed color on paper. Not too interesting, as you may imagine!

Miscellaneous Remarks: (1) Prissy isn't so bad after all, although you'd wince, too, if you saw her in that lurid, patch-worky dress. (2) My English class has so stimulated me that I'm chock-full of ideas for new poems. I can't wait to get time to write them down. I can't let Shakespeare get too far ahead of me, you know. (3) I have ideas for lots of paintings, too.

After starting high school, Plath would put aside her fairy tales and adventure fiction in favor of more mature themes—notably, coming-of-age stories and experiences suitable for teen and women's magazines (see Ill. 14 below). At a time when her numerous interests and talents were pulling her in many directions at once, the fiction she wrote for her high school assignments and literary contests often feature a female protagonist, not unlike herself, wrestling with conflicting life and career choices. Crockett's students were expected to make every effort to get their works published, and by her freshman year at Smith, Plath had tracked all stories, poems, and articles she submitted to various publications, starting with thirty poems she sent to *Seventeen Magazine* at age 16 and 17.

Essays Plath typed for her first year in Crockett's class demonstrate how her writing skills were steadily improving. 'Artistic Description' includes lyrical segments that incorporate some her favorite subjects: the effects of color in light, tools and media of her artwork, moody weather, and the Atlantic ocean, always described realistically as green or gray:[86]

Color

If a partially filled ink bottle is held closely before one eye and turned so that the sun's rays pass through it, the beholder is suddenly transported into a soft chamber of shifting cerulean tints, and his whole perspective is changed by this simple action. Objects viewed through the bluish light bend and waver in distorted masses, as if seen under water. The deep, royal-blue background is colored by areas of darker blue, almost verging on purple. Liquid blue-black pools tremble in the shadows, and thin lines of pale turquoise play over the indigo surface in capricious patterns. The circular white high light, shooting off in dazzling sparkles like a brilliant diamond, is the sun. It sets blinding white reflections dancing at the slightest motion of the bottle. The kaleidoscopic variety of blue tones and overtones is stimulating to the eye, but after a few enchanting moments the small blue world is placed on a dusty desk top beside a pair of raw, red erasers and forgotten until the pen again needs to be filled.

Sight

That evening at dusk, the Public Gardens were shrouded with fog, and the City-world outside was muffled by a gray, velvet wrapper. The distant buildings showed in a fuzzy blur against the sky, while the outlines of the surrounding foliage were so faint and indefinite that one could fancy one had stepped into a charcoal drawing. Through the misty twilight, their posts obscured by the smoky vapor, the globes of the street lamps seemed magically suspended in air. Shadows passed by vaguely human in shape, showing their hurried pace as they entered the Gardens. They, too, were caught in the mysterious spell of the foggy night.

Sea

On a warm, midsummer day, the sea reminds me of a green marble-top veined with white marker, or of dusky green parrot feathers on white lace. The bottom of the sea, seen through the translucent amber water near shore, is reminiscent of cobbled streets drifted over with yellow earth. The slimy fronds of seaplants undulate beneath the surface, and the fleeting shadows of clouds pass over the ocean floor, sending the fish slipping to safety among the rubbery ruffles of brown seaweed. Far out toward the horizon, the wind sends shivers across the water.

Along with lengthy critical papers on the works of male canonical authors written for English class, Plath submitted a four-page report on *Mrs. Dalloway*, the only academic essay she would ever do on the work of Virginia Woolf.[87] Written during the last semester of high school, this paper exhibits her reading technique, her use of personal voice for literary analysis, and her fondness for visual metaphors. But it also reveals an attraction to characters and subjects that would continue to fascinate her and show up in later writing—most notably, Woolf's treatment of the workings of the psyche and the unconscious. Plath's favorite character from the novel is Septimus Smith, a sensitive, insightful, and deeply troubled young man, who after suffering from terrible visions of his experience as a soldier in World War I, committed suicide at the novel's end. Plath's initial response of shock and confusion upon encountering *Mrs. Dalloway* became one of appreciation, as seen in comments on how Woolf has accurately portrayed the complex nature of the thought processes (a technique of creating an often disjointed internal dialogue Woolf had initially praised in the work of James Joyce). Plath began the essay with a summary of her first and second impressions of the novel, followed by an elegant defense of the author's startling methods. The rest of the paper focuses on what she called 'passages I could read over and over without tiring'.

To read Mrs. Dalloway is to have a startling experience. The method of presentation is unexpected, to say the least, and for one unaccustomed to the 'stream-of-consciousness' technique, the first encounter is electrifying.

. . . My immediate reactions, as I emerged after the fourth paragraph, was one of annoyance. How confusing! What fuzzy rambling sentences! What blurred impressions! I went back to the beginning and tried again. This time it went a little better. But even so, I asked myself, to what purpose all this bubbling of fragmentary thoughts. Only after I had read the book twice could I attempt to answer the questions. For Virginia Woolf cannot be assimilated in one brief, painless reading. She must be cultivated gradually, patiently.

As you read along, somewhat baffled by the unfamiliar way of writing, there comes a sudden flash of insight and you say, 'Here is something I have often thought!' or 'Here is a new, refreshing observation!' It is as if the sun were gradually illuminating a dusty, shaded room. At first you thought, 'What a jumbled conglomeration of vague shapes and shadows!' But as the faint light rose and increased, strange tints were revealed, and a glossy depth was apparent in the furnishing. There was substance and order where you had been able to discern none.

As mind after mind is laid bare, you jump about from one person's disconnected train of thought to another's. Imagine that you could peer into the brain of any passer-by at will. Would the thoughts be arranged in grammatical sentences, paragraphed with careful regard as a subject? Far from it. Our thoughts are inconstant and always changing—a kaleidoscopic shifting of images, recollections and impressions. So it is in Mrs. Dalloway.

At the time Plath was writing this essay, she was also learning to act on stage for the first time, playing the role of Lady Agatha in *The Admirable Crichton*. Crockett had the task of organizing the senior plays at the school, and after a good deal of hard work, the performance and Plath herself received positive reviews.

While Plath would continue her interests in attending plays and at times performing on stage during her college years, her main focus, encouraged largely by Crockett, continued to be writing. Most of her creative writing during high school is quite serious in tone as she struggled with the 'big issues' and sorted out who she was and who she would become. Yet her intense need to write was reiterated in many texts, including the final lines of her 1948 prose-poem titled 'Neither Moonlight Nor Starlight' that summarized this undeniable drive:[88]

> I write only because
> There is a voice within me
> That will not be still.

1. Illustrated letter to mother at age 7, page 1, 1940, mixed medium

△ **2**. Landscape with waterfall, 1943, crayon ▷ **3**. 'The Happy Camper' self-portrait, 1945, mixed medium

The

Happy

Camper

'Twas the night before Monday, and in the plath house every creature was stirring Including a mouse.

Both Grammy and mummy were baking with care In hopes that dear grampy soon would be there.

Warren was sitting On the edge of his bed, Practicing tunes That danced in his head

4. 'Twas the night before Monday' card to Grandfather, *c.*1943–7, mixed medium

5. 'Are you always working?' card to Grandmother, *c.*1943–7, mixed medium

◁ **6**. Snow White, *c.*1944–7, tempera

△ **7**. Mermaid and birds, *c.*1945–6, colored pencil

△ **8**. Backstage', 1946, tempera

▽ **9**. 1947 Diary, June 21 entry, mixed medium

Robin
David F.

up into the sky. The birches are blowing and shimmering in the cool, sweet wind. Just now a robin hopped up close to my chair, and, after standing motionless and eyeing me warily for a few minutes, he darted his beak into the ground, and after a few seconds came up with a juicy worm which he promptly devoured and thereupon flew away. Well, I must get back to my story writing, so I'll say bye-bye for now.

June 21 - David and Ruthie arrived shortly after lunch today. David is taller, better-looking, and oh, so much improved (I mean nice!) we spent the afternoon and warm afternoon sun. We are eating all of our meals out doors, and Ruthie and I both hope to receive glamorous tans by staying in the sun in our bathing suits before supper we sunbathed and afterwards all four of us played baseball till it was too dark to stay out. (114)

June 22 - Today Ruthie and I woke up at 9:00 after having a very peaceful night's sleep, which is somewhat unusual. After breakfast we donned our sunsuits and accompanied the boys to the beach since it was such a glorious day. Even though we both had a slight cold and couldn't go on a picnic, the boys do stunts for a while [him] an adorable lifeguard told us to climb up on the high dive with him, and then he did some fancy dives for us. He even offered to show us how, but we said politely (as (6) even politely) "No thanks, not now!" He lost his high diver, but I just grabbed her in time. He got kind of mad and tried to pull me off, but I held him, held him tight, and suddenly high... He went flying over backwards and landed hard on the dock, looking some what surprised, as you may imagine. He took us out for a ride in his "outboard" boat with a peke... and it was fun! we landed a little (2) damp from being splashed "plash!..." Ruthie and I really began to turn red (15)

10. Chinese jug with plate of fruit, 1947, pastel

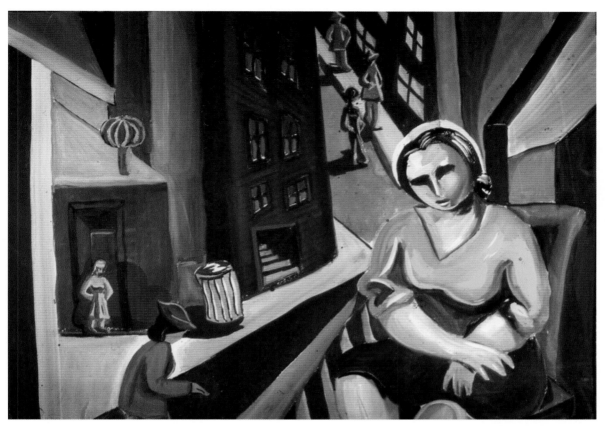

11. Street Scene with woman, c.1948–9, tempera

12. Three figures, c.1948–9, tempera

◁ **13**. Swaying cityscape, c.1947–50, tempera   △ **14**. Nativity scene, *c.*1948–50, tempera

15. 'Stella' and blonde cut-out dolls and outfits, 1945, mixed medium

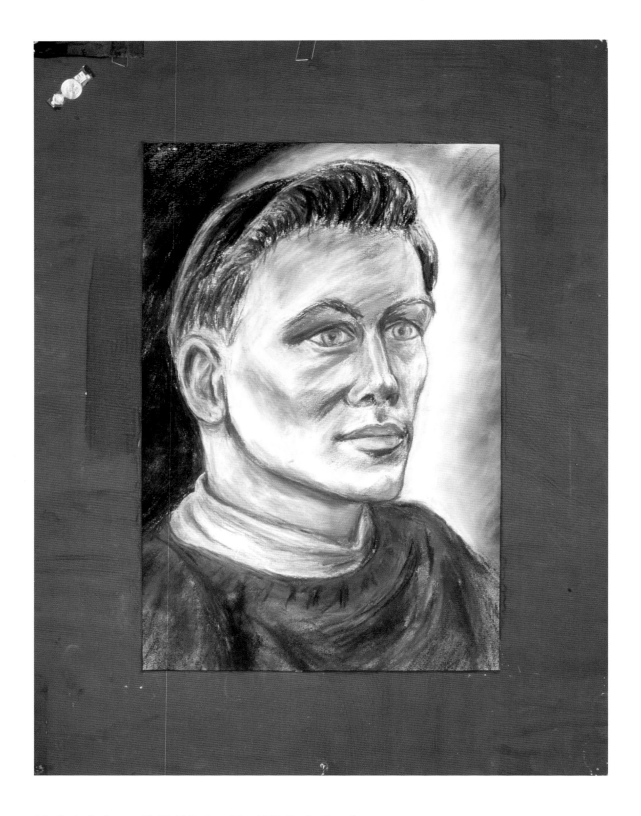

16. Portrait of man with 'Gold Key' medal, *c*.1946–7, mixed medium

17. Seascape at
Star Island, 1949,
water color

18. Camping at
Star Island, 1949,
water color

◁ **19**. Schoolgirl in a red sweater, eighth grade history
school book, 1946, mixed medium

△ **20**. 'SAVE HIM!', eighth grade history
school books, 1946

22. 'A War to End Wars' cover, eighth grade history school book, 1946, mixed medium

21. 'The World and the United States' cover, eighth grade history school book, 1946, mixed medium

11. Photo of Plath as Lady Agatha in 'The Admirable Crichton', 1950

The standard for writing 'sophisticated' humor in the early twentieth century was that of *The New Yorker* magazine, with influential contributors such as James Thurber and E. B. White creating works that championed this form of dry wit. The fact that one of Plath's story protagonists is named Louise Thurber implies she was aware of his work, and she had hoped to meet and possibly interview White during her guest editorship at *Mademoiselle*. She wrote numerous comical ditties, and her letters and diaries contain plenty of silly jokes and mild satire. But outright hilarity is rare in her texts, and most of her early experiments in writing focus on mastering traditional forms presented by the standards in popular and classical literature.

GARDENS AND MOODS OF NATURE

Flowers, gardens, and the beauty of nature are frequent topics in Plath's diary entries at age 12 and 13, and also show up regularly in her poetry, stories, school

essays, and art work. Her love and knowledge of flowers is evident in detailed diary descriptions of gardens and bouquets, at times accompanied by color illustrations. Just as her father had grown flowers at their Winthrop home, she kept a close eye on her own garden, where she planted violets and noted her obsession with pressing flowers into books.[89] In 1945 she chose to write of her garden scene for an Art Club assignment on the subject, 'From My Window', and the following year she wrote a poem called 'My Garden' into her diary.[90] The changing seasons and nature's beauty provided topics for writing throughout Plath's life, and the poems of Sara Teasdale, many of which she copied into her diary—'Late October', 'Full Moon', 'Autumn Dusk', 'Mountain Water', 'There Will Be Stars', 'Beautiful, Proud Sea'—influenced the nature poetry she was composing as a young teen.[91] In summer of 1946 she recorded her poem about a lake in her diary, intended for publication in the local paper. This untitled work presents the surface of the water as a mirror, an image of literal reflection she would develop to encompass the contemplation of remembrance, thought patterns, and clear-sighted self-reflection in later works.[92]

The lake is a creature
Quiet, yet wild,
Rough, and yet gentle,
An untamed child

Tranquil and blue
Where the boats slip by
Whirlpools of silver
Where the oars dip nigh

Emerald green
When the clouds scud-o
Whirlpools of silver
Gay white caps toss

The lake is really
The earth's clear eye
Where are mirrored the moods
Of the wind and the sky

Plath's treatment of landscapes and changing seasons had been expanding past the more bucolic descriptions of natural beauty seen in her earlier diaries. And since she was conscious of climate and weather phenomenon as important tools in

12. Photo of Plath in Wellesley garden, 1947

narrative writing, she learned to depict nature's variant moods with poetic flare and precision. She had noted her first experience with the extremely destructive side of weather while living in Winthrop at age 5, when a huge storm that hit the coast might have destroyed her grandparents' home on the oceanfront, if not for a sea wall her grandfather had constructed. In more than one text she recalled the incident, which her mother had portrayed to her children as the ancient Norse god Thor expressing his anger. Wind as a potentially destructive force with personal intent, often associated with masculine figures, would show up in Plath's writing thereafter, including her short stories, 'The Miraculous End of Miss Minton' written in 1947, and in 'The East Wind', its 1949 variation (see pp. 57–8). In her November 1949 diary entry, she wrote of 'the reprimanding sternness in the biting wind . . . there is no yielding. I see him sweep down the streets in a passion of righteousness like a staunch Puritan Minister.'[93]

Plath admitted to a lifelong worship of sunshine and ocean beaches, yet she also appreciated winter weather, at least while young. Her 1946 essay titled 'Snow-storms' started with the statement: 'I seem to be the only one in my family who really enjoys snowstorms.'[94] In a 1947 diary account of an unusual weather front, she detailed images of snow, ice, clouds, and mist, images she would continue to highlight in many of her mature texts:

> 1 FEBRUARY: Today certainly contained many freaks of Nature. During algebra the sky suddenly grew black and a kind of snow-hail came flying down from the clouds, driven furiously by the wind. The sky was dark with millions of flying specks of snow and ice. After a few minutes the squall subsided and the last lacy snowflakes floated gently to earth. The only sign of the snow squall was a bit of moisture on the sidewalk. So Nature's tantrum really amounted to nothing.

In another 1947 diary entry Plath was again experimenting with character setting as she wrote of the sounds coming from downstairs and the weather outside her window:

> 18 JUNE: I slept fitfully last night, and awoke at 10:00 this morning. I did hear grammy and Mary, the cleaning woman, accentuating their vehement statements denouncing Curley and Kelly by means of savage jabs of their mops and brooms. I shut my bedroom door, and in the comparative quietness I looked out my window. The sky was overcast with a low, cloudy fog. And the mists were rising over the hills in the distance. Wraith-like vapors rolled over the fields in the chilly calm of morning.

Amidst notes of her planned camp activities that summer, Plath wrote of her hopes that the delightful quaintness of the place would help her get ideas for the new mystery story she was planning. After commenting on how the early morning quiet provided good writing conditions, she offered the sense impressions of 'lonely' breezes, her unmade bed, and her color-coordinated outfit illustrated on the previous page. Her imagined dialogue with the diary itself, now more frequent in entries, is unusually direct in this passage [ellipses Plath's]:

> 27 JUNE: I have just a little time to write in you before Grammy gets up. You know that if anybody is bustling around the house it's so hard to write! . . . The cooling morning breezes are perfumed and they are lonely, too, I guess, from wandering around so long without anybody to keep them company except the birds. . . . The bedcovers are thrown back and the bottom sheet is all rumpled—just the way I slept on it. Of course I'll make the beds! Don't get so indignant—just a little while longer! I'm wearing my black skirt and white blouse with the black bows for the trip over (see page 103!)

Plath added the sense of taste to the narrative as she noted her breakfast and lunch, admitting to her hearty appetite: 'for lunch I had waffles, REAL MAPLE SYRUP AND DEERFOOT FARM SAUSAGES! Ah! how eating delights my little heart!!'

When Plath made up a story theme or personality she liked it might take on numerous incarnations before settling into its final form. The most notable example of this progression began in 1947 with a character sketch of a spinster who became the protagonist for the story with an 'awful lesson': 'The Miraculous End of Miss Minton'.[95] Just as water is central to other works of this period, Plath used the power of wind as her plot device in this story. Fascinated with the concept of unseen powers, she wrote that the idea for the Miss Minton character also came from the air, delivered by its invisible force that could manifest as either a soft, whispering breeze or a life-threatening storm:

> 10 FEBRUARY: By some trick of fate I wrote a few silly paragraphs about someone I thought of, the idea came whole out of the thin air, so I just put it down on paper. I have decided to copy it down here, and destroy the original papers. Listen now to the story of the . . . 'The Miraculous End of Miss Minton': Miss Minton walked with precise steps about her apartment living room, dusting each bit of antique furniture with care. It was spring. Against her will, Miss Minton had opened wide her front

window to give her apartment its annual airing. She felt an old softening in her heart, as ice must feel before a thaw. Rather uncomfortable, she thought. Suddenly Miss Minton felt a strange pang of loneliness. Odd that she, one who had always done her duty (no matter how hard), odd that she should feel lonely.

A soft breeze whispered through the open window and stirred the starched white curtains. It seemed to say something, Miss Minton thought guiltily, seemed to say that something was going to—to—

The breeze grew a little stronger, and rustled the stiff coverings on Miss Minton's treasured furniture. In fact the little breeze began to rush about in the once tidy room in a veritable gale. It knocked over pictures, lamps, vases, tables and chairs. Miss Minton stood paralyzed with horror—unable to cry out. The very rug beneath her feet was being lifted from the varnished floor by the raging wind! Miss Minton felt one terrible moment of being swept into the air like a bubble and spinning about upside down, nothing solid beneath her feet. Before she could regain her balance, she felt herself being blown outside, lifted right out of the open window, feather duster and all, into the warm spring air she fell down, down, all topsy turvy inside like you feel in dreams, only this wasn't a dream—oh no! Miss Minton flew so fast that no human eye could follow her; no human ear could hear her last breathless gasp of terror. There was one last moment of bright April sunshine and then there was darkness. The earth had opened, and had closed over the head of the terrible Miss Minton forever! Since this day the name of Miss Minton has never been heard again. But since we should never forget this awful lesson, this tale was sent to me by some unseen power to tell you.

The ominous gale that created so much havoc in 'The Miraculous End of Miss Minton' became the featured title for 'East Wind', written in 1949.[96] In this story Miss Minton is disturbed by the persistent rush of 'wind music' in her ears prior to encountering an 'elfin child' in the street. She soon finds herself being led by this child to the dark surface of a river, and is prevented from drowning by a sudden gust of wind that carries her into the sky toward an airy death. Knowing her end is near, she imagines being rid of her ugly cloak and 'drab apartment', no longer containing the treasured antiques, furniture, and starched white curtains of her earlier Miss Minton story. But when the wind shifts its course, her death is revealed to be a fantasy. She makes her way home in safety—though she has to step around a suspicious dark lump at the entrance to her apartment. Plath explored the possible life of this elfin child (who also turned out to be unreal) and the locale of Miss Minton's near drowning in another 1949 story titled 'The Dark River', a recurring image in numerous texts. Miss Minton's final incarnation is seen in Plath's first major prize-winning story, 'Sunday at the Mintons', published in *Mademoiselle* in 1952. This Miss Minton is an imaginative though sheltered woman, living a constricted life with her straight-thinking and badgering brother. During an afternoon outing he drowns in the sea, but this, too, is only a fantasy as he makes his way home with his sister in tow.

WRITING DRAMA AND ROMANCE

Fiction Plath wrote in her early teens includes attempts in Gothic horror, murder mystery, and fantasy genres that require serious drama. She was reading Poe at age 12, and his frightening themes can be seen in her 1946 story 'The Mummy's Tomb', a three-page thriller about a young heroine up against supernatural evil lurking in a museum. In 1947 she wrote a radio play entitled 'The White Mantle Murder', perhaps inspired by the 'Mystery Theater' radio programs she listened to as a child. She commented on one murderous story plot, stating, 'I plan to have some very mysterious, as well as romantic, parts in it, but it is quite hard to make up an interesting beginning when my best parts are in the middle!'[97] When imagined drama ran short, she also took the advice of the professionals to recreate it from the ordinary incidents in daily life. At age 14 she wrote a poem that her mother identified as the beginning of her tendency to embellish personal experience to create literature with 'tragic overtones'. Plath launched this venture in writing drama after her newly finished pastel drawing of a Chinese jug and plate of fruit was accidentally blurred by her grandmother[98] (see Pl. 10). She repaired the damage to her still life with no indication of being upset, but that evening she turned to poetry and her diary to write otherwise. The artistic dividend of the damaged 'best pastel yet' was her best poem yet, written in a style she judged to be contemporary:

> 30 MAY: In my art lesson today (which was private, as usual) I finished my picture of a Chinese jug and plate of grapes, cherries, and oranges. We both (Miss Hazelton and I) agree that it is my best pastel yet. I took it home proudly, and immediately showed it to mum, who was very pleased. However, someone accidentally rubbed a cloth against it and destroyed part of the clear coloring. I was heartbroken. I patched it up again, but you know, nothing like that is as good as new. However, I wrote a poem about it (my best one yet) in a very new, modern style.

'I Thought that I Could Not be Hurt'

I thought that I could not be hurt;
I thought that I must surely be
impervious to suffering—
immune to mental pain
or agony.

My world was warm with April sun
my thoughts were spangled green and gold;
my soul was filled up with joy, yet felt
the sharp, sweet pain that only joy
can hold.

 ★ ★ ★ ★ ★ ★ ★

Then suddenly my world turned gray
and darkness wiped aside my joy.
a dull and aching void was left
where careless hands had reached out to destroy

my silver web of happiness.
The hands then stopped in wonderment,
for, loving me, they wept to see
the tattered ruins of my firmament.

(How frail the human heart must be—
a throbbing pulse, a trembling thing—
a fragile, shining instrument
of crystal, which can either weep, or sing.)

'I Thought I Could Not Be Hurt' turned out to be a favorite among works she submitted the following year to her English teacher, Wilbury Crockett. He told Aurelia Plath that he had shared it with a colleague, who was amazed that one so young could have had such a devastating experience. When Mrs. Plath related this conversation to her daughter, she smiled and replied, 'Once a poem is made available to the public, the right of interpretation belongs to the reader.'[99] While Mrs. Plath suggested the many upbeat works rejected by *Seventeen* caused her daughter to explore 'the darker recesses of self' in writing, this interpretation does not address Sylvia Plath's real attraction to the macabre and Gothic idiom, and to high drama of all sorts.[100] One exceptionally dynamic poem she wrote at age 16, 'To Ariadne (Deserted by Theseus)', captures the classic drama of romantic tragedy, at a time when she was studying ancient Greek culture and art. In this poem she positioned Ariadne's 'white-hot rage' as she faces the sea—an image she would return to in October 1962 in planning a poem that almost certainly refers to her own 'white hot fury' after being left by her husband[101] (see p. 118). The last two stanzas of this 1949 poem show the heroine transiting from wrath to resignation in concordance with the moods of the sea, wind, and sky:

> The white-hot rage abates, and the—futility.
> You lean exhausted on the rock. The sea
> Begins to calm . . .
> . . . while the black clouds flee.
>
> ★　　★　　★　　★　　★　　★　　★
>
> Why do you stand and listen only to
> The sobbing of the wind along the sand?

In two consecutive entries written later that summer, Plath discussed various boys that held her interest, and the possibility of being in love. In one case she interrupted other work to write what she called, in code, 'quite passionate and rather lustful' pages of a new adventure story:

> 18 JULY: All the while I kept writing more of my mystery story. I must admit that I stopped once and quickly wrote four long pages of a planet story which I called 'Mission to Mars.' It was more or less in the middle, and was quobite pobassobi unobate and robath ober lobust fobul, if I do say so. I hid it away among my secret papers and commenced upon my mystery.

The next day she noted her brilliantly colored dreams, including one where she was having adventures similar to those of her story protagonists:

> In one of them I was the beautiful detective-ess who solved the ghostly murder of a young man. In another I rescued my friends from drowning on a huge ice glob in Antarctica. The other two were both very romantic.

Plath decorated three pages of one 1948 diary narrative with a wide, bright-colored rainbow around her script, and began the entry with a reference to it: 'Today was even more colorful and dreamy than this bright rainbow border.' She followed with a description of a school dance, offering one of her diary's most theatrical romantic anecdotes:

28 FEBRUARY: The ladies choice was the last dance, so seeing that Dave was picked first, I chose Tommy. He kept holding me tighter and tighter until I could hardly breath. I'm just so 'in love' with him that it hurts...I was just in dreamland. Tommy, Tommy, Tommy!!!—if you don't say you like me (this year!) I shall die of thwarted love. At least you know that I like you, but have plenty of other boyfriends for your competition. Ahh, Yes! I'm afraid I'm infatuated with Tommy Dugan.... Betsy can be kissed by him every day and twice on Sunday but I've had the one triumphant night!

Whether Plath saw the irony of being in love with her second choice for dance partner is uncertain, but by the time she was a senior in high school, her dates were steady enough to be recorded and organized onto lists—in one case, color-coded. They were also the subject of amusement, as seen in an illustrated note entitled 'Excuses for not dating'[102] (other date, babysitting, TB, cancer, turned communist), and a poem on adolescent love. 'Adolescence', likely written during her high school years, approaches the narrator's temporary love of 'every youth' with the mild sarcasm and self-mockery she cultivated in her writing. The third of five stanzas laments:

> My tears drop down into the dust
> For every lively lad
> I might have known and loved but if
> The chance I'd had.

Plath was enthralled with the possibilities of experiencing real romance and deep emotion, which she would dutifully capture in writing, most often in her diary, which continued to serve as her daily mirror and confidential friend. During her summer vacation on Martha's Vineyard at age 14, she wrote of having experiences where every moment was filled with the 'glory' of real living. The following fall when her new English teacher, Mr. Crockett, played a recording of Millay's 'The Ballad of the Harp Weaver' and 'Renaisance' spoken by the author, she described the poems as 'so beautiful, I could hardly keep from crying'.[103] After school she came home and wrote 'Alone and Alone in the Woods Was I', the first poem since 'May', which she described as 'long and deep', and 'of the two best I've ever written'. She also wrote another 'dramatic word-picture' and commented: 'I really out-poured my soul into these two, and will have a nice clean corner of my mind for storing up new impressions in the future!'

'My Memory Book', however, became less informative about her art and academic work as her interest in boys and romance began to take more of her attention. Her red scrapbook, with its photos, clippings, memorabilia, and running commentary, would eventually replace formal diaries as a record of important events during high school years. With four weekly painting classes at school, and another lesson at Miss Hazelton's house, she may have decided to reserve her diary for private thoughts and writing experiments, now more serious in tone after studying with Crockett. Drawings and doodles, however—most notably, her hour-glass-shaped women—still competed for space in her diary to the point that they were virtually banned. A week before turning fifteen, she complained that her 'scribblings' took up too much space, and that they showed the 'weak side' of her character.[104] Plath obviously considered them a more frivolous art form, not in keeping with the gravity of her writing, for on the following day she wrote across the top of the entry, 'Farewell to all drawings. There will be no such gay things herein! (SOB)'. At the first line of text, she drew an arrow pointing up to her farewell statement that said: 'Dear Diary: There! You see I have my resolution not to draw in here any longer'.[105] But the impulse to illustrate her writing, backed up by the long-time habit of mixing the mediums, proved to be irresistible. Within a month the drawings had made a full comeback in her diaries, with no further comments on the forgotten ban.

Facing Future

'I AM I'

'As for who am I? what am I? . . . that will preoccupy me til the day I die', Sylvia Plath wrote to new pen pal Eddie Cohen at age 17, two months after graduating from high school.[106] Another revelatory statement in this letter, however, makes it clear that she saw herself as a sophisticated young woman with strong intellectual and artistic leanings: 'When my little pals were trying out their first formals, I was reading Brave New World by Huxley and doing self-portraits in pencil.' Three years later she wrote the award-winning story 'Initiation', which follows her coming-of-age breakthrough in self-esteem and understanding. After struggling to be accepted socially during junior high, she finally achieved her goal to become 'popular' after

13. Self-portrait, *c.*1947–50, pencil

being asked to join a high school sorority. She pasted the sorority's invitation card into her high school scrapbook and added a note stating, 'I have been asked to join one of two sororities at high school! After squeaking through a grueling initiation week, I became a member of a Sub-Deb Club. It's amazing—but true.'[107] 'Initiation' features what she described in story notes as an imaginative, intelligent, and sensitive girl who observes the chattering group of sorority girls from the outside.[108] Her approach to outlining the story was to first draw the figure of the female protagonist, associated with the symbol of the heather-bird—'strong and proud in their freedom and their sometimes loneliness'—around which the plot line was written, an approach of drawing first and writing second she retained from her youth.

The series of progressively detailed sketches on the left side of the page may be depicting Millicent, the protagonist of 'Initiation', carrying a book, wearing flat shoes as she walks down the street—a more studious personality than the figure on the right, posed in high heels, who may represent the persona of Millicent after her social transformation, or one of the sorority girls described in the notes. Yet the heroine eventually rejects the opportunity to become a sorority member after meeting a man on a bus who talks of eating the eyebrows of heather-birds for breakfast, a bird that he says 'live on the mythological moors and fly about all day long'. Plath aligned her narrator's choice at the end of the story with allegiance to her close girl friend, not an initiate, whom she did not want to leave behind, as well as her 'new friend' who introduced her to this symbolic bird. And as in much of her earlier fiction, this personal identity is not defined in relation to the popular crowd, but formed from within, hinting at the qualities of the 'loner' she felt herself to be while in junior high. The last line of the story, 'And she knew that her own private initiation had begun,' presents the soul-searching of this mature 'initiate' in a manner that may have been informed by religious leaders and philosophies she was studying in high school and in her Smith classes. In draft essay notes for an introductory course on religion in spring 1952, she admitted that she was not a 'believer', and positioned her views within secular values: 'I don't consider myself one of those humanists . . . I am in favor of a healthy creative arrogance . . . I am an ardent pacifist.'[109] Yet the 'heather-bird' would continue to have a special meaning for Plath, serving as a form of totem, perhaps still associated with her personal identity as an artist and freethinker. Years after writing this story, she was horrified

14. 'Heather-Birds Eyebrows' story notes, 1952

when she witnessed her husband shoot a moorland grouse, a reaction that caused him to give up hunting.[110]

Stories like 'The Christmas Heart' and the 51-paged 'I Lied for Love' were written, according to Mrs. Plath's note, as an attempt to break into the 'True Story slicks'.[111] Yet many stories that explore boy–girl relationships reflect Plath's ambivalence and confusion about romance, and long-term worries about finding a mate who could live with her artistic habits. Self-explorations and relationships between women are far more common topics. 'Dialogue', an early 1953 story she wrote for a Smith English class, consists of 17 pages of heart-to-heart philosophical musings between two friends, Allison and Maureen. They talk of the purpose of life, whether the universe has order or evil spirits, and 'freaks of nature' they call 'grotesques'. To Maureen's statement, 'Psychologically, we are all grotesques,' Allison responds, 'Distortion has its uses. Artistic effect, you know.' This paper of pure dialogue concludes with Maureen asking her friend how she might affirm her life. Allison replies that she must try to 'figure out the most creative way to spend thirty million minutes, that's all, no opium, even if the hurt is bad.' Plath's high school stories often open with female narrators, poor or isolated, looking out their bedroom windows to people and scenes below, or out the windows of trains and buses during routine trips. Many 1948 stories such as 'Sarah', 'Allison', and 'Gramercy Park' present older women reminiscing about their past or brightening with new (female) friendships, while 'The Attic View' begins with a young woman in poor health who looks from her bed out at the 'bustling back street' of her boarding house in the 'shabby section of town'.[112] When a fellow office-worker tells her of a 'free secretarial night course for working class girls' the thought of 'sudden possibility of a future—of advancement' is likened to 'a glittering rainbow in her dismal world'. But while wondering about what life is like in the hereafter, she fades into unconsciousness and dies. The story ends with the landlady leading another tenant up the stairs to show the room, a young woman who also looks out the window to the view below.

A few stories Plath wrote at this time in her life connect images of water to luminous visions and fantasy, as she attempted to articulate the movement of her own imagination. As a junior she wrote 'The Brink' about a young woman named Janet who contemplated the 'unreal' passing landscape from a bus, where its 'shifting window pictures' formed 'something artificial ... prepared solely for her own amusement' that signified nothing.[113] When looking at her reflection in the window of a passing car, she thinks of how distanced it is, and watches her own thoughts 'eddying through' the 'deep pool that was her mind'. When she notices a patch of blooming forsythia, however, the vision creates 'tiny bubbles' that 'broke when they reached the pool's surface. The icy water tried to close over the bubbles but she would not let them.' Janet's view of the colorful flowers pulls her back from the brink of looking at life and people as insignificant and empty. In the 1949 story 'East Wind', an older woman living in a 'drab apartment' nearly drowns in the dark waters of a river, but is instead drawn into a gale that takes her whirling into the air. At the story's end the event is exposed as imaginary, while in 'The Dark River' Plath extends the theme further, incorporating elements from other stories. Her first-person narrator makes the acquaintance of a young woman as they sit watching the river waters.[114] This woman tells her, 'You will be the first to know the story of myself and the dark river,' and goes on to describe her youthful self as 'an elfin creature ... a lonely child with a story book in her lap', and her failed relationship with a young man she had loved. Using one of her most consistent plot devices of this period, Plath's final paragraph positions this encounter as an illusion:

The form of the young girl faded, and I found myself staring at the cloud patterns reflected in the river... but even as I looked up I knew that she, too, would be gone; for she was part of the river, and the radiance in her eyes had only been the sunlight dancing on the surface of the water.

Again recycling this concept, during the same period she wrote a poem called 'The Dark River' that explores love that is 'silent in its longing', but troubled by a dark river that 'runs between us... and oh, the crossing of it's vanquished | Braver ones than you or I'.[115] Plath's 1949 story entitled 'Among the Shadows Throng' came particularly close to depicting her position as an aspiring writer looking for exciting subject matter.[116] It begins with a description of another humble bedroom where 'a curious observer' reads a rejection notice from 'Youth Publications'. As two young women discuss their ambitions to get published, the main character, named Louise Thurber, questions her friend [ellipses Plath's]:

Do you ever have that feeling... that you'd like to subject yourself to every sort of situation and then write about it? I'd like to do that... to know all the feelings of a cripple, or of someone about to die, and yet be able to come back to myself again and write down my thoughts and emotions. I never wanted to be trapped in one personality... and I want to be everyone and still myself, too.

Louise Thurber's concept of overcoming the singularity of existence, while also cherishing the self, would be taken to a place beyond boundary when Plath expressed her famous desire to be omniscient and call herself God. After abandoning her regular diary writing for more than a year, Plath briefly used a new booklet to capture 'the rapture of being seventeen'—what she called the 'perfect' time of her life. This 13 November 1949 passage offers a careful distillation of topics she had explored extensively in her writing, most certainly recopied from notes, as seen in her 1947 diary statement on her first Miss Minton story: 'I have decided to copy it down here, and destroy the original papers.'[117] By the time she was composing this astonishing narrative, she had already been seriously analyzing her creative works for a full decade. Plath's heightened self-awareness and philosophical vision here offers a glimpse of the 'omniscient' perspective she now wished for. Her bedroom— no longer shared with her mother after her brother left for prep school—contained objects that identify her at the crossroads of past and future: her pictures of friends, the 'peaceful' colors and 'quiet lines' of her furniture, childhood books of poetry and fairy tales, and her desk facing the window, the spot from which she wrote. A description of wind moving down the street is again personified as an unruly force, although here it is a stern patriarch, a ghost from the nonexistent past who does not 'yield'—a persona that resonates with her own absent father. The first segment of this passage also contains three of Plath's more frequently quoted statements: 'I want, I think, to be omniscient,' 'I think I would like to call myself, "the girl who wanted to be God,"' and 'I am I—I am powerful.' Yet between the first two statements (not included in the *Letters Home* version), Plath mentioned her appreciation of the 'spark of divine insanity' she felt could help reshape humanity's 'crippled frame of existence', before protesting her potential destiny to be 'classified' and 'qualified' [ellipses Plath's]:

13 NOVEMBER: As of today I have decided to keep a diary again—just a place where I can write my thoughts and opinions when I have a moment. Somehow I have to keep and hold the rapture of being seventeen. Every day is so precious, I feel infinitely sad at the thought of all this time melting further and further away from me as I grow older. Now, now is the perfect time of my life. In reflecting back upon these last 16 years, I can see the tragedies and happiness, all relative—all unimportant now...fit only to smile upon a bit mistily. I still do not know myself. Perhaps I never will. But I feel free—unbound by responsibility. I still can come up to my own private room with my drawings hanging from the walls...with John Hodges and Bob Reedman and Rod and Bruce and Paul smiling at me from the pictures pinned up over my bureau. It is a room suited to me...tailored, uncluttered and peaceful. The colors are subdued— peach and gray, brown-gold maple—a highlight of maroon here and there. I love the quiet lines of the furniture—the two bookcases filled with poetry books and fairy tales saved from childhood. At the present moment I am very happy, sitting at my desk and looking out at the bare trees around the house across the street—the dull gray sky like a slate of icy marble propped against the hills. The leaves lie in little withered heaps, blown in pale orange piles in the gutters. There is a reprimanding sternness in the biting wind...there is no yielding. I see him sweep down the streets in a passion of righteousness like a staunch Puritan Minister...A ghost of the old days which never were. I could go on and on. Always I want to be an observer. I want to be affected by life deeply, but never so blinded that I cannot see my share of existence in a wry, humorous light—and mock myself as I mock others. I am afraid of getting older...I am afraid of getting married. Spare me from the relentless cage of routine and rote. I want to be free...free to know people and their backgrounds...free to move to different parts of the world so I may learn that there are other morals and

standpoints besides my own. I want, I think, to be omniscient—and a bit insane. That is the trouble with the world—(of course I can dictate from my judgment seat) not enough people have that spark of divine insanity that can retwist this crippled frame of existence which deforms all of us so horribly. I think I would like to call myself, 'The girl who wanted to be God.' Yet if I were not in this body, where would I be— perhaps I am destined to be classified and qualified. But, oh, I cry out against it. I am I—I am powerful—but to what extent? I am I.

The passage continues with Plath examining herself in the mirror, where she reflects on how her own idealized and cherished self-image might come into conflict with the one looking back at her. This passage anticipates her central concern with the relationship between the twin or double within herself, a theme she would study and develop in depth in later works. Plath made a few more commonplace entries in this diary that ended a few months later, but this 1949 narrative sets the tone for the new journals of Sylvia Plath that would begin the following fall. She graduated from Bradford Senior High School with a partial scholarship to attend Smith College in Northampton, Massachusetts, one of the country's most elite women's schools, and her first choice for undergraduate study. Plath expressed the shocking initiation the young high school graduate experienced upon leaving the sheltered world of home and schoolmates in an amusing and ironic cartoon illustration featured in the local newspaper. Spreading across the top of an article on high school graduation exercises, her drawing depicts a line-up of graduates in their black caps, with oversized heads (including one woman with a dog, also capped), happy with their achievements and accompanied by musical notes. The final two frames, however, are occupied by one realistically proportioned girl, diploma in hand, who walks through the academy's high Greek columns only to fall into the fires of the outside world—where her hair replicates the shape of the blazing flames.

FASHION STATEMENTS

'Closet Drama'

A bard named Shelly wrote about
the desire of moths for a star
describing how each winged lout
found food for thought afar.
Perhaps lean years have made this bug

15. 'Sylvia's view of graduation' drawing from *The Townsman*, 1948

a materialist—heaven knows
he now satisfies his hungry mug
by eating up my clothes![118]

Sylvia Plath loved to wear fine clothes, and her wardrobe provided a central focus for her evolving self-image. In illustrated letters home from camp as a young teen she began describing various outfits and costumes she admired or purchased, including those she had sewn herself, using a professional fashion vocabulary. She was taken up with the raging movie star culture of the forties, whose shapely, sultry actresses offered the standard models for female beauty and high fashion. Her diary entries discuss the performances of various stars of 'moving pictures' such as Ronald Colman, Marlene Deitrich, Judy Garland, and Margaret O'Brien, along with a letter she received from Hedy Lamarr and a signature from Bette Davis. She kept a collection of Greer Garson, Shirley Temple, and L'il Abner cut-out paper dolls, but their wardrobes could not compete with the wildly exotic and sexy outfits she was designing for two cut-out women dolls she made at age 12. Their eighty outfits—including hats, shoes, and accessories—confirm Plath's fascination with clothing design and its potential as a career.[119] One diary note describes a few dresses she was making for 'Stella' that include 'a pale blue evening gown, a Mexican costume and a suit-blue skirt, red jerkin and white long-sleeved sweater'.[120] These elaborate clothes also display her love of bright colors, flashy patterns, and attention to detail seen in much of her visual art, and her tendency to create in profusion once she fastened onto a topic or activity (see Pl. 15; Chapter 5, p. 191; Afterword, pp. 225, 228–9, 231–2).

As managing guest editor of *Mademoiselle* in June 1953, Plath was immersed in the world of high fashion with other college women from across the country. Regardless of this stressful experience (shortly before her first suicide attempt in August), she hoped to revisit this professional arena by entering the highly competitive 'Prix de Paris' contest *Vogue* magazine sponsored for college seniors. In fall 1954, with her post-graduation plans uncertain, the contest's first prize of a year in Paris working for *Vogue* sounded exciting. She was also keen to find a professional job. The contest rules required applicants to write a statement on why they entered the Prix de Paris, along with two longer essays on the subjects of fashion and the writer's impressions of the current American arts scene. Plath's draft statement of intent for the contest outlines her interest in 'writing articles, analyzing layouts and inventing feature and fashion displays that will attract the *Vogue* reader. This is not mere nebulous dreaming. This is practical experience.'[121] She also admitted her financial incentive, and talked of the Prix de Paris as 'the golden apple on top of the glass hill in the fairytale. I like riding up glass hills, only the golden apple crowning the whole venture gives it the requisite spice.'

Drafts Plath made for the contest's fashion essay, titled 'Party for a Princess', suggest a children's fashion presentation using a literary theme 'to hold the display together'. Drawing on favorite books from her own childhood, she used humorous quotes from *The Wind in the Willows,* along with savvy fashion journalism gained from her experience with *Mademoiselle*. These notes propose storybook settings for special events such as a birthday or tea, as well as outfits that would offer:

> that particular enchanted look for a party-goer. Here, a party dress that will bewitch the most discriminating young miss. A pale yellow dress of daffodil crisp nylon patterned with tiny white stars.
>
> Summertime goes with a shepherdess. A forest green cotton bodice that laces over a full-skirted frock of white, bordered with a print of laurel leaves. Straw hat ties with green bow, tilts back/wide brimmed, wreathed with daisies.
>
> Beach wear for the shore patrol.
>
> A picnic basket of fashion, both practical and pretty.
>
> On a Picnic We Will Go.
>
> 'There's cold chicken inside it,' replied the Rat briefly; 'coldtonguecoldhamcoldbeefpickledgherkinsaladfrenchrollscressandwidgespottedmeatgingerbeerlemonadesodawater...'

Plath abandoned the essay and instead submitted 'Wardrobe for Six Weeks in Europe', which offers advice to women planning a visit abroad—a topic she had already carefully considered. After receiving one of ten honorable mentions for her *Vogue* essays, Plath was awarded a Fulbright scholarship to attend Newnham College, Cambridge in fall 1955 for a Masters degree in English literature. While at Cambridge she wrote an article about touring the clothing stores and forecasting 'May Week Fashions' for the Cambridge literary newspaper, *Varsity*, which included four photographs of herself showing off the spring collection—including two poses in a polka-dot bathing suit. (see Chapter 3, p. 166).[122]

MIXING DISCIPLINES AT SMITH

In Sylvia Plath's entrance essay to Smith College, she wrote 'English and Art are my favorite courses,' stating it is 'the creative aspect of these subjects' that appealed to her.[123] While she dedicated much of her first two years at Smith College to visual art and writing, her study of literary technique and criticism resulted in steady progress and kudos not matched in her visual art. In journals and letters she made numerous references to the act of writing, which, unlike that of painting and drawing, could be experienced with the full force of all the senses. She was also drawn to writers who employed strong sensual and visually charged imagery. In the spring of 1951, when her art and writing began to interweave and overlap in all forms, she handed in an essay on an Amy Lowell poem entitled 'The Imagery in Patterns', identified as her 'personal favorite'.[124] In relating how Lowell used imagery to convey the 'sorrow and rebellion' of a woman who finds her lover had been killed in what Plath called 'a pattern called war', she touched upon her own fearful vision of women trapped in a cruel world designed by men. After offering a detailed analysis of the poem's imagery, focusing on 'the richly dressed lady walking up and down' what Lowell described as the 'patterned garden paths', Plath then contrasted the sensuous images of the woman's skin with the 'artificial stiffness' of her gown before stating her personal rebellion against the 'manmade' patterns such as a third world war.

Plath's final identification of the poem's 'clear imagery' that 'intensifies and answers' her own emotions demonstrates how she chose and developed her artistic and literary subjects. In a 1953 essay, 'Edith Sitwell and the Development of Her Poetry',[125] one of two class papers she wrote on Sitwell, Plath equated the poet's colorful, sensual language with that of Christina Rossetti's 'Goblin Market' before commenting on how a child might better respond to it.[126] She also likened Sitwell's 'acute and vivid observations' to that of a 'terribly clever and technically adroit child' who awakens in 'a very personal and intimate wonderland'—a child that sounds very much like the young Sylvia Plath. She went on to describe the other side of this 'bucolic world' where the 'storybook animals turn harsh and grunting and all is mired' in what Sitwell called 'heavy brutish greedy darkness'. She then quoted the poet's lines on how 'Destiny is befouled' in the darker side of nature in a stanza that ends: 'the country gentlemen wander, hunting for something, hunting'. Once again Plath's repugnance for the male world of wars and violence against nature was set in contrast to sensibilities of women and children, associated with renewal, hope, and the sustenance of life, and the fruitfulness of spring and summer seasons.

In a journal entry written in summer 1951 Plath detailed the process of composing her first sonnet in terms of unbounded senses, and the sheer pleasure of working with words:[127]

> 1 SEPTEMBER: Here follows my first sonnet, written during the hours of 9 to 1 a.m. on a Saturday night, which in pregnant delight I conceived my baby. Luxuriating in the feel and music of the words, I chose and rechose, singling out the color, the assonance and dissonance and musical effects I wished—lulling myself by supple 'I' 's and bland long 'a' 's and 'o' 's. God, I am happy—It's the first thing I've written for a year that has tasted wholly good to my eyes, ears and intellect.

'Sonnet: to Spring'

you deceive us with the crinkled green
of juvenile stars, and you beguile us with
a bland vanilla moon of maple cream:
again you tame us with your april myth.

last year you tricked us by the childish jingle
of your tinsel rains; again you try,
and find us credulous once more. A single
diabolic shower, and we cry

to see the honey flavored morning tilt
clear light across the watergilded lawn.
although another of our years is split
on avaricious earth, you lure us on:

> Again we are deluded and infer
> That some who we are younger than we were.

During the same period in summer 1951, when Plath was indulging the 'pregnant delight' of her sonnet to spring, she was creating another work based on the seasons that she considered one of her finest efforts, which she labeled as 'illogical, sensuous description'. This journal passage offers a uniquely close analysis of her own writing process, revealing her broad vocabulary and critical skills, and her interest in the visual-to-verbal, subconscious-to-conscious approach to word construction and associative color imagery that would be the hallmark of later works:

> (110): The wind has blown a warm yellow moon up over the sea; a bulbous moon, which sprouts in the soiled indigo sky, and spills bright winking petals of light on the quivering black water.
>
> (111): I am at my best in illogical, sensuous description. Witness the bit above. The wind could not possibly blow a moon up over the sea. Unconsciously, without words, the moon has been identified in my mind with a balloon, yellow, light, and bobbing about on the wind. The moon, according to my mood, is not slim, virginal and silver, but fat, yellow, fleshy and pregnant. Such is the distinction between April and August, my present physical state and my sometime-in-the-future physical state. Now the moon has undergone a rapid metamorphoses, made possible by the vague imprecise allusions in the first line, and become a tulip or crocus or aster bulb, whereupon comes the metaphor: the moon is 'bulbous', which is an adjective meaning fat, but suggesting 'bulb', since the visual image is a complex thing. The verb 'sprouts' intensifies the first hint of a vegetable quality about the moon. A tension, capable of infinite variations with every combination of words, is created by the phrase 'soiled indigo sky'. Instead of saying blatantly 'in the soil of the night sky', the adjective 'soiled' has a double focus: as a description of the smudged dark blue sky and again as a phantom noun 'soil', which intensified the metaphor of the moon being a bulb planted in the earth of the sky. Every word can be analyzed minutely—from a point of view of vowel and consonant shades, values, coolnesses, warmths, assonances and dissonances.

The passage continues with a reference to how writing relates to the disciplines of painting and music, subjects Plath spoke of as being outside of her areas of knowledge—most definitely not the case. It also expresses the nineteenth century gendered sense of authorship, as defined by Sandra M. Gilbert and Susan Gubar, when these female 'scribblers', generally dismissed as amateur upstarts by male critics, felt acute anxiety in comparing their works to that of men.[128] In examining the imaginative process and mechanics behind one line of verse, Plath concluded that her vocalization of the emotion and senses—her 'woman's world'—threatened to overwhelm her writing form, echoing her teenage diary tug-of-war between the more serious world of writing, associated with the literary canon, and her 'gay' diary scribblings, largely of women, that she felt revealed the 'weak side' of her character:

> Technically, I suppose the visual appearance and sound of words, taken alone, may be much like the mechanics of music or the color and texture in a painting. However, uneducated as I am in this field, I can only guess and experiment. But I do want to explain why I use words, each one chosen for a reason, perhaps not as yet the very best word for my purpose, but nevertheless, selected after much deliberation. For instance, the continuous motion of the waves makes the moonlight sparkle. To get a sense of fitful motion, the participle adjectives 'winking' (to suggest bright staccato sparks) and 'quivering' (to convey a more legato and tremulous movement) have been used. 'Bright' and 'black' are obvious contrasts of light an dark. My trouble—Not enough free thinking, fresh imagery. Too much subconscious clinging to clichés and downtrodden combinations. Not enough originality. Too much blind worship of modern poems and not enough analysis and practice. My purpose, which I mentioned quite nebulously a while back, is to draw certain attitudes, feelings and thoughts, into a pseudo-reality for the reader. ('Pseudo' of necessity.) Since my woman's world is perceived greatly through the emotions and the senses, I treat it that way in my writing—and am often over-weighted with heavy descriptive passages and a kaleidoscope of similes.

At age 18, Plath's habit of writing on her artistic progress had been deeply ingrained, as was her tendency to reuse effective themes or works in which she had invested time. Indulging a sense of nostalgia for her youth, which shows up in many of her texts during this period, Plath slightly revised the two lines that inspired this analysis into a poem for class, and for a paper entitled 'Suburban Nocturne'. This essay about a walk home at night concludes with comments on how her life has been formed from her experiences, likened to rooms or film frames she moved through, and what of her past has been lost:[129]

> Like Ulysses, I am part of all that I have met. But the film of my nights and days is wound tight in me, never to be rerun. The occasional flashbacks give me mere glimpses of the rooms that I have traveled through. One room says: Once the wind

blew a warm yellow moon up over the sea; a bulbous moon which sprouted in the soiled indigo sky and grew there forever like a tulip.

Plath's journal notes of summer 1951 also report her close observations of people around her. As a seasoned portrait artist and keen student of human nature, she was often able to capture nuance and personality in her drawing subjects, some of whom she identified by name. In one journal passage she described a woman who was most likely the subject of a pencil sketch:[130]

> A glance at Nancy, Jack's girl. Oblivious of my calculating stare, she walked across the stage, smiled friendly at someone I couldn't quite see, and stood down below, in the strange, half-curious, half-comical world on the terrace.

The figure of 'Big Sid' is not mentioned in her writing, yet his exaggerated proportions suggest he was an acquaintance she drew as a teenager. Plath's 'Johnny S' charcoal portrait could have been made in high school or college, and she later used this spelling of the name for her short story 'Johnny Panic and the Bible of Dreams'. Another ink sketch of her mother lounging on a lawn chair resembles many of the informal works she made on odd sheets or bits of paper, indicating her spontaneity in catching subjects with her ink pens and pencils.

After writing of her babysitting jobs for neighbors as a teenager, and her formal engagement as a live-in mother's helper in summer months following her freshman and sophomore years at Smith, Plath featured the care of young children and the domestic environment in all forms of creative disciplines. During her first summer of babysitting she was responsible for the care of three young children of a family living in the wealthy coastal-front community at Swampscott, Massachusetts. After a few weeks on the job, the strain of child care, meal preparation, and housework was alleviated when Marcia Brown, Plath's best friend and roommate from Smith, joined her in a babysitting job with a neighboring family. The friends met daily to take the children to the beach, and on days off they would get together to bike, swim, sail, and sunbathe—one of Plath's most cherished forms of relaxation. Plath made numerous loose sketches of these children in various poses, some of which were published with her article, 'As a Baby-Sitter Sees It', featured the following fall in the *Christian Science Monitor*.[131]

Plath first developed the topic in 1945 with 'From the Memoirs of a Babysitter', and after the Swampscott job, she composed 'Solo' for her poetry class. Ten years later

Nancy

17. 'Big Sid',
*c.*1946–50, pencil

she again returned to her 1951 summer experience for a new poem. 'The Babysitters', which included a more candid depiction of the job's downsides, and
transitioned from the singular subject of her best friend, Marcia Brown, to include
their common experiences.[132] The first draft features Brown positioned in
the domestic setting of 'wardrobes, bedsteads, chairs, tables, refrigerator and
ovens of her employer's house. The second draft of the poem, titled 'Madonna (of
the Refrigerator)', includes disturbing lines that Plath soon removed: 'the mother I
worked for | my boss | Wouldn't let me speak to Jews on the beach because of the
children' (though she had developed this theme in her 1952 story 'The Perfect Set-Up',
where a girl struggles with anti-semitism in her community). Plath maintained two lines
about Brown at the piano in the final draft: 'I remember you playing "Ja Da" in a pink

16. 'Nancy', *c.* 1950–2, pencil,

18. 'Johnny S', *c*. 1947–50, charcoal

pique dress | On the gameroom piano', which in the second draft led to the next line's loving reminiscence, also deleted from the final version: 'What has come over you now, my sister, my love!' This juncture marks the positioning of Brown over 'the map of America' at age thirty, with her twin children in her lap—still surrounded by iceboxes, washing machines, and sinks—now placed in a perspective of distance created by time and the Atlantic Ocean that separated them. Yet both figures are placed among 'glittering' white tools of domestic trade, household appliances likened to 'square white Alps' in this early draft. The final stanza of the finished version hints at the adventures of her beloved *Alice in Wonderland* as the narrator asks: 'what keyhole have we slipped through, what door has shut?' before concluding with a poignant sense of separation and unspoken loss: 'And from our opposite continents we wave and call. | Everything has happened'. Commemorating a high point of her summer experience, Plath pasted photographs she and Brown took of each other into her Smith College scrapbook, along with a drawing she made of her friend at the piano, images she commented on in the scrapbook, and the poem's drafts. Her notes on two of the photos indicate her effort to make them artful:

> Above: Cult of sunworshipping—me doing obeisance on altar of rocks of children's island—rowed to 2 miles out Marblehead Harbor on our day off. We packed a picnic, battled curious seagulls with driftwood, and explored the ramshackle deserted houses . . . Best friend, roommate, and confidante: Marty Brown—sketched playing a piano in Blodgett's rumpus room—snaps taken on day off at children's island— surrealistic aphrodite pose behind driftwood—figure head on dory we rowed 2 miles over.

In the third cycle of ten years for recording her experience with childcare as an adult, 'The Babysitters' would not be published until March 1971, when it appeared in *The New Yorker*.[133]

CAREER DECISIONS, BREAKDOWN, AND THE RETURN TO ART

Any progress Plath made in painting and drawing during the first two years at Smith could not approach the incredible success of her poems and stories. *Seventeen Magazine*, responsible for forty-five of her previous rejection notices, bought the story 'And Summer Will Not Come Again' for their August 1950 issue, and the

Mother

Sylvia Plath
August 23, '48

poem 'Ode on a Bitten Plum' that October. The magazine also gave her prizes for her stories, including a third place prize for 'Dens of Lions' in 1951, and second place for 'Initiation' in October 1952. They published 'The Perfect Set-up' that December, when The National Poetry Association accepted the poem 'Crossing the Equinox' for its anthology. 'Sunday at the Mintons' was published by *Mademoiselle* in August 1952 after winning one of two $500 prizes for its College Fiction Contest. Other poems published that year include 'The Suitcases are Packed Again', 'Twelfth Night', and 'Carnivale Nocturne' in *Seventeen* and 'Cinderella' in *Christian Science Monitor*. The fact that these works brought Plath over $750 in awards, in conjunction with her rare grade of 'B' for both semesters of sophomore art studios—after receiving A's for Art 13—must have influenced her choice of a literary career. The most she had asked for a painting was twenty-five dollars, while a few others had a sale price of five or ten dollars written onto their contest entry forms. There is no evidence that any of these were sold. Though Plath initially signed up for another art course at the beginning of her junior year, she decided writing was the more practical career option, and declared a major in honors English with a minor in Art. She would never again take fine art studios. Artworks she made after college, with few exceptions, were drawn from her environment, where her common subjects were interesting objects and scenes of cities or the countryside where she visited.

Despite Sylvia Plath's remarkable literary achievements as a young college student, doubts about her abilities came in recurring cycles. In February 1952, after receiving another rejection note from *Seventeen*, she wrote home about her growing sense of helplessness in achieving her artistic goals: 'I feel suddenly very untalented as I look at my slump of work in art and writing. Am I destined to deteriorate for the rest of my life?'[134] The next month Plath expressed a vague happiness with her classes in a letter to Ann Davidow: 'College is still fun—I love my courses—especially creative writing and painting.'[135] But the intensity of her academic schedule and social life left her routinely ill and exhausted, and periodically depressed. Although her correspondent and confidante Eddie Cohen suggested she receive psychiatric counseling to assuage her growing anxiety, she was resistant. One mocking poem she wrote at the time extends her insightful 1949 diary statement: 'Yet if I were not in this body, where would I be—perhaps I am destined to be classified and qualified. But, oh, I cry out against it':

19. 'Mother', 1948, ink

'The Complex Couch'

Psychiatrists provide each study
with a couch for love's dismembered body
where volcanic minds
erupt their rorschach-plotted past
to be tamed for cash and classified
neat as venetian blinds[136]

In early 1953, after breaking her leg in a skiing accident, she expressed doubt in her journal as to whether she had made a mistake in focusing on art and literature as an undergraduate, disciplines she would pursue in any case. She considered studying philosophy or psychology in graduate school, which would open new avenues for a career. And in contemplating what she called her 'still, stagnant, putridly and potentially rich sea' of her subconscious, she wrote of how she might put together the 'complex mosaic' of her childhood, the 'nebulous seething of memory' for uses in fiction.[137] While struggling with her broken leg, she stated in a February letter to her mother: 'Well, this will go down in history as Plath's Black Month'—an uncanny reference to the month of her suicide ten years later.[138] Yet when confessing unhappiness or serious obstacles she faced to friends and family, she often tried to make light of her suffering. She concluded the February letter home with a note on the consolation she found in her art:

> To make myself feel better I wrote two villanelles today and yesterday: a rigid French verse form I've never tried before, where the first and third line have to be repeated as refrains. They took my mind off my helpless misery and made me feel a good deal better. I think they are the best I've written yet, and of course sent them off blindly to *The Atlantic* and one to *The New Yorker*. Oh hell. Life is so difficult and tedious I could cry. But I won't; I'll just keep writing villanelles.

This letter has an 'omit' note by Aurelia Plath, who had initially considered it for *Letters Home*. Plath had fun with her poetry, as seen in an illustrated envelope she sent to her mother that winter that includes whimsical verse decorated with silly faces, resembling those she had sent to humor her as a child.[139]

Letters she wrote to quasi-boyfriends Myron Lotz and Gordon Lameyer, however, generally contain carefully composed anecdotal stories of her daily activities and literary chat, sometimes written neatly by hand and accompanied by colored

20. Marcia Brown playing piano, 1951, pencil

21. Plath's photo of Brown behind driftwood, 1951

22. Brown's photo of Plath sunbathing

drawings. In one letter she wrote to Lotz, she discussed a funny letter he sent her, coursework, and challenges she faced with certain subjects, and her appreciation of her teachers.[140] Set within narratives about her studies and the doctor who treated her broken leg after her skiing accident, she placed three carefully colored self-portraits, the last of which portrays her struggle with crutches in wintery weather. After talking about her excitement with an upcoming modern poetry unit and the thought of getting to know visiting poet W. H. Auden, she concluded this letter with an upbeat voice in discussing her priorities as a scholar and making fun of her broken leg:

> That is my first prerequisite for happiness: continued intellectual stimulation . . . what is as rewarding as a rich intellectual life? . . . me, I'll take my Roget's Thesaurus and be wrecked on a tropical isle. I am planning to have a Bacchanalian festival when I again can walk normally, involving a bonfire burning my crutches, and champagne will be

The Babysitters
Madonna (of the Refrigerator))

Tern + American: seen through the gilded cellophane
That takes the place of Dutch veneer.
It is ~~ten~~ adozen years since we rowed to the island, madonna, madonna.
The sun came straight down Not moon ~~~~ May the heart High Yen.
That summer we wore black glasses to hide our eyes
We were always crying in our spare rooms ~~the~~ ~~~~ sisters
In the two huge white handsome houses in Swampscott.
~~~~ I wrote in my diary about 'frog the color of fingernails',
~~And played the piano~~
It took us a lot of crying to get a day off.
Your children were older than mine: you had a supply of bourbon.
I remember you playing "Ta-ra" in a pink pique dress.
I hated babies + didn't know how to cook. I went to bed at eight.
And wrote in my diary, spitefully, ~~at length~~ till after midnight.

I hated babies, I didn't know how to cook, + ~~the man they I worked for~~
~~Wouldn't let me speak to Jews on the beach because of the children.~~
Nights, I wrote in my diary spitefully, till quite late.
~~You were better off,~~ you had a cook + a housemaid.
You knew where ~~my~~ Dunbar ~~+ could drive a car.~~
I remember you playing 'Ta-Da' in a pink pique dress.
What has come over you now, my sister, my love!
I ~~see you surrounded by~~ much through machinery
Iceboxes + washing machines at your back like square
                                                    white clips
You sit on the map of America; you are thirty
~~Iceboxes + washing machines~~, sinks in the middle distance
In your lap you hold twins, red-headed, with perfect teeth.
My voice rebounds among the washing machines, the refrigerators
How they glitter! whiter than the white caps that ~~july~~ day ~~~~
The island was deserted. The wood of the houses smelt dead
We beat the gulls off with driftwood + explored the porches
The stilled interiors, ~~~~ the wicker rockers the bald tables
I took a nice picture of you on the beach, lying on your
And   stomach
~~As if~~ growing out of the stones ~~legless~~ like a legless
                                        (figurehead.

served under the trees in the most original punch bowl yet: it will be long, white, and shaped like Sylvia's left leg. After which I will sell the fragments as either modern intrasubjective sculpture or relics of the Parthenon.

Plath's journal of this year, as usual, exhibits a darker picture and philosophical commentary on all of her difficulties and conflicting life choices, including the problem she had been addressing for years, now stated in tough language: how to manage a love affair as it becomes a long-term commitment. Her 1953 description of a once-adored mate and her own faults is both amusing and unusually cynical as she outlined an age-old dilemma:

> 5 MAY: . . . the fear is always there in my mind: tomorrow it will all be different—tomorrow I will hate the way he chuckles at a joke, or combs his hair with a dirty pocket comb. tomorrow he will see that my nose is fat and my skin is sallow, and we will both be two ugly, vain, selfish, hedonistic dissatisfied people, and the wine, and colored lights, and heated intelligent conversations will all be a fairy-tale inspired pipe dream, and the bitten apple of love will translate itself into discarded feces.

Pessimistic or not, Plath was an eloquent cultural critic who had the pulse of her society in outlining a dubious '50 year' marital bargain during which the wife will be required to:

> love your faults, honor your bestialities, obey your whimsies, ignore your mistresses, nurse your progeny, paper the walls of your home with flowers, and adore you as her dying mortal god, conceive babies and new recipes in labor and travail and remain faithful to you.[141]

As if to outline her own qualifications for the marriage market, Plath goes on to describe herself here as a 'potential minor poetess & story writer, one-time dilettante artist, reasonably healthy and attractive, alive, thinking, tall, sensuous, powerful, colorful white woman, age 21'. Although her ambitions as a writer went far beyond that of a 'potential minor' author, her acknowledgement of her new status as a dabbler of visual art instead of a potential professional, as well as her commanding personality and physicality, confirms her no-nonsense approach to analyzing her own strengths and weaknesses, and her prospects for literary success in a male-dominated field. During this landmark spring season, Plath was also occupied with preparation for her ambitious honors thesis on James Joyce's use of the double in *Ulysses* and *Finnegan's Wake*. Expressing doubts to Lameyer as to whether she might find anything original to say about the topic, she turned to him

23. 'The Babysitters' poem, draft 2

Dear mother:

Oh, bother!
Mrs. Bragg
(Alas, alag)
Is staying chez elle aujourd'hui
Eh bien, quelle ennui!

So I packed my books in a box
And for breakfast had Scotch on the
    Rocks
To give me that je ne sais quoi,
That gay la-de-dah
Attitude,
To give longitude and lattitude
To my bad high-hatted mood.
(On Braggs a pox
And some dirty sox!)

And so with a sandwich of roast beef.
I leef (by bus)   (aujus)
To face papers and etcetera
And polite rejection lettera
At Smith.

In the meantime, an abstract kith
To you for being my mother
Instead of the mother
Of somebody else or other.

Please call Mrs. Bragg to tell her
How much you wish well her
And won't be able to join her
    Saturday
On her trip to Smith because the
    latter day
Is the one that Kid Lotz and I will
    be away.
Tooralay!

If any unprecedented windfall
Should perchance befall
Me, I will call.
That is all.

Take good care of your health progress
While I am on my academic mission   ion
Because when I return in JUNE
I want you to be well in tune
For a gay pot shot
On my shocking pink yacht.

Love and laughter
From your daft daughter!
(who gets dafter & dafter!!)

for advice, and talked of reading Edmund Wilson's *'Axel's Castle'* in studying what she called her 'dearly loved Yeats, Joyce and Eliot', a book on symbolist writers she hoped would serve as a 'springboard' into Stein and Proust.[142]

Plath was writing an abundance of short fiction and poetry for her English classes, and she modeled her poetic techniques after her primary mentors: W. B. Yeats, W. H. Auden, T. S. Eliot, and Dylan Thomas, and among women, Marianne Moore, Elizabeth Bishop, and Edna St. Vincent Millay. While she was acutely aware of the poetry of Emily Dickinson, she rarely mentioned its influence on her work.[143] During her Smith years she wrote over 400 poems, most of which she would dismiss a few years later as miserable death-wishes. One sonnet that may fall into this category, written while Plath was at Lawrence House (1952–3), echoes Dickinson's contemplation of death in the figure of a 'white girl' framed in black:[144]

'White Girl between Yellow Curtains'

Across the narrow alleyway,
in the black square of a tall window
flanked by yellow curtains,
a white girl is making her white bed;

it strikes the bone this winter day
with a freezing innuendo
to see by inadvertance
a white girl making her white bed.

Snow fall, and the snow will stay
while the pale diminuendo
from the black square of the window
the violet twilight shortens
til the white girl goes to her white bed,
and the cold white grave is tenanted.

Plath's hard work during this stressful time paid off with more prizes. She succeeded in her bid for the highly competitive *Mademoiselle* guest editorship in spring 1953, and found her month at the magazine exhilarating and extremely demanding, a condition she usually thrived on. Though years later she would describe her experience in more negative terms, she wrote to Myron Lotz of the magazine's gala closing event in glowing detail on the sophisticated display of light and sound:[145]

> This week we had our big Guest Editors dinner dance and party on the St. Regis roof overlooking the city and sunset: table cloths, chairs, ceiling et. al. colored pink, the world arrayed with a rosy glow, and music continuous, with two bands that alternated, one sinking into the floor, the other rising and playing the same song so that no break was discernible, and outside the windows all the light of the city.

In describing the excitement and views of New York City in this letter, she stated that 'I never watch television.' She also noted the glamorous perks the assignment afforded in her Smith scrapbook, and her continued friendship with the Estonian refugee Ilo Pill (an artist who delivered her first violent kiss at age 17), when she visited in his Harlem apartment in Spring 1954 for a 'festive dinner' with family.

> Fantastic, fabulous, and all other inadequate adjectives go to describe the four gala and chaotic weeks I worked as a guest managing editor of Mlle under Cyrilly Abels—living in luxury at the Barbizon, I edited, met celebrities, was feted and feasted by a galaxy of UN delegates, simultaneous interpreters and artists—Ilo provided roses and wine in farewell.[146]

After returning home to Wellesley in July 1953, Plath's growing despondency was treated by poorly administered electroshock treatments at the local hospital. Her deteriorating mental state, and her struggle with reading and writing, culminated in extreme depression and a suicide attempt on 24 August 1953. After being successfully treated by Ruth Barnhouse Beuscher, however, a young psychiatrist at McLean Hospital, and with the patient language tutoring of Wilbury Crockett, Plath was well enough to be released in December. She was relieved that her analytical powers, and what her mother and a Smith friend had described as her 'fantastic' memory, were not compromised as a result of her illness and treatment. In 1961 she would recreate her entire *Mademoiselle* stint, breakdown, near-death experience, and full recovery for *The Bell Jar*, her only completed and published novel of three, all of which she based in biography.[147] But soon after returning to Smith, when she resumed her stellar academic career and active social life, she felt compelled to write about her brush with death. In the preface to 'The Devil's Advocate',[148] an essay on suicide and duality she wrote for her spring 1954 course on Tolstoy and Dostoyevsky, she talked of becoming 'dynamically involved in Dostoyevsky's ideas', explaining that 'the conflicts he poses in his novels are colored in my own mind; the dualisms he describes are reflected in my own attitudes.' She

25. Photo of Plath and mother of Ilo Pill in Harlem, 1954

took this opportunity to write of her own well-publicized suicide attempt, aligning her experience with the paper's thesis, stating: 'It was this conviction of oblivion after death, this disbelief in God and immortality that reassured me when I attempted, after two months of despair and reasoned premeditation, to commit suicide.' A year later Sylvia Plath would graduate *summa cum laude*, gaining three of Smith's top literary awards, including one for her honors thesis: 'The Magic Mirror: A Study of the Double in Two of Dostoevsky's Novels'—a more manageable and personally compelling topic than her intended thesis on the last novels of Joyce. At this time she also submitted 'Tongues of Stone' to a *Mademoiselle* fiction contest, a short story based on her McLean experience.[149] This story includes a lyrical retelling of her own suicide rescue, where she wrote: 'They had raised her like Lazarus from the mindless dead, corrupt already with the breath of the grave' and while at Cambridge, Plath noted in her journal, 'I feel like Lazarus—that story has such a fascination'[150]—early references to the figure of Lazarus that informed her stunning 1962 poem 'Lady Lazarus', a persona of rejuvenation she directly connected to this thwarted suicide.

Sylvia Plath resumed her abundant correspondence with friends and family upon her recovery (she left 696 letters with her family alone when she died), all of which was tailored for the recipient. Many of her letters to and from boyfriends reflect extensive literary exchanges, where the young men make every attempt to keep up with Plath, writing poems and critiques of books they studied and each others' work. In one case, Dick Norton (Plath's first love interest, who she felt was highly competitive with her) wrote an extensive spoof of Virginia Woolf's prose, also a topic of discussion with Gordon Lameyer and Myron Lotz. Language for her lover Richard Sassoon, a typed note, reflects their new physical intimacy as well as her self-conscious experimentation with 'cerebral' pillow talk:[151]

> to sassoon: wednesday, april 20: halfnakedly browning on natural mattresses of pine-needles we lolled luxuriant and cerebralized abominably about what all vitalistic people do...remembering: soft moonvaulted night, annoyed with a plethora of stars, climbing in hegelian dialictic spirals into the dark unknown

Plath's year-long love affair with Sassoon, a highly cultured Yale student who shared her intellectual interests and her enthusiasm for art, inspired some of the works she submitted for her final poetry tutorial at Smith. The couple made frequent visits to New York City where they ate at fancy restaurants, attended plays, music concerts, and films, as well as modern art museums and galleries. Plath wrote little of the classical art she had seen, and in letters of this period she mentioned viewing paintings of Sargent, Whistler, and Mary Cassatte, commenting: 'I must say my tastes in art are arrogantly modern'.[152]

Enthralled with seeing the famous works of the modern painters she had studied for years, Plath began writing her first batch of 'art poems', the second of which she would compose three years later. In a March 1955 letter home she enclosed a handful of poems inspired by a recent visit to the Whitney, and commented on her pleasure in receiving her mother's picture postcards of Gauguin's colorful paintings among her black and white rejection notices. The sonnet 'Midsummer Mobile', most certainly among this group of poems sent home, starts with a directive to follow the narrator, who acts as a form of tour guide. Allowing one stanza for each artist, Plath highlighted Dufy's and Seurat's placement of cool blues and white, sky and water, birds and fish, avoiding the mention of warm colors around the sun. The third stanza moves to Matisse's warm amber and orange of the ocean waves, inverting the more common association of water with cool temperatures and hues. The final couplet returns the poem to its title and theme, suggesting a Calder mobile as metaphor for the day's visit to the museum, while linking 'midsummer' to the seasonal sun, ocean, and blue sky of the paintings:

'Midsummer Mobile'

Begin by dipping your brush into clear light.
Then syncopate a sky of Dufy blue
With tilted stars of sloops revolved by white
Gulls in a feathered fugue of wings. Outdo

Seurat: fleck schooner flanks with sun and set
A tremolo of turquoise quivering in
The tessellated wave. Now nimbly let
A tinsel pizzicato on fish fin

Be plucked from waves of dappled amber where
A mermaid odalisque lolls at her ease
With orange scallops in wet hair,
Fresh from the mellow palette of Matisse:

Suspend this day, so singularly designed,
Like a rare Calder mobile in your mind.

Another poem inspired by this 1955 annual exhibit, 'Wayfaring at the Whitney: A Study in Sculptural Dimensions', addresses works by separate artists in three stanzas, the last of which she turned into a separate poem titled '"Three Caryatids without a Portico," by Hugo Robus: A Study in Sculptural Dimensions' (see Chapter 3, pp. 158–66). As was her habit, Plath made full use of her creative endeavors, and took a similar narrative approach in her 1955 arts essay assignment, first mentioned in a letter home:[153]

I am now in the finals for the Vogue Prix de Paris and must write a 'thesis' of over 10 pages—(at least) on 'Americana'; on my discoveries in the arts this year, what I've found most exciting in the American theater, books, music, etc.

The resulting essay, 'Arts in America: 1954. Collage of a Collegian', begins with the student planning her visit to the Whitney Museum, the 'mecca of modern art', where readers are led through the 'collage' of fine art offerings. In this paper she described the painting 'Pine Tree' by Gregorio Prestopino as 'a weird Rorschach-blot of twisted black on orange with the creaking rhythms of an amber plow in the foreground'. Applying a mimetic technique she favored in a poem based on this painting, 'Black Pine Tree in an Orange Light' duplicates the Rorschach test's method of spinning imaginative associations from visual imagery, and once again approaches readers directly, asking them to join in viewing and judging the work in the first and last stanzas of six. In between these stanzas, the Halloween theme and color scheme are underscored with related images of orange pumpkins and the black of devil's magic and the 'holy book', also echoing the ambiguity of their meaning, and implying the poet may be as clever as the painter in her approach to the subject :

> Tell me what you see in it:
> the pine tree like a Rorschach-blot
> black against the orange light:
>
> *   *   *   *   *   *   *
> . . . . how crafty the painter . . .
> to make orange and black ambiguous.

After reviewing paintings and sculptures, and a selection of the city's film, theater, and music offerings for her 'Arts in America' thesis, Plath positioned popular literary works within 'synesthesia', the full sensory encounter she strived to achieve in her writing:

> Another dimension of this world builds its facets from a spinning platter. Because we think in terms of synesthesia, we like to visualize and verbalize music. Our ear isn't tutored to hear music in its own terms alone; as we listen, tunes turn to color, chords vibrate into words.

Plath's adult interests in the fine arts, however, did not seem to include dance. As seen in her marginilia on assigned high school classroom readings on the 'fluidity' in various arts (by George Brandon Saul), she argued with the text that dance represents 'at best only momentary creation because of its fluidity. It is annoying in its degree of impermanence.'[154] Plath's need to 'capture', 'catch', 'clurch' and 'cling to' her own insights and experiences in writing (noted in her journal of 9 February 1958) and the social role of dance in high school, may have caused her to see it as a more negligible art form, just as she had considered her diary sketches when compared to her writing. Her acute awareness of the quick passage and loss of time, and her practical approach to managing what she had called the rest of her 'brief life', likely caused her to abandon her youthful 'shotgun' approach to creative endeavors. After winning a Fulbright for study at Cambridge, she indulged her love of theatre during her first semester, performing in college productions, but she gave it up to focus on her more serious interests in writing.

VIEWS OF THE CONTINENT

By the time Sylvia Plath went to read English literature at Newnham College, Cambridge in England, she was well on her way to becoming a seasoned professional. Yet she brought the brilliant world of modern art with her to England in books and art prints, and she continued to keep up with the art scene in visits to museums and informal study. Soon after her arrival in September 1955 she sent a postcard to Lameyer that featured a British Museum bust of the Buddha on the front. Her note said, 'Am continuing living in London cultivating buddha's calm directly opposite Ionic columns', and in a letter she wrote to him soon after, she made a rare and indirect reference to the art of van Gogh in describing her dorm room that contained:[155]

> enormous van Gogh-ish bouquets of yellow chrysanthemums, a flurry of vivid postcard modern art reproductions on door and wardrobe (memoirs of Art Galleries from New York City to Washington to London), a long, low coffee table, holding art books...Braque still life in fawns, rich russets, avocado green and highlights of yellow: forest green, sun yellow, chestnut brown, plus accents of black and white, are the colors I live among.

Plath used an equally broad range of painter's hues in her journal narratives, which she had started after a hiatus following her McLean hospital recovery. She returned to her use of journals as a storehouse for writing exercises and private musings, which she kept for future use in written compositions. Straightforward descriptions of colorful scenes, however, did not appeal to Plath as much as the subtle treatment of color tones and associate imagery in her work, skills she had acquired through years of painting, drawing, and analyzing art. She would utilize her artist's eye and analytical skills in addressing contemporary art and visual motifs in her poetry and prose, and in developing a limited color palette that eventually crystallized in *Ariel*. But as she discontinued her multi-medium art creations, her desire for color stimulation seemed to increase. One group of Plath's winter vacation notes exhibit her heavy manipulation of color symbol, set within contrasting depictions of light/dark, and cold/warm seasonal moods. On New Year's Eve 1955, she traveled with Richard Sassoon by train from Paris to Nice, with her portable Olivetti typewriter in tow. Her narrative strategy for these notes was to focus on the transition from a dark, cold, and color-neutral night into the brilliant landscape of the southern coast. Plath started the piece from her seat in the train station, with a question regarding the potential meaning or code, available to the 'initiate', of the rhythmic red, green, and blue flashing lights of a Christmas tree. After one other mention of turquoise blue, she began a complex progression of cold blacks, deep blues, whites, browns, and grays of the night train's passengers—including their clothes and the train's interior compartment—and the changing outdoor scenery. Warm tones in these first pages are strictly corralled to the point that objects such as the egg yokes and tangerines are not noted by color, and the one reference to 'red' identifies the type of wine without further elaboration. Upon the dawn arrival at their destination, however, the text breaks into a full-blown color description of the coastal town, as she watched the houses and street scenery slowly brighten. She later summed up her experience in letters to friends and family in statements such as:

> I gritted my eyes on pastel villas, orange and olive groves, snow-capped Alps Maritime, violently green pines, and that blissful blue blast of the sea. God, what a blissful change from the gray of Cambridge, London and even Paris! I was so hungry for color![156]

Plath's initial nine months as an American student in Europe would form the plot line for her first unpublished novel, *Falcon Yard*, where journals confirm her growing determination to put her life experience into novels. Intimidated by the thought, however, her initial approach to these Continental narratives was to start with stories, ideally published with her own illustrations. Soon after returning to England from France she wrote to her mother about her renewed efforts in fiction:[157]

20 JANUARY: I am starting a rather more serious and solitary life this term, giving up the very demanding, if stimulating, acting in the theater and writing at least 2 hours a day, no matter what. It is amazing how much better I feel doing this. I am building up creativity from inside out. Even though writing is difficult, often stilted at first, or rough, I firmly believe that if I work hard enough, long enough, some stories rising out of my rapidly growing perspective about people and places may be published. Somehow stories interest me more now than the narrower, more perfect form of poems.

What Plath was aiming for, however, was the more perfect form of prose, as seen in a similar letter she wrote to Lameyer the following day. She described her attempt to capture her visit to Matisse Chapel for a story, where she talked of 'still idolizing the intricate, polished style of *The New Yorker*, with its blend of intelligent wit and deep seriousness, excellent specific vocabulary (which I find hardest to cultivate)'.[158] She also admitted to reading while at Cambridge more than attending lectures, and stated, 'I get actually spiritually sick if I'm not writing.'

Sylvia Plath had hoped to meet up with Sassoon on her spring 1956 vacation in Paris, but he was out of town and she had to explore the city largely on her own. Her writing habits had her regularly typing letters and impressions of the city, this time on a borrowed Olivetti. She walked five to ten miles a day, and spent many afternoons making sketches of the city or copying works of art in museums and galleries. Viewing the famous works of artists she had studied greatly inspired her creativity. She wrote to her brother Warren that she was having fun sketching again, though she called her work 'stilted' and 'stiff' from lack of practice—just as she had described her prose to her mother. Plath's chronicles of her 1956 drawing experiences include a narrative on her creative technique, where she experienced sight through touch:

16 MARCH: Then, inspired, I took my sketch book and squatted in the sun at the very end of the Ile de la Cite in a little green park of Henri 4 du Vert Galant & began to draw the vista through the Pont Neuf; it was a good composition with the arches of the bridge framing trees & another bridge, and I was aware of people standing all around me watching but I didn't look at them—just hummed & went on sketching. It was not very good, too unsure & messily shaded, but I think I will do line drawings from now on in the easy style of Matisse. Felt I knew that view though, through the fiber of my hand.

Although Plath returned to drawing as a stimulating and enjoyable leisure activity, she reserved her more ambitious ink drawings to accompany published essays, some of which featured a visual art form in their titles. Instead of first writing on a topic that she would then look to illustrate, she commonly drew first and literally wrote around or about her subject afterwards. In a diary note of August 1957 she wrote about writing a couple of 'short colorful articles on Eastham' to go with drawings she had made at Cape Cod.[159] She also took this approach in drawings she made in Paris, the fishing village of Benidorm, Spain, and 'Wuthering Heights' territory, where illustrated articles of the subjects were published in the Cambridge newspapers *Cambridge Vistas* and *Varsity*, or the *Christian Science Monitor*. Her 'Spring Sketching in Paris' illustrated essay on the visit (published as *'An American in Paris'*) expressed her delight with the sounds and sights of the city, from its more famous art and tourist spots to obscure neighborhood streets. In a letter home she mentioned staying in 'the loveliest garret in Paris overlooking the rooftops & gables & artists skylight' with 'red & yellow sunshades on the windows like squares in a Mondrian painting'.[160] She recorded her more mundane activities (and despair at missing Sassoon) into a tiny journal, similar to her adolescent notes that include everything from boy chat, to what she ate and wore, and when she washed her hair. A journal entry she wrote nearly two years after this visit describes her viewing an exhibition of Nicholas de Stael's paintings, at the 'crumbling, scandalously falling-down new museum of modern art on the Seine'. In wondering about the artist's reasons for his recent suicide, Plath connected the heat of his painted colors to his 'vision of madness'—though the life and significance of Vincent van Gogh, the most notorious 'mad' painter-suicide of Europe, are not discussed in her existing journals:

> 21 DECEMBER: . . . viewed his painting, sitting, drawing line facsimiles & color notes of boats against a dark green sky, pale flavors and slender bumpy pears arranged, three, on a dark purple and green ground, blue squared Paris rooftops, black & white balancing brushstrokes, I adoring, alone, lonely, absorbing all that paint, reading how he jumped off a cliff at the Cap D'Antibes. What drove him? All those hot reds & blues and yellows spurting from his fingertips? What vision of madness in a mad world?

Sylvia Plath had serious doubts since her teen years about her ability to successfully combine a family and career, yet she eventually decided both were necessary for her personal fulfillment. On 14 June 1956 (Joyce's 'Bloomsday'), four months after meeting the British poet and ex-Cambridge student Ted Hughes, the two were married in a private ceremony witnessed by Aurelia Plath. Their six years together revolved around their common love of language and writing, and shared knowledge of literature. They critiqued each other's works, and Hughes regularly suggested story plots and subjects for Plath's fiction and poetry. As a strong advocate of an aural approach to writing, Hughes implored Plath to read her works aloud to determine their impact and value, and to depend less on her typically visual approach to writing. Yet he also encouraged what he considered to be her thera- peutic drawing habits, as he would later write of how nothing refreshed her more than sitting in front of some intricate pile of objects for hours, laboriously delin- eating each item. Plath's article 'Mosaics—An Afternoon of Discovery', written in 1958, presents her impressions of their Spanish honeymoon locale, when she made serious efforts to capture the local village scenes. In a letter to her mother written while on honeymoon, Plath described her 'sudden return' to sketching, comment- ing on her drawing style:[161]

> 28 AUGUST: Wait till you see these of Benidorm—the best I've ever done in my life, very heavily stylized shading and lines; very difficult subjects, too: the peasant market . . . a composition of three sardine boats on a bay with their elaborate lights, and a good one of the cliff-headland with the houses over the sea. I'm going to write an article for them and send them to the Monitor. I feel I'm developing a kind of primitive style of my own which I am very fond of. Wait till you see. The Cambridge sketch was nothing compared to these.

Along with detailed drawings Plath made during her two years at Cambridge, she sketched local scenes and individual objects in her journal notes and letters, as well as portraits of people in her environment. Onto her lecture notes about Yeats's 'Sailing to Byzantium' poem, she drew her own hand in the act of sketching the figure of F. R. Leavis at the podium, the renowned Cambridge don who was teaching the history and theory of literary criticism. She also mentioned him in a 1955 letter to Lameyer, stating, 'Twice a week I hear the pithy deadpan magnifi- cence of f.r. leavis, a tan devastating leprechaun of a man.'[162] Her sketch of Ted Hughes assumed her favored portrait stance, the profile.[163]

Sardine boats and lights patterned the beach during the daylight hours

Sketchbook of a Spanish Summer

By Sylvia Plath
Cambridge, England

After a bitter British winter, we sought the heart of sunlight in the small Spanish fishing village of Benidorm on the border of the Mediterranean for a summer of studying and sketching. Here, in spite of the tourist hotels along the waterfront, the natives live as simply and peacefully as they have for centuries, fishing, farming, and tending their chickens, rabbits, and goats.

We woke early each morning to hear the high, thin jangle of goat bells as the goatherd across the street led his flock of elegantly stepping black goats to pasture.

*   *   *

"Ya hoi!" came the cry of the little bread-woman as she strolled by with a great basket of fragrant fresh rolls over her arm. Daily, after breakfast, we walked downtown to shop at the peasant market.

Spanish kitchens are a far cry from those in America: only the wealthy possess iceboxes, which are proudly displayed in the livingroom; dishes are washed in cold water and scrubbed with tangles of straw; and a one-ring petrol stove must cope with everything.

The open-air peasant market begins at sunup. Natives set out their wares on little wooden tables or rush mats at a hilly crossroads between white pueblos that sparkle like salt crystal in the sun. Black-clad peasant women bargain with the vendors for watermelons, purple figs wrapped in their own scalloped leaves, yellow plums, green peppers, wreaths of garlic, and speckled cactus fruit. Two straw baskets hung on a balance serve as scales and rough stones are used for weights.

One woman holds a squawking, flapping black chicken while she calmly goes about the rest of her shopping. Strung up on wires against the peublo walls are gaudy striped beach towels, rope sandals, and delicate white cobwebs of handmade lace. Higher on the hill, a man is selling petrol stoves, earthenware jugs, and coat hangers.

*   *   *

The fish market is a fresh adventure every day, varying according to the previous night's catch. Every evening at dusk the lights of the sardine boats dip and shine out at sea like floating stars. In the morning counters are piled with silvery sardines, strewn with a few odd crabs and shells. Strange fish of all shapes and sizes lie side by side, speckled or striated, with a rainbow sheen on their fins. There are small fish with black streaks on shimmering pale blue scales, fish glinting pink and red, and a Moray eel with black eyes and a splendid yellow brocade patterning its dark back. We never quite had the courage to select our dinner from the pile of baby octopuses, their long legs tangled and twined like a heap of slippery worms.

*   *   *

All our food and drink came from the farms around us. When we needed extra milk for supper one evening, we crossed the street to wait for the goatherd. Soon a musical tinkling sounded in the distance, and the flock of aristocratic black goats rounded the wall of the corral, followed by the goatherd, who resembled a smiling Spanish leprechaun in patched, faded dungarees, rope sandals, and a sombrero. He invited us into the corral to watch the milking, clucking and shooing his goats into what he called "their little *casa*." Stepping after him into the dark, musky, pleas-

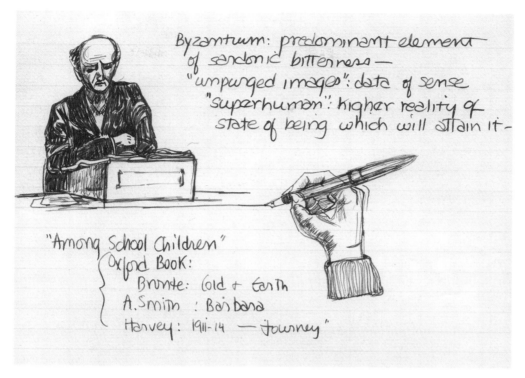

Byzantium: predominant element
of sardonic bitterness —
"unpurged images": data of sense
"superhuman": higher reality of
state of being which will attain it—

"Among School Children"
 Oxford Book:
     Bronte: Cold + Earth
   A. Smith : Barbara
   Harvey: 1911-14 — Journey"

27. Cambridge Don F. R. Leavis and class notes, *c.*1955–6, ink

The Professional

ART POEMS AND THE 'SPECTACULAR PROMISE'

Sylvia Plath and Ted Hughes returned to Northampton in the summer of 1957 to pursue teaching and writing professions. But a few months into her job as freshman English instructor at Smith College, Plath decided that a career as a professor was not worth pursuing. Anticipating her mother's objections to both her and Hughes's plans to drop their teaching jobs in favor of full-time writing, Plath wrote to her brother Warren of her disillusionment with teaching and the academy in general:[164]

> 5 NOVEMBER: I am simply not a career woman, and the sacrifice of energy and lifeblood I'm making for this job is all out of proportion to the good I'm doing in it. My idea of being a good teacher, writing a book on the side, and being an entertaining home-maker, cook and wife is rapidly evaporating. I wanted to write first, and being kept

26. 'Sketchbook of a Spanish Summer', *Christian Science Monitor*, Part 1, 1956

28. Ted Hughes, facsimile of ink sketch, 1956

apart from writing, from giving myself a chance to really devote myself to developing this 'spectacular promise' that the literary editors write me about when they reject my stories, is really very hard.

Also, I don't like meeting only students and teachers. That is the life here, and it is, in a way, airless...we need the stimulation of people, people from various backgrounds, for writing material. And I can't write about academics. We cast about for a place to live that wasn't New York and thought next year of living in Boston. Ted would get a job, not anything to do with a university, and I would write in the mornings and work part-time at odd jobs which would get me into meeting queer people and give me time to sketch and really work at writing. . . . this life is not the life of a writer. . . . I am needing to apprentice myself to my real trade. . . . How I long to write again! When I'm describing Henry James' use of metaphor to make emotional states vivid and concrete, I'm dying to be making up my own metaphors. When I hear a professor saying, 'Yes, the wood is shady, but it's a *green* shade—connotations of sickness, death, etc.', I feel like throwing up my books and writing my own bad poems

29. Photo of Ted Hughes, no date

and bad stories and living outside the neat, gray secondary air of the university. I don't like talking about D. H. Lawrence and about critics' views of him. I like reading him selfishly for an influence on my own life and my own writing.

The couple moved to Boston the following summer to pursue their writing careers, which for Plath included career plans as a freelance journalist, a short story writer for the major women's magazines, and a novelist. While teaching at Smith, however, she returned to the study of modern art by auditing a weekly course with Smith professor Mrs Van der Poel. A letter Plath received in early 1958 from *ARTnews,* asking her for a poem on art, propelled her into a new phase of poetry writing inspired by paintings and drawings of her favorite masters. The result would be eight 'art poems' that she felt allowed her to compete for the title of 'Poetess of America'. Calling on what she had been learning in class, she decided to first look to the works of Gauguin, Matisse, and Klee for ideas. In a two-page journal narrative, she noted the *ARTnews* letter and her trips to the library in search of art books.[165] The first page of the entry indulges her visions of color in the context of her interior environment in describing her dinner party. She noted the largely green- and red-colored food items and clothes of guests: green plants, pink skin, black dress, green salad, white and red wine, green stockings, red shoes, red and green skirt and top, tan yarn, pale blue mittens, and a red cape. While these red and green objects may have actually dominated the visual setting Plath described, her fondness for color groupings may have caused her to single them out for her journal notes. In the second page of her entry, she described a Matisse painting that necessarily engaged the full color palette:

> 4 FEBRUARY: . . . exploding in pink cloths and vibrant pink shadows, pale peach, pewter, smoky yellow lemons, violent orange tangerines & green limes, black-shadowed & the interiors: oriental flowery-pale lavendars & yellow walls with a window giving out onto Riviera blue—a bright blue double-pear-shape of a violin case—streaks of light from the sun outside, pale fingers—The boy at the scrolled piano with the green metronome shape of the outdoor world. color: a palm tree exploding outside a window in yellow & green & black jets, framed by rich black red-patterned draperies. A blue world of round blue trees, hatpins & a lamp.

Plath had always responded strongly to visual stimulus, and her long-term identity as a fruitful and successful writer was directly connected to the act of seeing art and her ability to record what she saw with accuracy and nuance. While working on her new art poems she discussed her craft in a BBC interview recorded with Hughes: 'I have a visual imagination. For instance, my inspiration is painting and not music when I go to some other art form. I see these things very clearly.'[166] Working with a sense of exaltation over the art books she was exploring, Plath would also analyze her new poems to be her best work to date, an important breakthrough she related in a letter home: [ellipses Plath's]:

> 22 MARCH: Just a note to say that I have at last burst into a spell of writing. I was rather stunned Thursday morning, my first real day off after a week of correcting 70 papers, averaging midterm grades and writing a report on another senior thesis, but I had about seven or eight paintings and etchings I wanted to write on as poem-subjects and bang! After the first one, 'Virgin in a Tree', after an early etching by Paul Klee, I ripped into another, probably the biggest and best poem I've ever written, on a magnificent etching by Klee titled 'Perseus, or the Triumph of Wit over Suffering'. A total of about 90 lines written in one day.
>
> Friday went just as well: with a little lyric fantasy on a lovely painting by Klee on the comic opera The Seafarer, a long and big one on his painting 'The Departure of the Ghost', and a little lyric on a cat with a bird-stigma between its eyebrows, a really mammoth magic cat-head. These are easily the best poems I've written and open up new material and a new voice. I've discovered my deepest source of inspiration, which is art: the art of primitives like Henri Rousseau, Gauguin, Paul Klee, and De Chirico. I have got piles of wonderful books from the Art Library (suggested by this fine Modern Art Course I'm auditing each week) and am overflowing with ideas and inspirations, as if I've been bottling up a geyser for a year. Once I start writing, it comes and comes. . . . If I can write, I don't care what happens. I feel like an idiot who has been obediently digging up pieces of coal in an immense mine and has just realized that there is no need to do this, but that one can fly all day and night on great wings in clear blue air through brightly colored magic and weird worlds.

This 'obedience' may have referred to her tendency to mimic poetic giants to the exclusion of developing her own original style. The 'magic and weird worlds' of the modernists certainly contain the rich and fantastical imagery that had always stimulated her creativity, yet it was de Chirico's early paintings and journal notes that offered a mix of prose-poetry and imagery that resonated with her own visionary leanings. Plath recorded her excitement in a journal entry that started with notes on her art poems and the intriguing de Chirico prose, and ended with her own free verse that incorporated objects from both. Her stimulus was again connected to a loosening of the imagination, linked to memory and the silent vocabulary of dreams, vision-quests, and tantalizing mysteries:

> 29 MARCH: We want to buy art books. de Chirico. Paul Klee. I have written two poems on paintings by de Chirico which seize my imagination—'The Disquieting Muses' and 'On the Decline of Oracles' (after his early painting, 'The Enigma of the Oracle') and two on paintings by Rousseau—a green & moody piece, 'Snakecharmer', & my last poem of the eight, as I've said, a sestina on Yadwigha of 'The Dream'. I shall copy here some quotations from a translated prose-poem by de Chirico, or from his diaries, which have unique power to move me, one of which, the first, is the epigraph to my poem 'On the Decline of Oracles':
>
> ① 'Inside a ruined temple the broken statue of a god spoke a mysterious language'.
> ② '"Ferrara" the old ghetto where one could find candy & cookies in exceedingly strange & metaphysical shapes'.
> ③ 'Day is breaking. This is the hour of the enigma. This also the hour of prehistory. The fancied song, the revelatory song of the last, morning dream of the prophet asleep at the foot of the sacred column, near the cold, white simulacrum of god'.
> ④ 'What shall I love unless it be the Enigma?'
> And everywhere in Chirico city, the trapped train puffing in a labyrinth of heavy arches, vaults, arcades. The statue, recumbent, of Ariadne, deserted, asleep in the center of empty mysteriously-shadowed squares. And the long shadows cast by unseen figures—human or of stone it is impossible to tell. [see Chapter 4, pp. 167–8]

This 'Chirico city' with its heavy arches and arcades that draw the viewer down its lanes, where statues speak and prophets dream, suggests a relationship with a work of art in human form, negotiated by gods and artists, that continued to intrigue Plath. Soon after starting work on several poems suitable for *ARTnews*, she decided on the title for the poetry collection she was planning. The book would be named after a poem she composed the previous year about her attempts to be rid of an earthenware bust made by her Smith classmate. Plath's journal entry explained how the visual appearance of this art object would work in the context of the poem's symbolic and personal meanings:

> 28 FEBRUARY: I had a vision in the dark art lecture room today of the title of my book of poems, commemorated above. It came to me suddenly with great clarity that 'The Earthenware Head' was the right title, the only title. It is derived, organically, from the title & subject of my poem 'The Lady & The Earthenware Head', and takes on the

compelling mystic aura of a sacred object, a terrible and holy token of identity sucking into itself magnet wise the farflung words which link & fuse to make up my own queer and grotesque world—out of earth, clay, matter, the head shapes its poems & prophecies, as the earth-flesh wears in time, the heed swells ponderous with gathered wisdoms. . . . At any rate, I see the earthenware head, rough, crude, powerful & radiant, of dusky orange-red terracotta color, flushed with vigor and its hair heavy, electric. Rough terracotta color, stamped with jazzed black and white designs, signifying earth, & the words which shape it.

Plath clearly envisioned the black, white, and orange-red terracotta of the earthenware head, yet in the poem's final draft of five stanzas, the color of the bust itself is revealed indirectly by its 'sanguine' and 'brickdust' complexion. The other two colors found in the poem accompany the sculpture on its final perch in a tree, both found in the fourth stanza: the green foliage and black feathers of birds:

> Fired in sanguine clay, the model head
> Fit nowhere: brickdust-complected, eye under a dense lid,
>
> *　　*　　*　　*　　*　　*　　*
>
> And resolved more ceremoniously to lodge
> The mimic head—in a crotched willow, green-
> Vaulted by foliage:
> Let bell-tongued birds descant in blackest feather

Sylvia Plath again explored the psycho-spiritual elements of sculptures after visiting the working studio of Leonard Baskin, a friend and Smith College professor. In 'Sculptor', her 1958 poem dedicated to Baskin, Plath focused on the qualities of the various dismembered 'bodies' of his works. This anthropomorphic approach to objects is common to many of her works, including her 1955 sculpture poem, ' "Three Caryatids without a Portico," by Hugo Robus: A Study in Sculptural Dimensions', which portrays the Robus torsos as three 'maidens' who are willing to support a portico, 'but such a trial is not granted by the gods' (see Chapter 3, pp. 157–8). In 'Sculptor' Plath also imagined invisible spirits at the mercy of their creator, hoping to take on human form, described here as a 'bald angel' who has agency and aggressively bargains with its maker, just as the earthenware head—the 'holy token of identity'—is presented as a form of parasite in 'sucking into itself magnet wise' her own 'queer and grotesque world'. The poem's opening lines set up the relationship:

> To this house the bodiless
> come to barter endlessly
> Vision, wisdom, for bodies . . .

Without their creator's cooperation, the sculptures are 'beggared | Of place, time, and their bodies'. Yet it is the bodiless here that serve as muses, holding the vision-wisdom that is offered the sculptor in exchange for bringing them to life. As seen in many of Plath's works that deal with co-dependent doubles, both have something to gain from the exchange. Her earlier choice of the earthenware head as the object of such collaboration, made by a student in Baskin's 1954 class, shifts into a grander scale as the teacher himself forms his full-bodied statues, creating a layered scenario between real and constructed life forms that may also be connected to the 'unseen figures' of Plath's Chirico's city, where it is impossible to determine whether they are human or stone. This faux-angel of 'Sculptor' negotiates its existence with the sculptor with an ironic form of hope that Plath sets in contrast to the plight of human beings, who perish with no option for physical mortality.

DIVINATION AND THE SUBCONSCIOUS IN VERSE

The exchange between artists and their creations was, in Plath's eye, always complex, and sometimes seamless in that the works serve to define the artists, or at least to dominate their lives. Yet for Plath, the artist's ability to understand her relationship to her own imagination and her past held the key to uncovering its deepest treasures. At the time Plath expressed her fascination with de Chirico's 'The Enigma of the Oracle', she was again exploring her own psyche in returned sessions with her McLean psychiatrist Ruth Beuscher. Much of what she wrote during this period deals with vexed family relationships and their resonances, and threads from these sessions became interwoven with divination experiments she was engaging with her husband—much of which was initiated to further their art.

Plath was aware of having clairvoyant abilities, yet she seemed to pay scant attention to the phenomenon. Hughes stated she had often mentioned intuitive flashes about unimportant matters, but that she generally ignored her psychic powers and any effect they may have had on others. Yet after meeting her husband, who had a long-standing interest in the occult, Plath began a more intensive if facile engagement with the mysteries, with an eye toward locating new ideas for writing as well as 'for fun'. In an attempt to ease Plath's debilitating 'writer's cramp', he employed his own methods of increasing creative stimulus from supernatural sources. Along with compiling lists of potential subjects for Plath's poems and stories, Hughes advised her on meditation techniques, and used hypnotism and their hand-made Ouija board on a regular basis. Calling these sessions 'magnificent fun',[167] Plath was intrigued by the concept of 'Pan', their main 'spirit contact' called on for advice on poetry subjects, and sometimes to get numbers for horse races. While they made no gains at the tracks, Plath was able to produce 'Dialogue over a Ouija Board', an unusual work she considered her first major poem in six months. In a journal entry of July 1957[168] she talked of her 'long lumbering dialogue' in visual terms, referring to it as

> more ambitious than anything I've very done, although I feel to be doing it like a patchwork quilt; without anything more than the general idea it should come out a rectangular shape, but not seeing how the logical varicolored pieces should fit.

Even while attempting to create a more casual speaking voice, Plath had no plans to abandon her complex play with language. Yet she hoped to overcome what she saw as a major deficiency of her 'small bad poems': an attempt at perfected technique that created what she called the 'slick shiny artificial look'[169] and lack of deeper content that had gotten her negative reviews by some Smith professors, Cambridge contemporaries, and other critics. Plath described the strategy behind her Ouija board dialogue in a letter home:

> 6 AUGUST: . . . a short verse dialogue which is supposed to sound just like conversation but is written in strict 7-line stanzas, rhyming acabcbc, but frees me from my writer's cramp and is at last a good subject—a dialogue over a Ouija board, which is both dramatic and philosophical.
>
> I really think I would like to write a verse play, now. If I practice enough on getting color into speech, I can write in quite elaborate rhymed and alliterative forms without sounding like the self-conscious poetry, but rather like conversation.

This extensive verse-poem, containing exchanges from an actual Ouija board session, records a discussion between the couple 'Sibyl' and 'Leroy' over the source, content, and value of the material supposedly provided by Pan. Plath's letters and the dialogue itself, however, imply that she saw the source of the Ouija messages as the couple's unconscious. As Sybil says to Leroy: 'I was perfectly right: Pan's a mere puppet | of our two intuitions' and 'our nerves are the sole nourishers' of his messages. She dismissed the role of Pan here, whom she felt played a false prophet: 'I would rather be staked for a witch, kindled and curled | to a cinder than meet a poor upstart of our nether | selves poaching as prophets'. Sybil also saw Pan as mocking Leroy's attempt to 'dredge up | pools, prophesies and such from the unfathomed | bottom of your brain'. In response to her skepticism, Leroy retorts: 'You need | nothing short of a miracle to nail | faith fast'. The space between these two personalities and diverging viewpoints, central to the dialogue, is put aside as the poem ends with a common statement the couple can agree on: 'When lights go out | May two real people breathe in a real room'.

Plath's 1957 poem 'Ouija' also portrays this divination process, while her poem 'Lorelei', written the following year, is based on a topic suggested by Pan. Referring to the spirit as an actual entity in journal notes and letters, she expressed amazement that it would have her write on the Lorelei, which she had never consciously considered as a subject.[170] The same July 1958 entry also mentions that three days earlier she had begun translating Grimms' fairy tales from German, her first work on the language in two years, effectively returning her creative process to themes that link memory to the unconscious:

> Pan said I should write on the poem-subject 'Lorelei' because they are my 'Own Kin'. So today, for fun, I did so, remembering the plaintive German song mother used to play & sing to us beginning 'Ich weiss nicht was soll es bedenten . . .' The subject appealed to me doubly (or triply): the German legend of the Rhine sirens, the Sea-Childhood symbol, and the death-wish involved in the song's beauty. The poem devoured my day, but I feel it is a book poem & am pleased with it.

The poem 'Lorelei', unlike earlier poems such as 'Aquatic Nocturne' that offers underwater scenarios in a range of colors, presents the 'death-wish' setting beneath moonlight, black and silver waters, and blue mist, with these cool colors placed only within the first two and final stanzas of twelve; Plath's narrowed color palette was now forming:

> It is no night to drown in:
> A full moon, river lapsing
> Black beneath bland mirror-sheen,
>
> The blue water-mists dropping
> Scrim after scrim like fishnets
> Though fishermen are sleeping,
> *   *   *   *   *   *   *

Deep in your flux of silver
Those great goddesses of peace
Stone, stone, ferry me down there.

Regardless of how Plath came upon her subject matter, she saw these processes and the act of writing itself as key to transforming the contents of her psyche into 'book' product. Hughes had introduced his wife to Robert Grave's *The White Goddess,* which explored a cosmology of symbols that connected women to poetry, and to the role of the moon goddess as Muse. While he insisted this book had a major impact on Plath, it may have been his gaze that placed her within this overarching myth system that intrigued her, along with the possibilities of trying out the White Goddess role in her planned novel. Touching upon Lawrence's notion of the 'bitch goddess', in sorting out the character of *The Bell Jar* protagonist, she wrote in her journal, 'who is that blond girl: she is a bitch: she is the white goddess'.[171] Hughes also exposed Plath to applied astrology and Tarot cards, whose depiction of universal forces in ordered, abstract diagrams and colorful imagery would have appealed to her. She planned to learn both divination forms, but like all the subjects she tried to master and gave up as unfruitful avenues, the best uses for these indulgences was in her writing. In 1960 she would accept Hughes's suggestion to write a poem about the 'clever student hanging from a tree'. 'The Hanging Man', based on the thirteenth card of the Tarot's Major Arcana, may have also been informed by Plath's book on Tarot, *The Painted Caravan*,[172] which offers a compelling portrayal of 'The Hanged Man' figure as 'Thief, Judas Card, Tau Cross, or Place of Sacrifice' that connected to her own life experience:

'The Hanging Man'

By the roots of my hair some god got hold of me.
I sizzled in his blue volts like a desert prophet.

The nights snapped out of sight like a lizard's eyelid:
A world of bald white days in a shadeless socket.

A vulturous boredom pinned me in this tree.
If he were I, he would do what I did.

Thought by readers to recall Plath's traumatic electroshock treatments of 1953, 'The Hanging Man' uses some of her now familiar color schematics—blue and white in this case—and the wry voice that would become perfected in late fiction and poetry. The concept of astrological influences on humankind, however, would show up most plaintively in her 1963 poem 'Words', the poem Hughes chose to conclude the *Ariel* collection against his wife's wishes, where the final lines, 'From the bottom of the pool, fixed stars | Govern a life', suggest the fatalistic 'Greek necessity' (per 'Edge') or inevitability of her final act.

FAVORITE COLORS IN ART AS IN LIFE

Sylvia Plath loved the color red, which she referred to as 'my color'.[173] And though she would also favor green and the metallics, her use of blue, black, and white were second to red in designing both her personal and literary environment after returning to England. She surrounded herself with these colors, which she felt had positive psychological effects, influencing her mood and comfort level. Her journal notes and letters are full of references to such objects, where she stated that she taught better wearing colors, as well as textures, that did not 'war' with her 'body & thought'.[174] Plath's favorite reading room at home had white walls and red curtains, furniture, and throw rugs, and the couple referred to a 'blue period' during their last years together. Hughes wrote of associating her with the red, white, and blue of the American flag, but red and black in particular ruled her wardrobe. For example, Plath requested that her mother send her red or black ballet shoes, and Hughes had written of her wearing a magnificent red velvet sleeveless dress at her 1956 birthday dinner. In a 1958 journal entry Plath described her image reflected in shop windows as she walked alone: 'lost, red-heeled, red-gloved, black-flowing coated . . . black-clad'.[175] In spring 1959 she noted her intention to write an article about Wuthering Heights country for 'red-shoes money', and recorded in her journal the sensual pleasure she felt in wearing her clothes and a new pair of red silk stockings:[176]

> 6 MAY: dressed, conscious of the color and the loveliness of being thin and feeling slink, swank and luxurious in good fits and rich materials. For the first time put on my red silk stockings with red shoes—they feel amazing, or, rather, the color feels amazing—almost incandescent fire silk—sheathing my legs: I can't stop looking—the stocking goes almost flesh-color, but gathers rose and glows at the edges of the leg as it cuts its shape on air, concentrating the crimson on the rounding-away, shifting as I shift. Quite satisfactory. I shall wear my white pleated wool skirt and deep lovely median blue jersey with the square neck to hear Robert Lowell this afternoon.

Plath's acute awareness of the role of color, texture, and line in fashion had always been central to her recurring cycles of self-improvement and renewal. Another 1958 journal note discusses her new life she would make from 'words, colors & feelings' and how she felt colors, rhythms, and words 'joining & moving in patterns' that pleased her ear and eye.[177] These renewals were inevitably connected to her professional identity as a woman writer—one who is successful, prolific, and famous—and how she would present herself in that arena. She talked of her body, her senses, and her writing in similar terms of fecundity and fertility, as if every part of her being was preparing for the rich harvest of her lifelong efforts. After reading a collection of *The New Yorker* stories, she wrote of feeling her own stories 'sprout', causing her to predict that she, in the 'fullness of time', would be among 'the poetesses, the authoresses' who had received recognition for their work.[178]

Color and its uses continued to influence much of Plath's writing as she further refined her craft, but at times she worried that her visual leanings overwhelmed her message. In her 1958 poem, 'Watercolor of Grantchester Meadows', she carefully corralled and limited her color references, an effect that became obvious in the poem's spring landscape of rich plant and animal life. Her symmetrical placement of colored objects within the text was also likely intentional. The last lines of the third stanza provide visceral images of floral life that are more aligned with the qualities of mammals mentioned in the poem, again undermining the distinctions between various forms of existence:

> Red clover gnaw beetroot
> Bellied on a nimbus of sun-glazed buttercup.
> Hedging meadows of benign
> Arcadian green
> The blood-berried hawthorn bides its spines with white.

Plath's journal entry of February 1959 expresses her sense of failure with the poem, largely in comparing it to the work of her contemporary Adrienne Cecil Rich, the poet she considered her main female rival: 'A misery. Wrote a Grantchester poem of pure description. I must get philosophy in. Until I do I shall lag behind ACR. A fury of frustration, some inhibition keeping me from writing what I really feel'.[179] But the poem was a success on some level, for a year later it was accepted by *The New Yorker*, after being written, she admitted, with that magazine in mind.

Sylvia Plath and Ted Hughes returned to London at the end of 1959 to pursue their increasingly successful writing careers and to set up house in anticipation of their first child. After selling *The Colossus and Other Poems* to Heinemann Publishers soon after, Plath expected her writing would be enhanced by the experience of motherhood, even if her artistic productivity would be necessarily reduced. After the home birth of her daughter Frieda Rebecca on 1 April, housekeeping and childcare duties caused frequent disruption of her writing, but her work gained a level of finesse that would continue to escalate. Regardless of the exhaustion of serving as wife, mother, hostess, and keeper of immaculate homes, Plath knew she had entered a new period of creativity and artistic achievement. After two decades of studying and experimenting with language, Plath now had all the tools needed to forge her own voice. She started writing *The Bell Jar* in early 1961, finished the novel in August, and published it under a pseudonym.

In March of that year she created her celebrated poem 'Tulips'—her first, according to Hughes, written without the use of the thesaurus she had depended on for vocabulary, and at great speed. Composed during a hospital stay for an appendectomy, this poem also marks the period when some of Plath's favorite colors, in this case red and white, came to impact her imagery in highly evolved forms that were free of the 'falsity' and 'rigidity' she felt had plagued her work. Plath had always been fascinated by the world of hospitals, doctors, and medical professions she had experienced in various capacities, and she wrote on the topic in all sorts of texts. 'Tulips' centers on contrasts in image and emotion, such as the bright red flowers versus the sterile, white hospital setting, self-concern versus family 'hooks', and a watery unconscious state versus the full breath of life—even if this breath is being appropriated by the red flowers. Composed on the same day, 'In Plaster' delves into the dialogue between her own self and 'other' with similar ambiguity.[180] This poem engages Plath's intrigue and study of the classic double in portraying the exchange between the 'old yellow' narrator and the 'absolutely white' figure encased in plaster—most certainly inspired by the woman in a full body cast who occupied a bed near hers. Plath's hopes to create a natural speaking voice based on daily life experiences was now achieved, while the tension between breakaway fantasy and droll, earthy witticism found in much of her mature poetry is sustained. The first two stanzas of eight set up the co-dependent relationship between the original and the double, which after again running through various contrasting stages of old/new, cold/warm, fear/love, is never resolved:

I shall never get out of this! There are two of me now:
This new absolutely white person and the old yellow one,
And the white person is certainly the superior one.
She doesn't need food, she is one of the real saints.
At the beginning I hated her, she had no personality—
She lay in bed with me like a dead body

And I was scared, because she was shaped just the way I was
Only much whiter and unbreakable and with no complaints.
I couldn't sleep for a week, she was so cold.
I blamed her for everything, but she didn't answer.
I couldn't understand her stupid behavior!
When I hit her she held still, like a true pacifist.
Then I realized what she wanted was for me to love her:
She began to warm up, and I saw her advantages.

Successive poetry drafts Plath started to collect after returning to England reveal her typically careful writing process, which had become more spontaneous. In looking at connections between journal entries, poems, art, and various other works, whether planned or executed, it is clear that she had control over a great deal of interrelated material. And with the creation of visual art serving as more of a 'consolation' and pleasure than an urgent need, her painterly eye continued to manifest in increasingly subtle forms. As Plath's preferred colors came to govern her poetic imagery, the rainbow palette seen in early works became largely relegated to descriptions of vibrant scenes of festivals, markets, and landscapes, and in describing her beloved flower gardens. In loose journal papers dated 9 October 1962 (the day she completed 'Wintering' and three days before finishing 'Daddy') she recorded her impressions of the 'incredible massed color of Clare gardens', indulging informally in what she had bemoaned as the purely descriptive qualities of 'Grantchester Meadow'.[181] The entry begins with 'sudden in a shaft of sunlight', a line from T. S. Eliot's 'Burnt Norton' that describes a deserted garden where 'There rises the hidden laughter | Of children in the foliage'. Plath took Eliot's lead in detailing her own luxuriant garden scene:[182]

'sudden in a shaft of sunlight'. All flowers incandescent: tall frilled red, yellow & white dahlias, lavendar & mauve starry asters (michaelmas daisies); little woman feeding gabbling hectic quadroons of ducks over queen's silver street bridge—air-plane view of shiny green mallard heads, speckled brown ladies & queer pure white duck; crossed ragged green meadows before Queens—graceful cinnamon grazing horses; purple clouded skies behind Kings chapel towers, showing stark white; dappled green ivy shade of path to clare.

In her next journal notes dated 21 October, Plath recorded dozens of fleeting word fragments for a planned poem. Placed within Dickinson-like dashes, her notes explore the heat of a woman's fury and 'small' will power set against the large, impersonal forces of nature. These conflicted emotions, which also appear in two poems she wrote the same day ('Amnesiac' and 'Lyonnesse'), are described in white and black, except for one reference to red coal fires:

Poem:

White hot fury—cold snow: Thick white moor—mist—lamps hanging, dim points—still: still: frozen leaves—bunked blackbird: rage—'one second more, the cat-hiss would come out'. Awareness of stifling smothering fury—walk in white blank world—symbol of shutting off from normal clear vision—futile outburst. human limits versus grand marmoreal vast power of cold, snow, stars & blackness . . . black stone fences . . . red coal fires, burning cheeks, cat under coal house . . . pose vast impersonal white world of Nature against small violent spark of will

For this person walking the moors, black, white, and red passions obscure the sense of 'normal clear vision' Plath valued, evocative colors she noted wearing in a March 1956 journal postscript about waiting for Hughes: 'Oh, the fury the fury . . . the panther wakes and stalks again . . . I wrote mad girl's love songs once in a mad mood like this when Mike didn't come and didn't come, and every time I dressed in black, white and red: violent, fierce colors'.[183] During Plath's final years, when she had mastered her art and turned her 'white hot fury' into powerful indictments against the stars and patriarchs that seemed to rule her fate, the lines between her two favorite disciplines—and between herself and her most influential female mentor—were again blurred.

Mastering Vision and Voice

VIRGINIA WOOLF AND THE 'HIDDEN' MENTORS

Many critics have written of Sylvia Plath's literary debt to Virginia Woolf. Sandra M. Gilbert has noted how Woolf's novel *The Waves* influenced Plath's poem 'Words' and her 1962 radio play 'Three Women'. Gilbert also stated that in another 1962 radio piece, 'A Comparison', Plath discussed the limits of poetry, stating she was envious of the novelist's art—this, supposedly, with Woolf in mind.[184] Tracy Brain revealed how Plath used *Mrs. Dalloway* and Charlotte Brontë's *Villette* as a template for *The Bell Jar*, as well as how Plath's 1952 story, 'A Day in June', is derivative of Clarissa Dalloway's stream-of-consciousness description of London in *Mrs. Dalloway*.[185] Steven Axelrod traced the ways in which Woolf, as Plath's 'literary mother', would withhold approval of her progeny's angry repertoire, and how Woolf's political texts—in particular, the feminist message found in *Three Guineas*—were problematic for Plath in light of her marriage, when she seemed relatively content to put her husband's career before her own. In discussing her response to Woolf's more passive, civil voice, Axelrod's focus on Plath's question 'What do we do with anger?' may touch upon a more veiled process here, and an answer to her question.[186] For it is Woolf's novels that may have led to Plath's formation of poetic personas of female empowerment so commanding, they seem to fly off the page and into the streets, as if to do her bidding. Yet like golem bodies of the Kabala, these beings may also be seen as a by-product of attainment—proof of stages on the path, not a deliberate end in their own right.

Determined to make her way as a fiction writer, in February 1957 Plath purchased the 'blessed diary' and novels of Virginia Woolf, which she called an 'excellent inspiration' for her own. While also looking to D. H. Lawrence, Henry James, and J. D. Salinger as mentors for novel-writing, Woolf's luminous, visually driven writing style and women-centered subject matter became the major models for what she saw as her own developing female voice. The two women had much in common. Both were highly skilled and competitive writers who worried about balancing their marriage and artistic careers. Woolf's sister and brother-in-law were painters, and her heightened awareness of visual and color effects is evident in all of her writing. While Plath noted their various differences, she felt an alignment with her 'idol' that had many personal parallels, including a love of cooking and suicidal urges, as noted in her journal:[187]

25 FEBRUARY: I was getting worried about becoming too happily stodgily practical: instead of studying Locke, for instance, or writing—I go make an apple pie, or study the Joy of Cooking, reading it like a rare novel. Whoa, I said to myself. You will escape into domesticity & stifle yourself by falling headfirst into a bowl of cookie batter. And

just now I pick up the blessed diary of Virginia Woolf which I bought with a battery of her novels saturday with Ted. And she works off her depression over rejections from Harper's (no less!—and I can hardly believe that the Big Ones get rejected, too!) by cleaning out the kitchen. And cooks haddock & sausage. Bless her. I feel my life linked to her, somehow. I love her—from reading Mrs. Dalloway for Mrs. Crockett—and I can still hear Elizabeth Drew's voice sending a shiver down my back in the huge Smith class-room, reading from To The Lighthouse. But her suicide, I felt I was reduplicating in that black summer of 1953. Only I couldn't drown. I suppose I'll always be over-vulnerable, slightly paranoid. But I'm so damned healthy & resilient. And apple-pie happy. Only I've got to write. I feel sick, this week, of having written nothing lately. The Novel got to be such a big idea, I got panicked.

Regardless of her nervousness, one month later Plath wrote in a letter home about progress she was making on the book, for which she had been gathering notes:[188]

> 25 MARCH: I grind daily on the rough draft of my 'novel'; only I know that it will cover nine months and be a soul-search, American girl-in-Cambridge, European vacations, etc. If I do my daily stint . . . I should have 300 single-spaced pages by the time we sail for home—a ragged, rough hunk to work on this summer. Once I see what happens myself, I'll start careful rewriting; probably chuck this and rewrite the whole mess.

The impact of Plath's mentor would be deep and long-lived, but her perspective on Woolf as author and woman vacillated between that of an amazed and admiring student to a critical competitor. In comparing their styles, Plath stated she was aiming to be 'Woolfish, but tough'.[189] In the first of two letters in 1955 to fellow student and poet Lynn Lawner, Plath wrote some of her sharpest words yet about Woolf's deficiencies. But in a letter to Lawner written in early 1959, Plath admitted that Woolf was still one of her idols:[190]

> I am ensconced between or among Henry James, Virginia Woolf (who palls, who never, I think, writes more than about tremendous party-dress emotions, except in the odd Mrs. Ramsay—who is, amazingly, often awkward and lumbering in her descriptions) and D. H. Lawrence . . .
> Ironically, I find that although I have always considered myself aware of the modern novel, my main awareness is of Henry James, Virginia Woolf and D. H. Lawrence. Formidable models and idols when confronting a blank page.

Plath recorded more back-and-forth judgments along these lines in her 1959 journals, where she referred to the luminosity of Woolf's novel *The Years* as apprehending both life and time: 'the descriptions, the observations, the feelings caught and let slip, are fine, a luminous web catching it all in, this is life, this is time'.[191] Yet one month later, Plath wrote of the unlikelihood of the novel's protagonist:

> 10 JUNE: Surely, this is not Life, not even real life: there is not even the Ladies' Magazine entrance into sustained loves, jealousies, boredoms. The recreation is that of the most superficial observer at a party of dull old women who have never spilt blood. That is what one misses in Woolf.[192]

Plath's comments on her metaphysical connection to Woolf, and the ways in which she studied her, were reserved for her journals. In an entry of February 1958, and another written soon after, Plath quoted Woolf about finding meaning in life as a writer, one that could capture the ephemeral moments of time and immortalize her name:[193]

> 23 FEBRUARY: I feel mystically that if I read Woolf, read Lawrence—(these two, why?— their vision, so different, is so like mine)—I can be itched and kindled to a great work: burgeoning, fat with the texture & substance of life: this my call, my work; this gives my being a name, a meaning: 'to make of the moment something permanent'.
>
> 2 MARCH: But what is the psychic equivalent of the whole experience: how does Woolf do it? How does Lawrence do it? I come down to learn of those two, Lawrence, because of the rich physical passion—field of force—and the real presence of leaves and earth and beast and, sap-rich, and Woolf because of that almost sexless, neurotic luminousness . . . infusion of radiance: a shimmer of the plasm that is life. I cannot & must not copy either.

Although resolved not to copy Woolf's prose, dramatic imagery from the novels *Mrs. Dalloway* and *The Waves* seems to appear not only in Plath's poem 'Words', but also in 'Lady Lazarus' and 'Ariel', where she indeed managed to create the psychic doubles of Woolf's characters. In *Mrs. Dalloway*, as seen in many of Plath's high school stories, the characters are in transit or view the world from windows. The novel begins with Clarissa Dalloway's view of a motorcar which passes silently and unseen through the London streets, carrying an unknown person that would be revealed as the Prime Minister. The chapter soon moves to a bus ride through the city on a June day, where Dalloway imagines what will be discovered by 'future antiquaries' while 'sifting the ruins of time'. This image of a future audience, sorting through human remnants in hopes of discovering an elusive truth, is written into 'Lady Lazarus'. A handful of objects in this poem also found in Woolf's prose include bones, wedding rings, gold fillings/stoppings, and dust/ash—as well as a male patriarch connected to Empire and death:

> when London is a grass-grown path and all those hurrying along the pavement this Wednesday morning are but bones and a few wedding rings mixed up in their dust and the gold stoppings of innumerable decayed teeth. Then the face in the motorcar will then be known.

*   *   *   *   *

> Ash, ash—
> You poke and stir.
> Flesh, bone, there is nothing there—
>
> A cake of soap,
> A wedding ring,
> A gold filling.

While working out the characters of *The Bell Jar*, Plath's journal entry describes Woolf as an enabler, who must eventually be superseded by the child—possibly herself as Esther Greenwood, a persona likely informed by de Chirico's fascination with 'Enigma' as well as Hughes's infatuation with Robert Graves' *The White Goddess*:[194]

> Virginia Woolf helps. Her novels make mine possible: I find myself describing episodes: you don't have to follow your Judith Greenwood to breakfast, lunch or dinner, or tell about her train rides, unless the flash forwards her, reveals her. Make her enigmatic: who is that blond girl: she is a bitch: she is the white goddess. Make her a statement of the generation.

As Axelrod points out, the fact that *The Bell Jar* protagonist was originally called 'Judith' may elude to the another imagined figure, that of 'Judith Shakespeare'—the tragic sister of William—that Woolf wrote of in her famous text *A Room of One's Own*,[195] a book that Plath did not mention in journals nor annotate with her usual markings and marginalia. In fact, within the huge body of works Plath left behind, it is her surprising silences on certain subjects that are worth examining, as well as the role her diaries and journals played as an imaginary friend of sorts, to whom she would share her secrets. In one case she extended this entity to the realm of the sacred, where she disclosed in her journal 'and I alone am escaped to tell thee'.[196] Plath's comment on how she liked reading D. H. Lawrence 'selfishly' for his influence on her own life and writing offers a clue on her own somewhat 'secret' uses of important mentors. For example, while Plath admitted to her mother how she used Emily Dickinson as a model for poetry she was writing, her general lack of commentary on Dickinson's poetry might be seen in the context of distancing herself from what Aurelia Plath called her own 'bible'; Plath wrote instead of her admiration for the sensual imagery of Rossetti, Lowell, Sitwell, and Lawrence. The absence of direct commentary on the works or life of Vincent van Gogh, or discussion of the novels of the Brontë sisters (her earliest reference was a diary note at age 11 about seeing the movie 'Jane Eyre' twice in a row), the horrors of World War II, the 'feminist' cause, and Woolf's *A Room of One's Own* and *Three Guineas* (also unmarked by Plath) may 'speak volumes' even if Plath did not directly reference them. For these hidden topics ultimately found voice in her poetry, making a presence in some of her more electrifying *Ariel* personas—most notoriously, 'Lady Lazarus' who consumes men, the possibly Jewish daughter and victim of the Nazi figure in 'Daddy', and the fearless rider of 'Ariel', the Hebrew lioness of God—indeed, women capable of spilling blood. While in *Three Guineas* Woolf's narrator suggests flaming the word 'feminist' out of existence, it seems as if Plath pulled it out of the ashes and resurrected it par excellence in her own 'statement of the generation' voiced by the 'blond bitch' and directed to the entire system of patriarchal privilege, without ever writing the word. This particular brat, however, has an unabashedly American voice that deliberately avoids what Plath saw as the constricting gentility of British writing—a voice she characterized as 'fresh, brazen, colloquial'.[197]

The outward expression of feminist vengeance that Woolf suppressed may be embodied most directly in the pre-feminist era, phoenix-like figure of 'Lady Lazarus' who mocks 'Herr God, Herr Enemy'. It is the figure of male dominance—represented in the Prime Minister, the generals of war, and the figure of death—that Woolf also continually confronted in her life and work. Both Woolf and Plath described death as a desirous seducer, often the enemy, associated with the cycle of degeneration and renewal, and in certain cases, with the vehicle of the horse. Gilbert noted how Neville's passage cited above ('Words and words and words, how they gallop') resonates in Plath's Ariel poem 'Words'—which ends with the fatalistic view of a life ruled by the stars.

> Echoes traveling
> Off from the center like horses
>
> ★   ★   ★   ★   ★   ★   ★
>
> Words dry and riderless,
> The indefatigable hoof-taps.

This connection may be confirmed in Plath's copy of *The Waves*, where she underlined sections from the speeches of characters Neville and Bernard that bring together narratives and objects she would also employ in 'Ariel':[198]

> I am a poet, yes. Surely I am a great poet. Boats and youth passing and distant trees...Words and words and words, how they gallop—how they lash their long manes and tails, but for some fault in me I cannot give myself to their backs; I cannot fly with them, scattering women and string bags. There is some flaw in me—some fatal hesitancy, which, if I pass it over, turns to foam and falsity.[199]

> Death is the enemy. It is death against whom I rise with my spear couched and my hair flying back like a young man's, like Percival's, when he galloped in India. I strike spurs into my horse. Against you I will fling myself, unvanquished and unyielding, O Death![200]

The name 'Ariel', which may have represented both the spirit-horse in *The Tempest* and the actual horse of that name that Plath was riding in lessons at the time, has numerous links to these same two passages in *The Waves:* foam, strings, hair flying, the view over water of the human world left behind, the arch of the horse's back as the rider flies upward, and the inability of the rider to control the thrust of the animal. In 'Ariel' the narrator ascends to the skies on her horse in a liberating, irrepressible drive towards the sun and annihilation, duplicating Woolf's words and imagery in phrases such as 'brown arc | Of the neck I cannot catch . . . hair; | Flakes from my heels', 'dead stingencies . . . I | Foam to wheat', 'dew that flies | Suicidal . . . | into the red | Eye . . . of morning'.

Yet it is the final passage of *The Waves* that seems to have taken Plath to her roots as a poet. In the rider of 'Ariel', Plath indeed created the 'psychic equivalent' of Woolf's character Bernard, who stated: 'Surely I am a great poet' before flying toward his death, like the Greek youth Icarus who flew too close to the sun against his father's advice. The horse-rider deaths of Woolf and Plath both pose a deliberate and defiant 'unyielding' to the finality of death. For one may, it is asserted, find immortality in the written word, with the high ground being held, per tradition, by the poet. Five months after purchasing Woolf's novels and memoirs in England,

and right after carting them back to Massachusetts, Plath offered her most detailed and illuminating commentary on *The Waves*. This lengthy journal entry of 1957, written the day after she finished the novel, encapsulates many of her thoughts on life, writing, and the issue of motherhood, crystallized in the context of her own journey—and an underlined quote of William Blake:[201]

> 7 JULY: Last night: finished 'The Waves', which disturbed, almost angered by the endless sun, waves, birds, and the strange unevenness of description—a heavy, ungainly sentence next to a fluent, pure running one. But then, the hair-raising fineness of the last 50 pages: Bernard's summary, an essay on life, on the problem: the deadness of a being to whom nothing can happen, who no longer creates, creates, against the casting down. . . . My life, I feel, will not be lived until there are books and stories which relive it perpetually in time. I forget too easily how it was, and shrink to the horror of the here and now, with no past and no future. <u>Writing breaks open the vaults of the dead and the skies behind which the prophesying angels hide</u>.

As Plath had hoped, the 'here and now' did not contain her. If we extend this affiliation of lineage to its farther edges, and engage in what Jacqueline Rose identifies as the creative 'fantasy' that Plath embodies,[202] we might play with some questions: In underlining the words of Blake on oracles coming from writers of the past, might Plath also be placing herself in a lineage of seers whose writing would overtake death? Might the visionary/visual lineage of the painter Blake also extend to Yeats, who had intended to follow his father's career as a painter, and whose brother, like Woolf's sister, was also a professional painter? Gilbert referred to Plath's literary inheritance in the context of the 'House of Yeats'[203] where she literally ended her life, in an essay on the topic that quotes the final lines of Yeats's poem 'To Dorothy Wellesley' for its epitaph:

> *Climb to your chamber full of books and wait,*
> *No books upon the knee, and no one there*
> *But a Great Dane that cannot bay the moon*
> *And now lies sunk in sleep.*
> *What climbs the stair?*
> *Nothing that common women ponder on*
> *If you are worth my hope! Neither Content*
> *Nor satisfied Conscience, but that great family*
> *Some ancient famous authors misrepresent,*
> *The proud Furies each with her torch on high.*

Can we also look to this high chamber of books Yeats writes of, and see the sleeping 'Great Dane' who cannot bay at the moon as Shakespeare's Hamlet, whose beloved Ophelia commits suicide in a manner similar to Virginia Woolf's? May we look to Yeats in the context of Plath's visionary inheritance that passed through literary threads—or torches—per Blake's realm of angelic prophesy? Is Yeats's figure who waits at the top of the stairs connected to the vision-induced figure of H.D.'s 'Tribute to the Angels' who stands in the same place, holding her book that contains the 'unwritten pages of the new' which is also a 'tale of a jar'?[204] And is this figure in turn related to Woolf's young Judith Shakespeare who kills herself at a London crossroads after being betrayed by her colleague and lover, a man of the theatre? In a final stage of rebellion against her literary mother, may Plath be seen to 'bust windows' for the sake of breathing fresh air, just as Woolf accused Joyce of doing after reading *Ulysses*?[205] In fact, is Joyce Plath's real literary parent? The one who tied inspiration to memory, the barnburner who blazed the old school of writing, just as Woolf suggested in *Three Guineas* that the old school for women—their fathers' libraries of male-authored classics—may be best burnt down? Like Joyce, Plath not only rejected Woolf's approach of avoiding the display of blatant ego, self-absorption, and anger, she used these tools to reforge a new language of classics, per the tradition of H.D., as well as multiple personas she created that spoke directly to *her* generation. As if employing a form of sympathetic magic, Plath's confluence of character names and personal identities speak to how she saw her life, work, and literary afterlife interwoven with that of Virginia Woolf and other mentors, hinting at how these resonances may in turn extend to her readers. Yet this form of 'magic' bypasses the mere divinational powers of the tarot cards wielded by the gypsy daughter of 'Daddy' to encompass the transformational power of human language—the realm of sound and words also inhabited by bards, visionaries, healers, and yogis throughout the ages.

In traversing these 'star paths' lit by predecessors, however, Plath kept one foot on common ground. While there was a certain romance in aligning herself with Woolf, she admitted to having another 'literary mother' who wrote for the popular audience, but whose potential influence on her own writing went largely un-acknowledged. The American novelist and Smith alumni Olive Higgins Prouty endowed scholarships that supported Plath's study at Smith, and she also paid most of her hospital bills in 1953. Although Plath came to deride Prouty in letters home and in her biting portrayal of her as a character in *The Bell Jar*, this initially secret sponsor had much in common with Plath as well as Woolf. Prouty started publishing her novels in 1913, years before the women's suffrage movement of the twenties, the 'first wave' of twentieth-century feminism. Her stories portray the difficulties American women faced in trying to find a life of independence and integrity, despite the extremely limited roles afforded them by Victorian and prewar society. Although her mother was superintendent of the Sunday school at a conservative Congregational church, Prouty, when asked by the minister whether she believed in Jesus Christ, replied 'I guess so.'[206] As a teenager she dreamed of becoming a writer, and worried that marriage would be the end of her hopes for a professional life. Although her husband encouraged her writing, Prouty was constantly torn between her responsibilities to her family and her craft, which she felt she had to practice, with admitted deceit, as if it was only a 'hobby'. Two of her three children died while young, and two years after losing her infant daughter she suffered what she called a 'nervous breakdown'. Her psychiatrist advised her to get a room of her own outside her house so that she could work regularly as a professional writer. She would later describe her experience at her doctor's sanitarium as 'an educational institution from which I "graduated"', and her story of breakdown and recovery would be incorporated into two of her novels.[207] When Prouty's novels became successful, she donated most of her proceeds to charity. She wrote her last novel in 1951, the year of her husband's death and Plath's early study at Smith. Ten years later, when Prouty tried to find a publisher for her memoirs (in 1961, the year *The Bell Jar* was being written), her reputation as a writer had fallen off, and she was forced to publish the book at her own expense.

After being turned into a play and a Hollywood movie, *Stella Dallas,* Prouty's most famous novel, was made into a radio serial that aired weekdays for eighteen years. The author, however, who had not consented to the sale of the rights, was appalled that her protagonist had been turned into a melodramatic and sentimental heroine. She tried without success to stop it from being broadcast. Yet in 1958, facing her career as a writer, Sylvia Plath had readily acknowledged her intentions to create emotionally wrought stories that featured such heroines. After publishing her first book of poems in 1960, Plath would continue her plans to create stories for women's magazines, as well as more 'potboiler' novels, as she described *The Bell Jar* in a letter home. But the figure of Prouty as a living role model, so closely aligned with her own mother, may have been too close for Plath's comfort. And as self-absorbed as Plath was in her own development as an artist, she may have been unaware or uninterested in Prouty's early courage in forging her identity as a writer of substance.

WRITING ACROSS THE GROUNDS OF YADDO

While composing poems for Robert Lowell's poetry workshop in 1958, Sylvia Plath was also taking children's books from the library in preparation for writing one of her own. After composing an eight-page poem titled 'The Bed Book', she wrote in her journal that she was very pleased with the work, and would rather publish this book than a poetry collection. The following year, however, after surgery that allowed her to become pregnant, the prospect of motherhood became a unique stimulus for poetry that would extend beyond her and her husband's eleven-week autumn stay at Yaddo, the renowned artist's colony in Saratoga Springs, New York. After leaving her teaching job, and with nearly three months devoted to writing ahead of her, the pressure was on to produce 'book poems'—as distinguished from 'exercise poems'—for her planned collection, while also publishing as many singular works as possible.

Unburdened by household duties, and with plans to move back to England in December for the early spring birth of their child, Plath had time to write, read, draw, and explore the Yaddo estate grounds at her leisure. Soon after arriving she wrote to her mother, 'I particularly love the scenic beauty of the estate: the rose gardens, goldfish pools, marble statuary everywhere, wood walks, little lakes', objects that would become central to her writing over the fall.[208] She was feeling more confident after achieving her long-lived ambition to get her work into *The New Yorker*, which had accepted her poems 'Mussel Hunter at Rock Harbor' and 'Nocturne' (renamed 'Hardcastle Crags') in June 1958. While Plath had nearly a dozen essays published in the *Christian Science Monitor* during the Boston and Yaddo period, she called the publication 'smalltime' and wrote in her Yaddo journal of having 'dreams of grandeur': *The New Yorker* accepting her illustrations along with her written works—'giving sanction to my running about drawing chairs and baskets'.[209] In the meanwhile, she kept track of what the *Monitor* was publishing. In a letter to her mother,[210] Plath mentioned having 'two little exercise poems' accepted by their Home Forum Page, and a week later she wrote again asking:[211]

Explorations Lead to Interesting Discoveries

By Sylvia Plath
Saratoga Springs, N. Y.

Outworn objects have a way of keeping strange company. Whether in barns or basements, attics or antique shops, they leave behind their natural environment and form nodding oblongs, knobs and wheels, legs and handles.

There, four feet planted firmly in the crab grass and purple vetch, a rusted iron stove stood, subject to any whim of the weather. A stippling of orangey red warmed the once-black surface against the weathered, oyster-white shingles of the garage had seen their heyday and come to rest, unsung, dimly remembered by their owner, if at all; and yet, not without a certain shapeliness, an honorable patina conferred by time and wear.

Here I found an old-fashioned sleigh on holiday, its snow-cutting runners framing the scrolls and plumes of summer greenery, bearing no wind-nipped children of the nineties, but a crew of jugs and tins. The jugs of sturdy earthenware, mottled gray, buff, and a glossy molasses-brown, perched fat and complacent on the back of the sleigh as on any pantry shelf.

Once one becomes a hunter of odds and ends, of "shoes and ships and sealing wax," or whatever may turn up, no long-neglected corner is safe from the curious eye. Each object has a line, a tint, a character of its own—the older and odder the better.

One does not need to become a buyer of antiques to savor these age-polished, wear-smoothed jugs, and barrows and boxes and stoves and sleighs. One can try to capture them with a few lines of the pen, or, lacking cupboard space, store them in a niche of words.

Drawings by the author

A colorful pattern of rounds and oblongs, knobs and wheels, legs and handles

acquaintances with all manner of strangers.

While exploring in the country one summer day, I rounded the corner of a weed-grown garage long fallen out of use and discovered, near a large pile of quahog shells, a whole clan of these once-serviceable, discarded objects basking in the bright sunlight. Jumbled together with apparent abandon they formed a colorful pattern of rounds and face to a glow worthy of an oil painter.

Next to the stove a sun-silvered wooden chest took the air, empty now, but stirring the imagination: what had it held and guarded in its day? Fine linens, a carpenter's tools, a pirate's coins? And how did it come at last to sit beside a rubber tire, round as a doughnut, an upended wheelbarrow, and a pump?

All of these objects silhouetted

The value of these objects is sometimes only in the eyes of the beholder. However, the choicest of them often appear—still in motley company but with a price tag matching their age and rarity—in antique shops.

Dear Youth Section

In a recent issue in the Youth Section a contributor told of using the blower attachment of her vacuum cleaner to aid in defrosting the refrigerator. Today I used the same method and I have never defrosted so well, so quickly, so easily before. I wish to thank your contributor for the suggestion and The Christian Science Monitor for printing it.

(Mrs.) Louise Dunn
Los Angeles, Calif.

"Each object has a line, a tint, a character of its own—the older and odder the better."

Household Hint in Rhyme

If you're one of those people who do not enjoy
Cleaning silver, here's what you must do:
Make a polishing cloth from instruction below,
It's so simple and timesaving, too.
Take an old piece of toweling, eighteen-inches square,
Stitch the edges so that they won't fray,
Then into a bowl put the following things
And mix them all up straightaway.
Of household ammonia, two tablespoons,
Two teaspoons of plate-powder, too,
Two cups of warm water is all that you need,
Soak your towel, and dry it; then you
Simply wash all your silver in hot soapy suds,
And use this cloth to rub the things dry,
Then your silver will always keep gleaming and
    bright,
It's so easy to do. Why not try?

RUTH WILDING

Have you seen my two sets of drawings on the Youth Page of the Monitor these last Mondays—the 12th & 19th? Do save them, because I would like copies of the drawings which came out well. The paragraphs were only written to glue them together and give them more likelihood of being printed. Have either my Yaddo or Magnolia Shoals poem come out on the Home Forum Page yet?

That year Plath published two illustrated articles in *Christian Science Monitor* that offered an artist's perspective on the sights she drew: 'Mosaics—An Afternoon of Discovery' and 'Explorations Lead to Interesting Discoveries'.[212] The first essay details her efforts to draw the vibrant scenery of the Spanish fishing village where she had spent her honeymoon. As always, she considered the act of creating art and her subject matter equally worthy of analysis. Plath began this essay by pointing out the obvious advantages of a 'motionless subject to a person rather slow with pen and pencil . . . the pattern is a constant one, changing only with the light, as shadows shorten or lengthen, emphasizing line or mass'. Since the cows and villagers were never still for long, she used the 'mosaics' formed by the various windows, balconies, doors, and chimneys of buildings for her drawing subject. The second essay discusses an odd assortment of items she had come across in the countryside, where each object 'has a line, a tine, a character of its own—the older and odder the better'. She described them as offering:

> a colorful pattern of rounds and oblongs, knobs and wheels, legs and handles, tumbled together with apparent abandon that formed a rusted iron stove as a strippling of orangey red that warmed the once-black surface to a glow worthy of an oil painter.

Perhaps because Plath had already published her only appropriate kitchen drawing in the 'Mosaics' essay, and she was not comfortable drawing from memory, another essay published by the *Monitor* that year was not illustrated. But this lack was compensated by Plath's visually rich and lyrical language that evoked her pleasurable cooking experiences in a style she felt was suited to the magazine's 'Home Forum Page' readers. In 'Kitchen of the Fig Tree' she compared three kitchens she had cooked in as a married woman—including her Boston 'Kitchen with a View' and English 'Kitchen of the Four Doors', so named for its four doors that led to other rooms.[213] The essay first presents the view outside Plath's kitchen window in Boston, opening with the statement that while others may like 'a room with a view', she would rather have a kitchen with a view. After all, Plath loved to work while looking out windows, and she spent a good deal of time cooking elaborate meals. She complained about the inconveniences of the English kitchen in this and other texts, and named her Spanish 'Kitchen of the Fig Tree' as her favorite for the fruit it offered outside the door, to be eaten straight from its branches.

Reflecting her preference to draw from models, Plath generally used her daily experiences, past and current, for writing material. If she didn't record her impressions on the spot, she was known to return from an outing and immediately take to her journal to describe what she had seen and heard. Plath mentioned her inertia in starting stories at Yaddo, and the same journal entry that notes her dreams of grandeur also contain a reminder to herself to 'Send for diary'—meaning, remind her mother to send it from her Wellesley home. Just as this childhood home served as a storehouse of memories and past works Mrs. Plath kept religiously and would send off when beckoned, Plath's Yaddo experience would provide images and texts upon which she drew for the rest of her life. Borrowings from the Yaddo journals, poems, and pictures, in fact, can be detected in some of her most influential late poetry.

An intricate drawing she made, along with its description in a Yaddo journal entry, confirms Plath's sense of drawing as therapy and inspiration for writing. She described the first 'ambitious seeds' of a poem on a birthday (her own coming five days later) that would be 'a dwelling on madhouse, nature: meanings of tools, greenhouses, florist shops, tunnels, vivid and disjointed. An adventure. Never over. Developing. Rebirth, Despair, Old women. Block it out.' This same entry indicates that many of the greenhouse objects she drew formed the basis of 'Who', the first segment the seven-part 'Poem for a Birthday':

22 OCTOBER: Drew a surgical picture of a greenhouse stove yesterday and a few flowerpots. An amazing consolation. Must get more intimate with it. That greenhouse is a mine of subjects. Watering cans, gourds and squashes and pumpkins. Beheaded cabbages inverted from the rafters, wormy purple outer leaves. Tools: rakes, hoes, brooms, shovels. The superb identity, selfhood of things.

> 1. 'Who'
> The month of flowering's finished. The fruit's in,
> Eaten or rotten. I am all mouth.

October's the month for storage.
This shed's fusty as a mummy's stomach;
Old tools, handles and rusty tusks.
I am at home here among the dead heads.

Let me sit in a flowerpot,
The spiders won't notice.
My heart is a stopped geranium.

If only the wind would leave my lungs alone.
Dogbody noses the petals. They bloom upside down.
They rattle like hydrangea bushes.

Moldering heads console me,
Nailed to the rafters yesterday:
Inmates who don't hibernate.

Cabbageheads: wormy purple, silver-glaze,
A dressing of mule ears, mothy pelts, but green-hearted,
Their veins white as porkfat.

O the beauty of usage!
The orange pumpkins have no eyes.
These halls are full of women who think they are birds.

This segment and its title indeed address what Plath identified in her journal as 'the superb identity, selfhood of things', as well as the 'never-over' adventure of exploring the psyche. Admittedly designed as a 'pastiche' based on the poetry of Theodore Roethke (who wrote of greenhouses owned by his father, Otto), the entire seven-part sequence was accepted for *The Colossus and Other Poems,* first published in England. But when *The Colossus* was published in the United States, Plath suspected the American intolerance for the 'macabre' may have resulted in the rejection of the poem by editors—one of whom was Marianne Moore. At Plath's insistence, however, two of seven sections, '*Who*' not among them, were retained in the second published version of 'Poem for a Birthday', a work many critics see as the initial signs of her awakening *Ariel* voice.

Plath's recycling of material from her Yaddo texts is evident in her 1961 poem 'Private Ground' (originally titled 'First Frost'), one of the many poems she wrote about the art colony. The last two lines of the poem's third stanza use her common technique of giving natural or inanimate objects an emotional life:

> Flatten the doped snakes to ribbons. In here, the grasses
> Unload their griefs on my shoes

Months later Plath felt the concept of grieving grasses was worth recapturing for 'The Moon and the Yew Tree', which has the image slightly reformulated and placed significantly in the poem's third line:

> The grasses unload their griefs on my feet as if I were God

One of Plath's most celebrated poems, 'The Moon and the Yew Tree' was written in October 1961, five days before her 29th birthday—always a productive month for Plath, as it would be again in 1962, when many of her powerful *Ariel* poems were composed. This four-stanza poem reveals Plath's late color preferences—minus red—and careful manipulation of dark and light contrasts in relation to associative color imagery, opening with two lines that reveal the narrator's internalized thought:

> This is the light of the mind, cold and planetary.
> The trees of the mind are black. The light is blue.

Set in cool shades that reflect the season, only the trees are noted as black in this second and final line: 'And the message of the yew tree is blackness, blackness and silence', while the moon's face in the second stanza is 'White as a knuckle'. The color blue, however, is placed throughout, where the blue light of the mind is followed by the moon-mother's cloud coverings of the third stanza: 'Her blue garments unloose small bats and owls', and the clouds and robes of the saints in the last stanza: 'Clouds are flowering | Blue and mystical over the face of the stars. | Inside the church, the saints will all be blue'. The effect is that of a spooky outdoor scene: a round pagan moon illuminating jagged night creatures and tree branches through its moving clouds, set in contrast to the Christian saints stilled and contained in the church, also floating like clouds, yet with 'hands and faces stiff with holiness'. Plath again recreated here what she called the 'bleak geometric tension of color and form', the term she used to describe the 'ugliness' of Hopkins House, where she imagined the 'brittle bony branches squeaking hideously as the wind stirs them' against the house.

Other poems Plath wrote on her remarkable Yaddo experience, most notably 'Medallion' and 'Private Ground', as well as her journal of the period, seem to have directly contributed to 'Edge', one of two final poems written six days before her death on 11 February 1963. A Yaddo journal entry begins with the description of frost on the plants and grass, the 'dead red' petals of the roses, and the white statues that were being shut into huts for the season:

> 1 NOVEMBER: Frost stiffened and outlines the grassblades with white, and the whorls and rosettes of leaves and weeds. The rose garden shone in the sun, the thorny stems, with dead red leaves, bound together. The white statues are all encased in little wooden huts, like out-houses, against the raves of winter and vandals.

The first stanza of 'Private Ground' contains many of these images, as did 'Edge', where the 'stiffened' rose garden, white objects, and a dead woman associated with a Greek figure are prominent:

> First frost, and I walk among the rose-fruit, the marble toes
> Of the Greek beauties you brought
> Off Europe's relic heap
> To sweeten your neck of the New York woods.
> Soon each white lady will be boarded up
> Against the crackling climate.

> **'Edge'**
> The woman is perfected.
> Her dead
>
> Body wears the smile of accomplishment,
> The illusion of a Greek necessity
>
> Flows in the scrolls of her toga,
> Her bare
>
> Feet seem to be saying:
> We have come so far, it is over.
>
> Each dead child coiled, a white serpent,
> One at each little
>
> Pitcher of milk, now empty.
> She has folded
>
> Them back into her body as petals
> Of a rose close when the garden

Stiffens and odors bleed
From the sweet, deep throats of the night flower.
The moon has nothing to be sad about,
Staring from her hood of bone.
She is used to this sort of thing.
Her blacks crackle and drag.

The despairing moon in 'The Moon and the Yew Tree' sees nothing of the church interior, offering her observant daughter no tenderness, and the moon in 'Edge' stares down in nonchalance, bringing the poems to similar endings. Yet the acceptance or inevitability of death expressed in 'Edge', also found in the last lines of 'Private Ground' (see below), has caused many readers to see this poem as pointedly autobiographical in referencing the death of the 'woman perfected' so close to her own suicide. While this interpretation has foundation, it may be more of a reading in hindsight instead of planning on Plath's part. The last extant letter she wrote, a week before her death, was addressed to her close friend and college roommate Marcia Brown, whom she had invited to visit, stating her wishes to show off her two beautiful children. In 'Edge', the representation of a dead mother who enfolds her dead children into her body 'as petals of a rose close', and the two dead children as serpents, are some of the poem's most provocative images. But they may be related not so much to Plath's own story of loss and death, but to that Yaddo's founders—notably, Mrs. Katrina Trask, a poet and mystic who was interred in a tomb at Yaddo surrounded by roses—as well as her own anxiety about birthing a healthy child. The connections between these various texts are dizzying in their abundance and inter-related imagery, creating the sense of falling into a labyrinth of connecting links. Yet as seen in 'Private Ground', these impressions were originally addressed to the mistress of Yaddo, who left her symbol, a rose, carved on the building's lintels and mantels. Plath placed the line: 'Eleven weeks, and I know your estate so well' prominently in the poem's first drafts as well as the final draft, while she excised another significant line: 'I am the daughter of your melancholy'. Plath also removed two stanzas that explore the personal qualities of Mrs. Trask at the end of the draft process, including references to her similarity to the 'dreaming woman' of a Fuseli painting, her body being laid after death in quicklime 'like a criminal', her having 'One foot in the Tyrol, the other stuck somewhere | In manic-depressive Prussia', and the 'ghost of Wagner' and German beer—though the 'The snows of the Tyrol, the clear beer of Vienna' would show up in 'Daddy'.

The Yaddo estate was dominated by its magnificent and extensive rose gardens, but also by the tragic story and images of the Trask family, who were depicted in portraits throughout the manor. All four of the Trask children died from diphtheria while young, and Mrs. Trask dedicated the artist colony (named by a daughter) and one of its statues, to their memory. Plath's Yaddo poems are infused by the scent of fading roses and twin images of sleeping figures and dead baby creatures, including the two dead moles of 'Blue Moles'; the 'incense of death' coming from the fading fall roses in 'Manor Garden' (which seems to speak to her own developing child through its fetal phases and family inheritances, including suicides, which she notes on the father's side); the two sleeping figures of 'The Sleepers' (who 'among petals pale as death . . . they sleep on, mouth to mouth', and to which 'no harm' can come); and the 'dead baby snake' she saw on the grounds, noted in journal notes. Plath's early Yaddo journals identify 'Medallion' as the 'one good poem' she had written since coming to the estate, which she described as 'an imagist piece on the dead snake'.[214] Indeed, 'Medallion' contains many words and concepts found in 'Edge'. It features a dead snake with a 'rose-colored tongue' whose opaque belly recalls 'milk glass' around which 'white maggots coil'. And the final lines present the laugh of the snake being 'perfected' in death, just as the first line of 'Edge' posits a woman perfected in death. And where the 'throats' of roses bleed sweetness in 'Edge', it is the white statues in 'Private Ground' that serve to 'sweeten' Mrs. Trask's 'neck' of the New York woods. The first of fourteen drafts of the poem, in fact, begins with an address to Mrs. Trask with few changes:

> First frost, and I walk among the rose hips, the marble toes
> Of the Greek beauties you brought by ship
> From Europe's relic heap
> To sweeten your neck of the New York Woods.
> Soon each white lady will be boarded up

The second stanza ends with a reference to the dead carp the narrator gathers from the Yaddo ponds, but the inclusion of the word 'baby' also makes their presence seem more human: 'The baby carp | Litter the mud like orangepeel' (while the dead snake in 'Medallion' was positioned in 'peeled orange wood'). In the final lines of the fourth and last stanza, the narrator dispassionately likens the pool of water to a morgue that holds the small lives, similar to that of the moon in 'Edge' who is 'used to that sort of thing'—the cycle of life and death:

> The woods creak and ache, and the day forgets itself
> I bend over this drained basin where the small fish
> Flex as the mud freezes.
> They glitter like eyes, and I collect them all.
> Morgue of old logs and old images, the lake
> Opens and shuts, accepting them among its reflections.

This 'morgue of old logs and old images' that accepts the glittering eyes of lives that pass through it may be connected to Plath's own reservoir of visual images, interlocking memories, and fears of motherhood in relation to her own pregnancy, contributing to some of the ground-breaking poems that would surface during her final months. Yet the revelatory edges of the unconscious and the psyche that Plath and Hughes shared so closely and incorporated into their art must also be taken into account in looking at the Yaddo experience. Hughes was working on an intensive study of *The Tibetan Book of the Dead* and its central *bhardo* experience— the liminal space between death and rebirth wherein the departed spirit journeys for seven weeks. Plath was also contemplating realms between worlds during her last months in America. While preparing her first book of poetry for publication, and after mentioning her best poem about the dead snake in journal notes, she commented, 'my book poems <u>are</u> all about ghosts and otherworldly miasmas.'[215] In gathering all the 'glittering eyes' from the Yaddo lake, this eleven-week journey may have created the conditions in which Plath was able to experience some form of visionary awakening, a Joycean epiphany that positioned her past, current, and future works in alignment with her metaphysical identity as a cultural and literary phenomenon *to be*. Two years earlier, when looking to demarcate her ultimate voice, she wrote in her journal, 'I must be a word artist. The heroine. Like Stephen Dedalus walking by the sea', sounding on the bird-girl's 'petticoats'.[216] On the private grounds of Yaddo, the portrait Sylvia Plath was painting of herself as a sea-bitten artist-heroine, looking both backward and forward, was coming into focus.

THE CHILD'S EYE, THE WOMAN'S HEART IN *ARIEL*

Sylvia Plath used the visually rich 'intimate wonderland' of her youth as a creative touchstone all her life. But it was the act of listening to poetry—her 'new way of being happy' she experienced as a child—that formed her approach to the *Ariel* poems. In 1962, during her last year of life, Plath was writing reviews of children's literature, reading to her children, and regularly listening to and recording her own BBC radio recordings. Adopting Hughes's long-term advice to write poems meant to be read out loud, she used the chanting rhythms, rhymes, and loopy word play of children's literature in some of her more important poetry. Two of Plath's most influential works, 'Daddy' and 'Lady Lazarus', reflect some of the heavy rhyming, repetition, and simple iambic pentameter rhythms found in the books of Dr. Suess, one of Plath's favorite childhood authors. (She had reviewed his *Cat in the Hat* book, and was surely aware of *Green Eggs and Ham*, published in 1960.) The Lady Lazarus persona, a multifaceted frightener long in forming, extends a heavy toll for the 'hearing of the heart' as well as the viewing of her scars. While composing for sound, however, Plath never abandoned her visual repertoire; the red flame of the Lady's hair and the black shoe of 'Daddy' are surely among the more formidable color images found in modern poetry. Written the same month as these two ground-breaking poems, on Plath's final birthday of 27 October, 'Poppies in October' drafts demonstrate how the artist's highly developed color strategies and language inversions deliver mood with subtlety and force. The final version mentions only the color red, but this red is not used to describe the late blooming poppies, but the woman's heart, while it is the flowers that wear skirts:

> **'Poppies in October'**
>
> Even the sun-clouds this morning cannot manage such skirts.
> Nor the woman in the ambulance
> Whose red heart blooms through her coat so astoundingly—
>
> A gift, a love gift
> Utterly unasked for
> By a sky
>
> Palely and flamily
> Igniting its carbon monoxides, by eyes
> Dulled to a halt under bowlers.

31. Photo of Plath with daughter Frieda, 1961

> O my God, what am I
> That these late mouths should cry open
> In a forest of frost, in a dawn of cornflowers.

Set against the cool, assumed black of bowler hats, the frost at dawn, and the blue of cornflowers, is the urgency of a medical emergency. A draft version of the poem shows how Plath eventually reduced the event to its simplest form, free of excessive adjectives, objects, or exposition.[217] Between the ambulance and the red heart, she initially placed two lines using the colors white and grey, here associated with the death of a male and a state of linear distance that silently mimics the distinctive sound of a retreating ambulance:

> The white, decorous hearse,
> . . . will roll him forever
> In to the diminishing grey architectural perspectives of limbo

The deletion of these lines moves the poem away from Plath's Chircio city-like liminal spaces of uncertain existence, returning the focus to red, to human life, to the woman whose heart beats and opens like a flower.

In Plath's final poems inspired by the experience of motherhood, some likely intended for her volume following *Ariel,*[218] she incorporated brightly colored objects, including toys, to evoke the child's place within the domestic space. And even in late texts where direct references to colors or emotion rarely surface, their presence is felt. In the poem 'Child', written two weeks before her death, the word 'color' is followed by objects associated with certain colors that contrast the unhappy darkness without being noted: (yellow) ducks, (white) snowdrops, (green) stalks, and (blue) pools.[219] Yet the color red, used to emote anger, fire, and passion, is absent. The poem starts with a reference to the eye of the child, most likely that of her daughter Frieda, who had surprised both parents by inheriting the light blue eyes of her grandfather, Otto Plath:

'Child'

Your clear eye is the one absolutely beautiful thing.
I want to fill it with color and ducks,
The zoo of the new

Whose names you mediate—

April snowdrop, Indian pipe,
Little

Stalk without wrinkle,
Pool in which images
Should be grand and classical

Not this troublous
Wringing of hands, this dark
Ceiling without a star.

This last stanza replaces earlier lines Plath wrote in a draft: 'not this | Grubby dishcloth . . . this black paper, without moon or stars'. The removal of direct reference to black and dreary domesticity softens the poem's starker setting into grayer tones, where the movement of hands changes from the handling of a dirty dishcloth to a poignant gesture of worry. The vision of a child's clear eye, associated with what Plath referred to as 'blue days' of a cloudless sky, is here replaced with an encaged state of darkness she had feared for herself and which she now fears for her daughter. Plath repeatedly returned to images of seeing, clarity, watery reflections, and traveling through air in works about the child, also represented in the poem she wrote at age thirteen about a lake personified as the untamed child who serves as (mother) earth's mirror to the sky. In this poem pools of water are again connected to childhood innocence, self-reflection, and memory, in turn associated with a 'quiet' gaze of the mother on the wild roughness of youth. The final stanza offers the metaphor of the lake as 'the earth's clear eye | Where are mirrored the moods | Of the wind and the sky'—the gentle and loving look of the mother at the child.

The sound of the child is the subject of 'Morning Song', written in February 1961, when Frieda was eight months old. Planned as the opening poem for *Ariel*, the narrator begins with the statement: 'Love set you going like a fat gold watch', where the last three syllables in particular evoke the rhythm of ticking. The passage of time is also implied in the final stanza wherein the walls of the room, possibly decorated with 'flat' pink roses, are brightened with the coming of dawn that:

Whitens and swallows its dull stars. And now you try
Your handful of notes;
The clear vowels rise like balloons

The simile of 'clear vowels' as rising balloons and similar uses of the letter 'o' may also be found in Plath's 1958 poem 'The Disquieting Muses', based on the de Chirico painting of the same name.[220] This poem confronts the child's realization of a mother's misleading presentation of reality, one that has obscured clarity of vision, giving no warning of its darker powers. The visual sport or 'eye rhymes' that Vendler associated with *Ariel* is fully evident here in the 'cookies and Ovaltine' that mimic the shape of de Chircio's bald, featureless heads, along with the 'boom boom boom!' and other double-o, double-b, and double-d words in this poem: foot, wooden, stood, schoolgirl, glowworm, bobbed, bubble, oddly. These words repeatedly evoke the shape of the balloon, the soap bubble, and the mother's mouth as she calls the child to come—a word that again forms an 'o'. In the sixth of seven stanzas, the narrator views the mother floating on a green balloon, before identifying her real traveling companions, the disquieting muses:

> I woke one day to see you, mother,
> Floating above me in bluest air
> On a green balloon bright with a million
> flowers and bluebirds that never were
> Never, never found anywhere.
> Like a soap bubble as you called: Come here!
> And I faced my traveling companions

The child grows up to face a cruel reality; the bubble pops as does the balloon. Plath's hearkening back at age 18 to the magical worlds of children's books with their 'faultless illustrations', and 'the beautiful dark haired child (who was you) winging through the midnight sky on a star path in her mother's box of reels', is here reversed. The mother's bright colored promises belong to a world that never was, a statement similar to Plath's diary passage after turning 17 that seems to reference the patriarchal father in the form of invisible wind, likened to a unyielding and 'staunch Puritan Minister', who is also 'a ghost of the old days which never were'.

Written the same day as 'Edge', the poem 'Balloons' centers around colorful 'globes' that are real yet transient, like the soap bubble.[221] In this poem, many of the words used to describe the young brother's domain again have 'o' vowels, including those that evoke its round shape and movement: oval soul, scooting, moons, globes.

It also contains the pink of 'Morning Song', as well as the primary colors of 'Child': yellow cathead, blue fish, and 'these traveling | Globes of thin air, red, green'—one of which 'has been popped by this bite'. As in 'Child' and the untitled lake poem, the clear world of 'Balloons' is connected to the world of light, made up of the full color spectrum, presented in the poem's final stanza:

> Then sits
> Back, fat jug
> Contemplating a world clear as weather.
> A red
> Shred in his little fist.

In considering endings for these poems, in the final lines of 'Balloons' as well as 'Child', the parent looks to the child and imagines a new world that is clear and free of clouds and dark coverings, hoping yet perhaps doubting whether she may protect them from the troubled realities and disorder of the future. The inevitability of death and promise of new life is assured in much of Plath's poetry, but the level of indifference to these forces fluctuates between feeling insignificant and powerless against the 'vast impersonal white world' and self-assertion in 'the small violent spark of will' mentioned in her 'Poem' notes about a walk on the moors, made during a deeply traumatic yet crucial period in her life as a writer. The challenge of negotiating human existence and the process of renewal within an impersonal and changing universe—and broken families—is not easily met. One cannot always take the approach of the speaker in 'Private Ground', who surrounded by portraits of children lost to disease, and fading life overtaken by frost, appears as impassive to this cosmic cycle as the moon in 'Edge'.

Divisions between statue and human, plant and animal life in these mature poems are often obscured in clouds, smoke, or mist, shifting their shapes into different perspectives and new ways of being. Yet the worlds of the adult and the child remain separate. The shock of the 'red shred' in the fist of a baby boy after taking his empty bite, the process of learning truths with age, may become the lack of wonder of dull-eyed men under bowler hats, and a sky poisoned by carbon monoxides, who see bright summer flowers in the fall. We are reminded here that life is dangerous, yet one can survive against the odds. And while it is never clear what part an overarching God plays in these lives, if any at all, blessings and sublime meanings are read in signs, invisible traces, and the splendor of nature—that of the interior mind as well as flora and fauna. Regarding the 'late mouths' of the flowers that 'cry open', the narrator of 'Poppies in October' states in wonder: 'O my God, what am I' to see them—turning the scene inward, looking and listening for clues, suggesting the interdependency of viewer and viewed in quantum observation, the unifed sense impluse of a mystical state, or her own late flowering in *Ariel*. This crying out also recalls Plath's statement at age 17 about the questions 'Who am I? what am I?' that will preoccupy her until the day she dies.

The de Chiricoesque 'perspectives of limbo', however, removed from the final draft of this October poem, do not diminish with time. Addressing the wonderment in small lives of the domicile, of children and flowers, the woman/mother in 'Kindness' also balances tenuously within an existence that might overwhelm her without warning. Just as Plath recalls the 'love gift' of late-blooming poppies, the narrator of this late poem (written ten days before her death) envisions the figure of 'Dame Kindness' who glides around the home like a balloon, with her smoky blue and red jeweled rings, bringing uncertain smiles. The mood is similar to a line from 'The Moon and the Yew Tree': 'How I would like to believe in tenderness', while wishing the saints, 'gentled by candles', might look upon her with mildness. The soulfulness of the child's cry and the healing sweetness of sugar are positioned as innate to existence, before the narrator admits her plight: the 'desperate butterflies' of her Japanese silks may be pinned and anesthetized at any moment. Neither grace, nor the breath of life, is guaranteed.

Yet the poet's understanding of herself as an artist is firm. Situated between the offer of steaming tea and the poem's final gifts, a legendary statement identifies the first true love, the primary life force, of Sylvia Plath:

> The blood jet is poetry,
> There is no stopping it.

The mother here is helpless as a child in trying to stall a force as natural and inevitable as the changing seasons. She is poised between her eternal and earthly ties, feeling the cyclical, stalled, floating, and forward motions around her all at once. The movement of this family and the hopeful kindnesses that sustain them is framed delicately and tentatively within the text, but these two lines streak red against the page with a certainty that indeed promises something permanent from this poet's moment in time. As if in a theatrical aside, Sylvia Plath reminds her readers of her bequest to us, her 'unstill' voice and its place in our existence, before acknowledging another love gift of new flowering life: 'You give me two children, two roses.'

2

Plath at War

LANGDON HAMMER

Even if it were not the work of the thirteen-year-old Sylvia Plath, it would be an arresting, disturbing image (Pl. 20).[1] The image depicts a schoolgirl in a red sweater, neat blue skirt, and red ankle socks, with a red bow in her wavy blonde hair. She sits at a table, partly turned away from us, her chair on a rag rug. She leans over an open book. Her chin is propped on her bent right arm, indicating thought. Scrubbed and prim, her knees and ankles together (her long legs perfectly parallel), she is a model of mid-twentieth-century, middle-class American girlhood. A thought-bubble, a device she sees every day in the comics, rises above her in the space over the table. Inside the crowded bubble, sagging like a heavy cloud about to spill its bad contents, we see a trench, the bloody body of a dead soldier, and another soldier firing a howitzer. In the distance small figures run across the battlefield escaping an explosion. A big blue tear rolls down the girl's cheek. Behind her is a broad red curtain; it frames this little drama of reading and thought, and converts the domestic scene to a stage-set. Above the bubble are the words 'World War I'. Above that are other words in red pencil in another hand: A+ Excellent!

This is the first page of a report written by Plath for her eighth-grade social studies class in February 1946. She uses an initial, decorative page to explore what she otherwise cannot speak of in the impersonal format of the report: the experience of reading and thinking about war as she assembled the information in the pages that follow it. Her picture silently insists that that experience is part of the report. But it is not so clear what part it has. She presents the problem in the form of an hallucinatory montage, a kind of surrealist collage: on the one hand, the perfect, proper American girl; on the other, the violence and misery of war—bleeding men, exploding bombs. What do they have to do with each other?

The artist's hand is steady and careful: the watercolors do not run; the lines of the table and chair are set at precise angles and establish an abstract design at the center of the picture; the curtain and the girl's body and clothes are firmly contained in their pencilled-in borders. And the child seems just as much in control as the artist who depicts her. Everything about the picture's composition (the girl's poise, the table's geometry, the stability of the four chair legs on the rug that encircles her, cozy and domestic) says that she is safe and the master of her thoughts. (The A+ confirms Plath's self-image and reveals the disciplined effort behind it.) Yet we sense the child's subjection to those mental images. War literally hangs over her. It is alien and strange, but it belongs to her too, linked to her by that train of soft blue bubbles. World War I is remote in time and space, but it is also there in the room with her, going on in the present. Her bowed head expresses concentration and probably grief. Does it also express contrition, or even some hint of guilt? Is there any sense in which she might be responsible for war in a far country, or war in the past? Or war in her mind? What can she do about war? What has it done—what is it doing and what will it do—to her?

War, actual or imminent, was always in the background of Plath's life. When she was writing about World War I, World War II had just ended. With a father born in the contested Polish Corridor of Germany[2] and maternal grandparents born in Austria, she must have been aware of World War II as something that concerned her close-knit family from the beginning of it; once the United States entered the war in 1941, war news was simply part of daily life. At the end of the war, like other American children suddenly faced with the horrors of World War II,[3] Plath was frightened by footage of the concentration camps that she saw in newsreels at the movies.[4] Plath was aware too of the American bombing of Hiroshima and Nagasaki. Later, from 1946 on, war between the United States and the Soviet Union arose, which would have meant a total, mutually annhilating war, was a continuing threat. Plath brooded on nuclear warfare and on the Korean War in her journals and letters. Her mother had made her aware—and proud—of her father's pacifism;

she worked out, while still a high school student, her own committed, reasoned position as a pacifist. And yet Plath's attitude toward war was not one of simple opposition. War inspired in her horror, dread, outrage, disgust. It also inspired curiosity: she wanted to know what war is like, and to that extent, she wanted to experience it. She actively envisioned, as the vivid images in her school report show, the experience of individual soldiers—the soldier firing the howitzer and the one lying dead beside him.[5]

In 'Daddy' and other poems from late in her career, Plath brought the historical violence of World War II and the Holocaust into troubling, unexpected conjunction with the domestic relationships between father and daughter and husband and wife.[6] Her World War I report shows her doing something similar while yet a child. The continuity between the child's vision and that of the mature poet implies a long-term imaginative project. Throughout her life, Plath struggled intellectually and creatively to address what Marianna Torgovnick has called 'the war complex' in modern and contemporary American culture. Torgovnick's term names 'the difficulty of confronting the fact of mass, sometimes simultaneous, death caused by human volition under state or other political auspices, in shorter and shorter periods of time, and affecting not just the military but also, and even more, civilians: a fact urged on us insistently by World War II, but as insistently deflected'.[7] The 'war complex', Torgovnick continues, produces 'gaps and ellipses in public discourse'[8] that register how mass death and responsibility for it are forgotten, 'deflected', or disclaimed. To repair those 'gaps and ellipses'—which is both a cognitive challenge and a moral one—requires a kind of imaginative or poetic work. The goal is to bring 'the harsh realities of war' into focus for the individual and, through 'an ethics of identification',[9] to reject the 'othering' of the enemy in war, making it possible, Torgovnick argues, to see the self in the other and vice versa.

This essay will explore Plath's confrontation with 'the war complex' as we find it in her school reports and in some of her late poems, with attention along the way to passages in her letters and journals where war appears as Plath's subject matter or as material for metaphor. Already as a child, Plath was engaged in the type of ethical imagining that Torgovnick calls for. She engages in a version of it in her school report on World War I by insisting that she is part of the history she reports on, and that it is part of her. Interestingly, her capacity to picture the battlefield and soldiers is connected to the act of representing herself. Self-consciousness and consciousness of war take shape at the same moment and in relation to each other in this case. Plath seems to understand, exactly in her impulse to foreground reading and fantasy in the way she does, that the girl at home and the soldiers in battle occupy related, gendered positions that together constitute some larger whole, a system of relations in which distant, disassociated elements define each other. The idea anticipates the arguments of feminist anti-militarists such as Cynthia Enloe, who maintains that female stereotypes support the ideological system that produces war.[10] The idea is linked to Plath's recognition, as she develops as a writer and a thinker, that she carries warring emotions within her. And this kind of mental warfare is apparent, as we will see, in her attitude of opposition and attraction to war itself.

Battlefield and home: these disparate spaces of experience are signified in Plath's school report on World War I by two mirroring shapes. Beneath the girl's chair is the rag rug, cheery and snug; above her is the thought-bubble, full of war. Each is self-contained and circular: they are like a schematic representation of the so-called separate spheres of men's and women's activity. Yet they are both composed of the same colors (a blue border with red, brown, green, and yellow inside it). It is as if the battlefield and home, for all their differences, were composed of the same material, revealing a fundamental connection between them.

The rug itself is a rich symbol. Traditionally, the rag rug is made in the home out of cloth or fabric too old or worn to use in other ways. The cords are made strong by being pulled tight and braided, one wound around another. It is an expression of women's force, art, and thrift, and their power to shape the world of the home. It signifies self-sufficiency, self-containment, and inventiveness.

The rug in the picture may refer to a specific rug in Plath's childhood home. We know that, thirteen years later, she worked on a rag rug of her own, and that rug suggests a way to understand the one in her earlier picture. When she and Ted Hughes lived in Boston in 1959, Plath wrote in her journal about rug-making, which was at the time for her an important symbolic act of home-making, on a visit to the home of a female friend, a new mother:

Amazingly happy afternoon with Shirley yesterday. . . Brought my bundle of woolens and began to make the braided rug: immense pleasure cutting the good thick stuffs, wrestling with the material and getting a braid begun. Talked easily about babies, fertility, amazingly frank and pleasant. Have always wanted to 'make something' by hand, where other women sew and knit and embroider, and this I feel is my thing . . . Felt part of young womanhood.[11]

Cutting, wrestling, and braiding, Plath exerts herself. It is women's work, and it gives her a chance to speak about 'babies, fertility', while it requires and releases a kind of physical force that is usually seen as masculine. The suggestion of aggression here comes out in another journal entry about the same rug: 'Braided violently on the rug . . . and felt anger flow harmlessly away into the cords of bright soft colored wool. It will be not a prayer rug but an anger rug.'[12]

Perhaps the rug in Plath's school report is 'an anger rug' into which her mental images of war 'flow harmlessly'. Or, it may be that the energy passes the other way, and the contents of the bubble draw out and make visible a violence worked into the tight, intricate design of the rug. Plath places herself in the composition between the rug and the bubble; she is the conduit and mediator who joins them; it is as if the colors that are found in each of them flowed from reservoirs of emotion within her. Indeed, in her clothes, the red and blue mixed or braided with each other and with other colors above and below her appear in simple, unmixed blocks: red sweater, blue skirt; red socks, blue shoes. In each case, the red is up, the blue down. The girl's hair is decorated by a red ribbon, a hot little halo, above which, tracing a diagonal line from her bowed head, the howitzer fires a burst of red into the sky. The cover of the history book she is reading is red, linking history and fire, while her demure blue skirt is draped across her legs, hanging down. The two colors are of course suggestive of specific emotions. They imply a visual representation of ambivalence: at once angry and sad, Plath seems to be, as we say, seeing red and feeling blue. Her anger (if that is what the red signifies) links her to the violent scene above her, while the sadness implied by the blue pools in ripples, like tears, in the rag rug below. The schoolgirl is learning to see and represent herself as divided, the center of warring emotions.

The cover of the report (Pl. 21) introduces other motifs of opposition and division. The report title appears on a heraldic shield: 'A War to End Wars'. Plath wants to see this war in the best possible light by emphasizing its idealistic justification. But the failure of World War I to end war must have struck her forcibly as she reflected on the war that had just ended. She must have grasped too the contradiction of trying to wage war against war. The construction paper she chose for the report cover is blood red: it is as if the red stage curtain that will be pulled back to reveal the girl reading on the next page is still drawn. The symbols of war and peace, sketched in ink, cross each other behind the shield: the laurel branch and the sword. (Plath's decorative shaping of the 'W's in the title phrase 'World War I' picks up the design of the clashing swords on the report's next page.) The crossing of the laurel branch and the sword (which treats the laurel branch as if it *were* a sword) implies a debate, a clash of arms, in which neither side has had the last word. But the sword drips blood on the laurel branch, staining it. Plath seems to acknowledge that, so long as peace and war are at war, war goes on. She is learning that pacificism itself entails combat, and that, to oppose war, she must make war. The whole page is red.

We can observe Plath's thinking about war develop and take on multiple dimensions in her schoolwork, letters, and journals from the late 1940s and 1950s when, increasingly, war enters into her erotic imagination, and is in this way associated with intense pleasure as well as pain. The motif of the bloody sword reappears on the cover of a social studies report Plath submitted in the spring of 1946, 'The World and the United States' (Pl. 22). It is a report on the nation's political role in the post-war world, and Plath cut out and pasted on her cover an image of the American flag and a globe. On the globe, turned to show the Pacific Ocean with a spotlight on the United States, a sword is plunged into a calendar page for December 7, 1941, marking the Japanese attack on Pearl Harbor. The handle of the blade is marked with a red swastika, merging the Japanese aggression and that of Nazi Germany; the tip drips blood. The choice of image for the report cover makes it clear that memories of World War II color Plath's sense of the post-war world.

Of course, the threat of world war persisted. The opening section of this school report consists of newspaper clippings about conflict between the United States and the Soviet Union over oil in Iran. In the next section Plath asks, 'Can the UNO Prevent Another World War?' In another section with the title, 'The US Faces Postwar Problems', she writes: 'Some people are yet oblivious of the fact that world peace is still a long way off.' She continues: 'The US is about the only country fitted to supply food for the wartorn lands. Millions are dying; millions have died, and many more are slowly starving. We must forget ourselves in our effort to send all we can overseas.' As if to bring out the human dimensions of this crisis, Plath includes a poster she has made for the Red Cross. Beneath the organization's symbol, a man lies bleeding with wounds to his head and chest (Pl. 23). 'SAVE HIM!' block letters implore us. 'Give Now! You may save your loved ones.' When we step back from the information and images of the report, a general view emerges. The threat of war for Plath is urgent and diffuse at the same time, close and far away. On the one hand, Americans are 'oblivious' to the suffering of others, insulated in their comfortable middle-class lives; on the other hand, they must act to save their 'loved ones'. Everyone is in danger.

Plath developed her pacificist views, which were strongly associated with her father, under the guidance of her high school English teacher Wilbury Crockett, who emphasized social responsibility and made writing a means to advance it.[13] With her classmate Perry Norton, Plath wrote the short statement 'Youth's Plea for World Peace', which appeared in *Christian Science Monitor* in 1950. Opposing President Truman's directive to develop the hydrogen bomb, Plath and Norton stress the central contradiction of the Cold War arms race—that the escalation of military threat as a strategy of defense precisely increases the threat that the strategy is intended to defend against. As few public statements in 1950 did (and for that matter, as few public statements have since that time), the statement acknowledges the fact of America's mass destruction of enemy civilians in World War II. Plath and Norton argue:

> At first glance it seems inconsistent to undertake the construction of a weapon designed to kill more people efficiently, and yet maintain that this plan of action is consistent with the objections of our program of peace and security. . . . Already we have succeeded in killing and crippling a good part of humanity, and destruction, unfortunately, is always mutual.

The point is that war is a system of action and reaction in which aggression against one side is at the same time aggression against the other.

Also under the influence of Crockett, who believed that understanding between people of former enemy nations would promote peace, Plath corresponded with a student in West Germany named Hans-Joachim Neuport. This fascinating correspondence, which began in 1947 and continued until 1951, repeatedly returns to the topic of war. As she puts it in her first letter to Neuport, Plath was acutely aware that 'I, personally, do not know what war is like,' whereas her correspondent did.[14]

She was frankly bothered by her insulation from 'history' and by the comfort of her American life, in contrast to the hardships which Neuport had known, and which emphasized to him, as Plath admiringly put it, 'the seriousness of life'. During 'the last war', she had 'felt nothing', she told him, and the war itself was 'as unreal as a fairy tale'.[15]

The curiosity that Plath expresses about Neuport's experience of war returns in other forms in her journals. These passages introduce feelings about war less rational and harder to approve. In 1950, for example, in her first year at Smith College, Plath narrated a date with a United States army veteran. The entry is well on its way to becoming a short story, and it gives a glimpse of the way in which war and the erotic came into conjunction in Plath's imagination. When Bill, the veteran, dances with Plath's narrator, he says to her, 'Sylvy, oh, Sylvy. You know, we're an awful lot alike'; aware that she is at the same time fighting for and against this former soldier on the dance floor, she says to herself, 'You've scored a beachhead.' They sit down and move close to each other. She pats 'his shoulder maternally' and urges him: 'Tell me. About the war.' She has heard that 'He was disabled. You wonder if he has a wooden leg and think how noble you would be if he had one.' He tells her about his injury (where or what it is she doesn't specify). Then she asks: 'What's it like to fight? to kill someone? (Your curiosity is aflame. Granted you can't be a man, but he can tell you how it was).'[16] Soon Bill too grows enflamed; and when, outside in the dark, he 'fights' with her, pushing her down on the ground for sex, she fights back—and successfully drives him off.[17] Excluded from battle, she finds her fight behind the fraternity house, and becomes a kind of soldier, a veteran too.

War and the erotic return together elsewhere in Plath's journals: Writing in 1955 about her passionate love for Richard Sassoon (who was—significantly for Plath—a distant relative of the English World War I poet Siegfried Sassoon), she reflects: 'I know it is too simple to wish for war, for open battle but one cannot help but wish for those situations that make us heroic, living to the hilt of our total resources.' In another entry concerning Sassoon, she returns to the same metaphor: 'I have a great deal of that desire to use myself to the hilt, and where, for men, fighting is a cause, for women, fighting is for men.'[18] Here Plath is explicit that sexuality is woman's battlefield, and, called to erotic fight, she wants to become a weapon, a sword, and use herself 'to the hilt'. The link between sexual desire and aggression reappears in probably the most famous of her journal entries, when, describing her intense first encounter with Ted Hughes, she writes: 'And when he kissed my neck I bit him long and hard on the cheek, and when we came out of the room, blood was running down his face ... Such violence, and I can see how women lie down for artists.'[19]

What is the relationship between Plath's earnest, rational pacificism (a political and ethical position to which she remained committed from high school to the end of her life) and the role of war in her imagination, where a desire to know about war merges with a desire to experience it and with sexual desire? Summarizing Freud's thinking about war, Jacqueline Rose suggests a perspective relevant to Plath:

> War does not only threaten civilization, it can also advance it. By tending toward the conglomeration of nations, it operates less like death than like eros which strives to unify. . . . If, therefore, war neither simply threatens nor simply advances the cause of civilization, it is because it mimics or participates in the fundamental ambivalence of civilization itself.[20]

By 'ambivalence' Rose means the co-presence of contending emotions, rather than the dearth of strong investments, the state of 'mixed feelings', that we often use that word to mean. Her point, following Freud, is that the psychological condition of ambivalence is fundamental both to war and to the constitution of the self.

Even as a schoolgirl, Plath grasped these ideas, at least insofar as her picture of herself reading about World War I implies them. Later, influenced by her reading in psychology and her own psychotherapy, Plath became explicit and self-conscious about her interest in the condition of psychological ambivalence. In her book *The Haunting of Sylvia Plath*, where she brings psychoanalytic ideas to a comprehensive reading of Plath, Rose argues that Plath used her writing to conduct an improvised psychoanalysis of her warring affective investments.[21] For example, in 'The Rabbit Catcher', as in other late poems that Rose treats, 'Plath sits on the edge of two contrary analyses of women's relationship to patriarchal power,' simultaneously showing women's oppression by patriarchal power and their willing, even desirous participation in it.[22] In an interview, Rose generalizes about this quality of Plath's work and praises her capacity to 'articulate together in the space of her writing—in a single text, a poem, a line of a poem—on the one hand a strong, articulate protest against social institutions such as medicine and psychiatry and marriage, while on the other and at the same time acknowledging women's complex and sometimes self-defeatingly pleasurable engagement in the very structures against which they protest'.[23] Plath's double attitude toward war, combining protest and 'pleasurable engagement', demonstrates the same capacity.

Plath's famous provocation in 'Daddy'—'Every woman adores a Fascist'—is an example of it, since the line could express protest (when we hear a savage irony in it) or a frank declaration of sexual pleasure. 'The problem', Rose remarks in her comments on the passage, 'is only compounded' by the lines following: 'Every woman adores a Fascist, | The boot in the face, the brute | Brute heart of a brute like you'.[24] 'Who', Rose asks, 'is putting the boot in the face? The fascist certainly... But, since the agency of these lines is not specified, don't they also allow that it might be the woman herself (identification *with* the fascist being what every woman desires)?'[25] This reading is reenforced by the fact that Plath's female speaker calls the father a 'black shoe | In which I have lived like a foot'. Daddy's daughter is both foot and face, the aggressor and victim. She is herself and him.

By taking on and exploring competing identifications as she contemplates historical violence, then, Plath, or her surrogate-speaker, seems to divide in 'Daddy', to split into two parts or selves. When, conversely, she ponders self-division, she finds historical violence active within her. This is what happens in 'Cut', a powerful poem, full of wild fantasy, that was written twelve days after 'Daddy', to which it is clearly related. The poem returns to motifs and impulses we saw in Plath's school reports, and demonstrates the continuity between her earlier and later imaginings of war.

'Cut' arose from a domestic incident in late October 1962: Plath cut her thumb badly while preparing food in the kitchen of her home. She dedicated it to Susan O'Neill Roe, her housekeeper and nanny in this period. The scene of the accident—the kitchen—locates the poem in that space of the home most clearly associated with the feminine, and the dedication to Roe emphasizes women's work. The poem takes place, then, in a version of the domestic space marked by the rag rug in Plath's school report; and again, scenes of war enter that space through Plath's mental images. The poem begins:

What a thrill—
My thumb instead of an onion.
The top quite gone
Except for a sort of hinge

Of skin,
A flap like a hat,
Dead white.
Then that red plush.

Little pilgrim,
The Indian's axed your scalp.
Your turkey wattle
Carpet rolls

Straight from the heart.[26]

As if part of a game a child might play with her hand, the poet immediately sees her thumb as a little man, although in this case a wounded one. The 'flap' of skin at the tip suggests to her a white 'hat', so white in fact that the man appears dead: red, the color of war and of wounds, is also the color of life, of blood. Then, in the first of several fantastic conceits, the poet hails the dead man as a pilgrim an Indian has scalped. Next, the poet compares her flowing blood to the wattle of a turkey, whose throat will be slit for Thanksgiving dinner.

The rush of blood, signifying strong feeling, comes 'Straight from the heart'. The characters that follow—pilgrim, Indian, turkey—come straight from a child's book of American history (a set of characters that would be especially vivid to a child, like Plath, who had grown up in Massachusetts). As the poem progresses, it moves ahead in time to the Revolutionary War: 'Out of a gap | A million soldiers run, | Redcoats, every one'. That all of this is inside the poet, ready to burst out (like the images of World War I straining at the borders of the schoolgirl's thought-bubble), suggests that we carry history as an otherness within us, under pressure, only provisionally sealed.

It is not simply that history came into the home when the child brought it back from school, however. It is not simply something that has been internalized, like ideology. Rather, the poem is about discovering a structure of division in the self that is also in war. The cut in this poem recalls the swords in Plath's World War I school report and the red blade plunged into the calendar page for December 7, 1941 (Pl. 22). To cut oneself is to declare war on the self, to turn against the self, and so to become both the Fascist's foot and the woman's face, aggressor and victim. The cut is an emblem of a psychological split that, in Rose's words, 'mimics and participates in the fundamental ambivalence of civilization itself'. 'Whose side are they on?' Plath asks of the Redcoats as they run. She could ask the same question of herself—Whose side am I on?—when one hand wounds the other, releasing and expressing a perhaps unconscious wish for self-destruction. To be on two sides at once—to be both the hand that cuts and the one that is cut (the title, which could be read as a verb or a noun, includes both ideas)—is the essence of ambivalence. That idea is emphasized in the next turn of Plath's fancy: 'Saboteur, | Kamikaze man—', she calls her wounded thumb. The wound signifies sabotage and self-subversion, a suicidal, 'Kamikaze' impulse.

Taken together, the further implication of these images is that, if ambivalence is a form of war, war is a form of ambivalence. War is the 'cut' that generates the opposition between self and other within the larger unity of civilization. That opposition, which makes it possible for nations to inflict mass death on their enemies and to disown it, defines 'the war complex' Torgovnik describes. Plath rebels against it in 'Cut'—rebels against the generalized forgetting of mass death and the disowning of responsibility for it in public discourse—through an hallucinatory fantasy that links the sword of war and the cooking knife, and thus brings history into the kitchen, where aggression is recognized as part of the poet's relation to herself.[27]

In the closing stanzas of 'Cut', the poet applies a bandage, and the wounded thumb becomes not a 'Homunuclus' but a menstruating girl, perhaps a memory of the eighth-grader who created Plath's World War I report:

> The stain on your
> Gauze Ku Klux Klan
> Babushka
> Darkens and tarnishes and when
>
> The balled
> Pulp of your heart
> Confronts its small
> Mill of silence
>
> How you jump—
> Trepanned veteran,
> Dirty girl,
> Thumb stump.

The bandage is described first as the white sheet of the Ku Klux Klan, calling up the masked member of a lynch mob—another figure from American history, this one scarier than the story book pilgrim and redcoat, but equally familiar to the imagination of an American girl in the 1950s. As the bandage 'Darkens and tarnishes', it suggests to the poet a Russian woman's red headscarf. With the shift in gender the finger's blood is represented next as menstrual flow ('The balled/Pulp of your heart'), an idea reenforced by the shaming phrase, 'Dirty girl'. Now the cut becomes a figure for the female sex; the genital opening is a war wound that turns the girl into a 'Trepanned veteran'—or an amputee, since the wounded thumb is a 'stump'.

This final configuration of images, in which the female genitals become the sign of an amputation (what must surely be a castration, following Freud's view of female subjectivity, which Plath would have known), is a version of the fantasy ground on which the Smith College student's sexual struggle with Bill, the veteran, took place; and her identification there with the wounded soldier, which drew her to him, desiring to know what war is like, is in a curious way confirmed. These associations, however, were already in place for Plath long before this and related poems in the final year of her life. The closing lines of 'Cut', like Plath's eighth-grade report on World War I, say that the schoolgirl reading about war, imagining war, was already at war herself.

3

Plath, Hughes, and Three Caryatids

DIANE MIDDLEBROOK

Almost everyone who consults this book will have heard the story about the night in February 1956 when Ted Hughes attended a rowdy party at Cambridge University, met the poet Sylvia Plath, and kissed her, with enormous consequences for the future of poetry. But few will know that deep in the background of this momentous conjunction of two of the twentieth century's most notorious literary figures was a poem Plath had written a year earlier, during her senior year at Smith College. It had a very long title: ' "Three Caryatids without a Portico", by Hugo Robus. A Study in Sculptural Dimensions'.

In late autumn 1954, during Plath's last year at Smith College, she decided to enter a competition sponsored by *Vogue* magazine, the Prix de Paris, for which the winner would receive $1000 and a trip to Paris. During the winter months of her senior year Plath was applying for every grant, fellowship, and prize that might help her fulfill her aspiration to get to Europe as soon as she graduated from Smith. By January 1955, Plath had made it as far as the finals for *Vogue's* Prix de Paris, and was required to submit a 10-page essay on the arts. Plath wrote about a visit she had made in March 1954 to the Whitney Museum's Annual Exhibition of American Art. She structured her essay as a guided tour that begins on the Museum's first floor, with an exhibition of sculpture. Among the pieces Plath describes is 'Three

32. Photo of 'Three Caryatids without a Portico', Hugo Robus sculpture, *c.*1953–54

Caryatids without a Portico', by Hugo Robus. This was a plaster cast of three linked torsos with vase-like necks, standing 34½ in. high. The figures, Plath said, 'curve with the lyric calm of plaster, a trio of supple pillared maidens'.[1]

Caryatids, of course, *are* pillars: female figures used as columns to support the entablature of a building. According to ancient historians,[2] the Caryatides were priestesses of Artemis in the village of Caryae in Laconia. When Greek armies destroyed Caryae they captured and enslaved the women, requiring them to retain the dress that would identify their origin. The use of female figures in flowing dress as architectural supports on a famous temple at Athens, the Erechtheum, was said to commemorate this victory. One of the six caryatids from the Erechtheum was among the Parthenon sculptures sold to the British Museum in 1816 by Lord Elgin, and its image has been widely reproduced.

The title of Hugo Robus's sculpture evokes the tradition of this architectural use of the female figure; but his caryatids bear no weight, and they have neither heads nor arms. Robus later explained:

> 'I was first attracted to the female form without arms, by noticing the line and form produced by the 'halter' top bathing suit . . . The important pattern I had in mind was the endless playing of silhouettes against one another as the viewer moved about the group. The head forms were a hindrance and so I eliminated them.[3]

Something about the radical disfigurement of those caryatids prompted Plath to return to them in March 1955, a few months after completing her essay for *Vogue*. This time she wrote them into a poem:

> In this tercet of torsos, breast and thigh
> slope with Greek serenity
>   though decapitated
>
> each body forms a virgin vase
> curving with the classic grace
>   of tranquil plaster;
>
> these maidens would support with valor
> portico that weighed the pillar
>   of lyric sister
>
> but such a trial is not granted
> by the gods: behold three daunted
>   caryatids.

This version of the poem shows Plath struggling for an apt description of the headlessness of Robus's female figures. She decided on humor, and shaped the poem as a slightly satirical riddle containing its own answer. What is a caryatid without an entablature? 'Daunted'. Plath may have been imitating the style of Phyllis McGinley, whose light verse she saw regularly in the pages of the *Saturday Evening Post*, for Plath's letters home that spring show her determination to make a living from her writing: 'I am going to SELL,'[4] she assured her mother.

Plath's essay ' Collage of a Collegian' didn't win the Prix de Paris from *Vogue*, but she got to Europe anyway: in September 1955 she embarked for England to study literature on a Fulbright Fellowship at Cambridge. She also hoped to achieve some recognition as a writer while she was in England, and brought along some of her unpublished manuscripts. Plath submitted the poem about caryatids to a small literary journal published at Cambridge, called *Chequer*.[5] Her journals show that she was already familiar with *Chequer*—in fact it is arguable that its pages, not the dance floor of the St Botolph's party, provided Plath's first meeting ground with Hughes. Before laying eyes on the man, she had seen the poems he published in *Chequer* titled 'The Jaguar' and 'The Casualty'.

And something about the poetry she read in earlier issues of *Chequer* prompted her to revise ' "Three Caryatids without a Portico", by Hugo Robus. A Study in Sculptural Dimensions' before submitting it. She retained the ungainly title, but, with just a bit of retouching that didn't disturb the rhyme scheme, she elevated the poem's mood, shifting from light humor to slightly pensive observation. Significantly, she now provided the caryatids with heads. Here is the version printed in *Chequer*, with Plath's revisions in boldface:

> In this tercet of torsos, breast and thigh
> slope with **the** Greek serenity
> > **of tranquil plaster**;
> each body forms a virgin vase,
> > **while all raise high with regal** grace
> > **aristocratic heads**;
> these maidens would support with valor
> a portico that weighed the pillar
> > of **classic** sister,
> but such a trial is not granted
> by the gods: behold three daunted
> > caryatids.[6]

The issue of *Chequer* containing Plath's 'Three Caryatids' was published in January 1956. To Plath's immense surprise, her poetry was immediately singled out for a sneering review in another student publication called *Broadsheet*. Plath had unknowingly wandered onto a battlefield in a collegiate poetry war, and turned out to be on the wrong side. The reviewer dismissed Plath's style as 'quaint and eclectic artfulness', then added, 'My better half tells me "Fraud, fraud," but I will not say so; who am I to know how beautiful she may be.'[7]

The mimeographed pages of *Broadsheet* looked amateurish, but they were widely read and discussed. As she wrote to her mother, 'there are 10 critics to each poem . . . using clever devastating turns of phrase to show off their own brilliance . . . [But] the deep parts of me are not affected, and I cheerfully go on writing.'[8] The deep parts of her were affected, though, as her journals show. Plath well understood the problem posed by her desire to SELL: it greatly influenced the voice in her writing. Yes, she wanted Phyllis McGinley's type of commercial success, but she also longed for acceptance as a peer by the serious (male) poets around her. And though Plath was mortified by the manhandling she received in *Broadsheet*, the rhetoric 'how beautiful she may be' gave her an opening. When the first issue of a new journal by these same poets, *St Botolph's Review*,[9] was released on 25 February, Plath bought a copy and was invited to the launch party to be held that night. Nervous about the social challenge, she fortified herself beforehand with several whiskies. But before getting drunk she had fortified herself another way, too: she had memorized some of the poems in *St Botolph's Review.*

Once she arrived at the party, Plath started working the room, trying to charm these prickly student literati. One in particular caught her attention, the tall black-clad fellow off in a dark corner of the party she recognized as Ted Hughes. To her delight, he noticed her as well, slouched across the room, and stood staring into her eyes. She began yelling over the loud dance music words that he recognized were lines from a poem he had written. Pleased, he shouted back, 'You like?' He took her aside into an adjoining room and re-filled her glass with brandy. Plath later noted in her journal that, while chatting her up, Hughes made a rather lame defense of the *Broadsheet* review that called her 'Fraud'. Then he kissed her, hard, and she bit him on the cheek until blood ran.[10]

This is *the* origin story in the legend of Hughes and Plath: the famous party that set up the kiss that caused the bite that prompted the tryst that led to the sex that became the passion that fueled the marriage that led to the poems of Plath and Hughes. But what had that fuss over 'Three Caryatids' been all about, in the first place?

The poets with whom Ted Hughes identified were ideologically opposed to the kind of well-made verse at which Sylvia Plath was adept. All of the *St Botolph's* poets were devotees of the theories Robert Graves put forward in his book *The White Goddess,* the book he described as a 'grammar of the language of poetic myth'.

Graves argues in *The White Goddess* that poetry has a religious function in society; it keeps alive the primordial myths and ancient rituals that affirm man's animal instincts. By the 1950s, *The White Goddess* had become a cult book at Cambridge, and the year before Plath arrived, Graves himself had reinforced its influence by giving, at Cambridge, an outrageous series of lectures, in which he debunked the poetry at the peak of current literary fashion. Gerard Manley Hopkins, D. H. Lawrence, W. B. Yeats, Ezra Pound, Eliot, W. H. Auden, Dylan Thomas—all were ridiculed as 'false' poets.[11] The *St Botolph's* poets took the same line in reviews they wrote for *Broadsheet*. That is why they were so hard on Sylvia Plath. 'Three Caryatids' referred to a work of modern sculpture, not to the instincts—that would have been its first flaw. Worse, the poem was written in rhymed stanzas, indicating that it was 'artful' rather than inspired—those were its other flaws. But the reviewer had also asked, 'Who am I to know how beautiful she may be?'[12] This remark could strike us as blokish insolence, but we would be mistaken. It is a feature of Graves's theory that the 'true' poet is male and that he receives his creative affiliation with the power of the White Goddess by falling obsessionally in love with an actual woman. The goddess 'demanded that man should pay woman spiritual and sexual homage',[13] Graves said. In his passionate sexual embrace of the woman who inspired his love, a poet would reach through that female person to the dreadful power she embodied.

This theory of poetry had great importance for Ted Hughes at the time he met Sylvia Plath, and it is evident from the way he later wrote about Plath that, for Hughes, Plath embodied something of what he understood about the power of the White Goddess. At the end of his life, in *Birthday Letters*, he cites his contact with Plath's 'Three Caryatids' as a defining moment in his vocation, in two poems that stand at the opening of the book on facing pages, like double doors through which we pass to reach the theatre where his drama with Plath will be staged.[14] The poems are titled 'Caryatids (1)' and 'Caryatids (2)', and they immediately follow the poem 'Fulbright Scholar'; their position is important, because all three of these opening poems show Hughes meeting Plath in print (first in a newspaper photo, then on the pages of a literary journal) before he meets her in person.

The 'Caryatids' poems look back on the role Hughes had played with the other *St Botolph's* poets, in ganging up to mock Plath's 'Three Caryatids' in *Broadsheet*. He did not write the review, but he shared the attitude. Here is 'Caryatids (1)';

Hughes is thinking about the lack of curiosity he brought to Plath's poem when he first saw it in *Chequer*:

> What were those caryatids bearing?
> It was the first poem of yours I had seen.
> It was the only poem you ever wrote
> That I disliked through the eyes of a stranger.
> It seemed thin and brittle, the lines cold . . .
> I felt no interest. No stirring
> Of omen . . .
> So missed everything
> In the white, blindfolded, rigid faces
> Of those women. I felt their frailty, yes:
> Friable, burnt aluminum.
> Fragile, like the mantle of a gas-lamp.
> But made nothing
> Of that massive, starless, mid-fall, falling
> Heaven of granite
>   Stopped, as if in a snapshot,
> By their hair.

Hughes's poem is a revisionary misreading of Plath's. As you will have noticed, Plath tells us that Hugo Robus's sculpture is made of plaster, whereas Hughes refers to the material as 'granite', and as 'Friable, burnt aluminum. | Fragile, like the mantle of a gas-lamp'. Plath depicts the figures as vase-like; Hughes depicts them as massive and in a falling position, with streaming hair. Most significantly, Hughes puts blindfolds on their faces. His poem implies, I think, that Plath's 'Three Caryatids' was a harbinger of the female vision that was Plath's contribution to twentieth-century poetry. Moreover, his references to omens and a gaslamp implies that it was a tragic vision, and associated with Plath's suicide.

Hughes's 'Caryatids (2)' is a reflection on the causes of his <u>own</u> blindness to the subject matter of Plath's poem. He now understands that what stood in the way of his ability to read her with imaginative empathy was the tightness of his youthful bonds with his male Cambridge friends:

> Stupid with confidence, in the playclothes
> Of still growing, still reclining
>   In the cushioned palanquin . . .

> three of us, four, five, six . . .
> A dramaturgy of whim,
> That was our education . . .
> All roads lay too open, opened too deeply
> Every degree of the compass.
> Here at the center of the web, at the crossroads,
> You published your poem
> About Caryatids . . .
> 　　　　　we concocted
> An attack, a dismemberment, laughing.

One of the major contributors to the education of these young men, as we have noted, was the male-centered theory of poetic inspiration they absorbed from Robert Graves. Is Hughes implying that none of the lads could recognize the visionary content of a poem that had been written by a woman? Interestingly, in 1981 Hughes omitted Plath's 'Three Caryatids' from his edition of Plath's *Collected Poems*—in 1981, we might say, he was still 'stupid with confidence' about the implications of Plath's imagery. But by the time of publishing *Birthday Letters*, he is ready to see this meeting with Plath's poem as a crossroads in his life, and in 'Caryatids (2)' he walks us with him across an intersection that separates his youth from his manhood.

Is Hughes right in having second thoughts about 'Three Caryatids'? Was there a lot more to Plath's poem than the *St Botolph's* gang noticed? In retrospect we can say with confidence both yes and no.

Yes, because 'Three Caryatids' shows traces of Plath's preoccupations with women as makers of art, a subject that Robert Graves does not give much attention to in *The White Goddess*. Possibly, Plath was being witty when she chose the stanza form of 'Three Caryatids': she may have been alluding to the poetic meter called 'sapphics',[15] after the ancient Greek poet Sappho, when she put the opening lines into trochees and dactyls, and ended each stanza with a short line. To make a poem properly in sapphics, though, she would have written four-line stanzas, and employed dactylic and trochaic meter consistently. So she may not have been alluding to Sappho; nonetheless, 'Three Caryatids' is the first poem by Plath that makes use of classical sculpture of the idealized female body as a symbolic legacy with daunting relevance to the female onlooker.

As we noticed, Hugo Robus's sculptured caryatids didn't have heads; but in revising her poem at Cambridge, Plath gave them heads <u>and</u> a point of view. Ironically, five months after the publication of 'Three Caryatids' in *Chequer*, Plath was photographed in a halter-top swimsuit for a story about spring fashions published in *Varsity*, the Cambridge University newspaper for which she worked briefly as a reporter during the spring term in 1956. Plath is acting out the role of the 'headless' woman, so to speak, letting the camera look at her haltered body while she looks away. But her <u>poem</u> endowed the female 'object' with a consciousness, a subjectivity. It was one of the earliest moments in Plath's poetry when the legacy of male dominance in art was seized and shaken up by the question, 'What's in it for me?' In Plath's poetry, sculptural 'classic sisters' are always negative images, idealized female bodies that repudiate female fertility along with female consciousness. They appear frequently in Plath's later poems,[16] where they shimmer with Plath's ambivalence about the successful professional woman who avoids or fails at childbearing. This symbolism reaches its culmination in Plath's very last poem, 'Edge': the solitary, aged female moon stares down at a woman who resembles a classical statue, 'perfected' by her death; and she has folded her children back into her body.

So Ted Hughes, in *Birthday Letters*, was justified in viewing Plath's 'Three Caryatids' as an overture to a significant and specifically female symbolism in Plath's work. Yes; but also no. Those aspects of Plath's 'Three Caryatids' could not have been noticeable in 1956, because they exist only in the totality of her work, including her journals and letters; and they come into focus only in her last and greatest poems.

4

Conversation amongst the Ruins
Plath and de Chirico

CHRISTINA BRITZOLAKIS

On 29 March 1958, Sylvia Plath notes in her *Journals*: 'I have written two poems on paintings by de Chirico which seize my imagination—"The Disquieting Muses" and "On the Decline of Oracles" (after his early painting "The Enigma of the Oracle")'.[1] In this passage, Plath goes on to transcribe some quotations from de Chirico's writings, noting their 'unique power to move [her]':

① 'Inside a ruined temple the broken statue of a god spoke a mysterious language.'
② ' "Ferrara": the old ghetto where one could find candy and cookies in exceedingly strange and metaphysical shapes.'
③ 'Day is breaking. This is the hour of the enigma. This is also the hour of prehistory. The fancied song, the revelatory song of the last, morning dream of the prophet asleep at the foot of the sacred column, near the cold, white simulacrum of god.'
④ 'What shall I love unless it be the Enigma?'

These hermetic prose fragments, which Plath found reproduced in James Thrall Soby's monograph, *Giorgio de Chirico*, become legible only in the context of his so-called 'metaphysical paintings', or *pittura metaphysica*, the most famous of which are dated between 1912 and 1919, and the aesthetic theorizing which accompanied them.[2] Their poetry of ruins, labyrinths, and fragments is placed under the sign of the 'classical', though it simultaneously highlights the discovery, or 'revelation' of the strange or numinous within the familiar or everyday. The implications of Plath's engagement with de Chirico's pictorial language for her poetics have been largely neglected.[3] Yet that engagement is clearly far more than a matter of inert 'allusion', being central to her evolving conception of the poem as a theatre of repressed memory, and to the construction of the 'daughter-in-mourning' persona, first hinted at in 'The Disquieting Muses'. Nor is it limited to 1958–9, the period of the *Journal* allusions, during which she was writing a number of poems on paintings, by Rousseau and Klee as well as de Chirico.[4] Plath had been aware of De Chirico's paintings as a source of inspiration since at least 1956; Ted Hughes, in his notes to the *Collected Poems*, links the first poem selected for the volume, 'Conversation amongst the Ruins', with the De Chirico painting, *Interview* (1927), 'a postcard reproduction of which', he notes, 'was pinned to the door of the poet's room.'[5]

Plath's response to de Chirico's work is played out in both iconographic and thematic terms. His *oeuvre*, like hers, is structured as a catalogue of obsessively repeated motifs, many of which are reiterated by Plath.[6] Her 1958 *Journal* entry attempts a prose evocation of his urban landscapes: 'everywhere in Chirico city, the trapped train puffing its cloud in a labyrinth of heavy arches, vaults, arcades. The statue, recumbent, of Ariadne, deserted, asleep, in the center of empty, mysteriously shadowed squares. And the long shadows cast by unseen figures—human or of stone it is impossible to tell.'[7] A number of Plath's poems revolve around de Chiricoesque conceits such as the abandoned statue ('The Colossus', 'Barren Woman'), the defaced, sightless mannequin ('The Disquieting Muses', 'The Munich Mannequins'), the physical diminution of the speaker-figure ('Electra on Azalea Path', 'The Colossus', 'The Beekeeper's Daughter'), and the casting of shadows ('The Disquieting Muses', 'The Colossus'). De Chirico's early 'metaphysical' phase of 1912–19, referred to by a contemporary of the painter's, Ardegno Soffici, as a form of 'dream writing',[8] is often cited as a precursor of Surrealism. It was succeeded by a highly controversial turn toward a more conservative classicism, accompanied by a programmatic plundering of his earlier work in the form of multiple reproductions.[9] In the United States, he was recognized as a key modernist as early as 1936, when the Museum of Modern Art displayed seventeen of his paintings and nine of his drawings in its pathbreaking exhibition, 'Fantastic Art, Dada, Surrealism'; accordingly, his works influenced many painters from the United

States coming of age between the two World Wars.[10] James Thrall Soby, the Museum's curator and collector, whose magisterial 1955 monograph Plath read, played a major part in introducing the paintings to an American public. Her formation as a poet coincides with the point at which modernism began, in the 1950s, to be canonized and institutionalized within the Anglo-American academy. De Chirico's poetic of ruins and fragments, I shall argue, prompted her to reflect upon her relationship to a modernism in the process of being institutionalized, tapping into her longstanding concern with questions of 'influence', or inheritance, both textual and psychic.

De Chirico's 'metaphysical' style, though seemingly undertaken in the name of a neoclassical revival of the Renaissance heritage of architectural perspective, is a potent source of estrangement effects. As William Rubin points out, de Chirican perspective, rather than projecting the illusion of a secure, rationally measurable space, immerses the viewer in 'a network of conflicting spatial tensions that undermine, psychologically speaking, any initial impression of quietude or stability'.[11] Foreshortened or tilted planes, multiple and conflicting vanishing points, and the use of pseudo-modeling (flattened or low relief) all tend to dislocate the viewer and provoke spatial anxiety. The metaphysical still lifes, which alternate with the urban landscapes, deploy a more abstract, collage-like melange of mediums, surface textures, and notational techniques, including the use of inset perspective boxes. In De Chirico's subversive formalism, then, linear or geometrical perspective 'remains a purely schematic scaffolding'.[12] It harnesses a legacy of classical urbanism, embodied in the squares and arcades of Italian cities such as Turin and Florence, for intensely subjective, even hallucinatory atmospheric effects. In these silent, evacuated urban spaces, bodies are almost invariably absent, marked only by their shadows, or mimicked by statues and mannequins. From the outset, these paintings were described by commentators as 'oneiric', poised on a frontier between dream and waking consciousness. De Chirico's repeated references, in the painting titles and in his prose, to 'the Enigma', reinforce a prevailing sense of the uncanny or phantasmatic, in which ordinary objects are rendered ominous by the return of the repressed.

Anachronism is crucial to the aesthetic of *pittura metaphysica*; archaic or classical references—sculptural or architectural, such as statues, fragments of statuary or ruins—are juxtaposed with images of urban modernity such as trains, railway stations, or store mannequins. 'Chirico city' is littered with images of an unchanging classical tradition, relics of a lost cultural authority, whose meanings, though only partly legible, continue to haunt the present. It anticipates Freud's use of the archaeological trope, in *Civilization and its Discontents*, to suggest that, 'in mental life, nothing that has once taken shape can be lost, that everything is somehow preserved and can be retrieved under the right circumstances.'[13] The preoccupation with the method of the 'old masters' and the citation of pre-existing works, as in the motif of the 'abandoned' classical statue, stages a dialogue with the museum in terms of the 'other scene' of the unconscious. For example, several of the statues depict the mythological figure of Ariadne, asleep on the island of Naxos, where she had been abandoned by Theseus; first featured in the painting, 'Melancholy' (1912), she appears in no less than seven pictures in 1913. The repetition of the image, as much as its mythological associations, points to states of emotional suspension and arrest such as nostalgia or homesickness. 'Melancolia' (more precisely an Italianate variant, *melanconia*), the inscription at the base of the statue, which like 'enigma' appears in many of de Chirico's titles, is arguably the psychic trope which governs the static, repetitive world of his paintings.

The symbolism of the statue of Ariadne, mentioned by Plath in the 1958 *Journal* entry cited above, may well have offered a visual correlative for the recurrent periods of creative paralysis and blockage documented in the *Journals* of the period. However, de Chirico also provides a model of a fragmentary 'dream writing' of extraordinary metaphorical richness organized around these very tropes of psychic obstruction or the 'unspeakable'. In a self-penned entry in the Museum of Modern Art volume *Twentieth-Century Italian Art* (1949), he writes that his early art 'appeals directly to the counter-logic of the subconscious, to those swamp-like regions at the edge of the mind where ecstasies bloom white and the roots of fear are cypress-black and deep'.[14] De Chirico's optics of dream and the uncanny enables Plath to recover the resources of modernism within the empirical-formalist protocols of the New Criticism, reshaping the latter into a surrealist method based less on narrative sequence than on a sequence of disjointed and psychically overdetermined images. Her remodeling of the formalist lyric, I shall argue, parallels the process which Hal Foster identifies at work in de Chirico's paintings, whereby 'psychic time . . . corrupts . . . pictorial space.'[15]

Shadows Cast by Unseen Figures

For both Plath and de Chirico, a thematic of lost or obscured origins, of memory and forgetting, is played out in a familial iconography. Each suffered from the early loss of a father, mythologized this event as a pivotal moment in the artist's creative life, and converted it into an iconographic and narrative resource. The 1958 poems written by Plath, 'On the Decline of Oracles' and 'The Disquieting Muses', represent something of a turning point in this respect; the former was the first of her 'lost father' poems, while the latter was the first to focus upon her relationship with her mother. De Chirico commemorated his father, a railroad engineer, not only through the architectural environment of his cities—the smokestacks, towers, and of course trains—but also, in his still lifes, through the frequent inclusion of draughtsman's implements, and blackboards covered with geometrical diagrams. In the famous painting 'The Child's Brain' (1913) (see pl. 39), originally entitled 'The Spectre', he depicts the father through the prism of the child's obsession as a looming, enigmatic presence, suspended between adult memory and infant fantasy. His naked torso, with its childlike shape and flabby, pallid texture, almost fills the picture frame, while the curtain-like fluted column, with its suggestion of partial concealment or veiling, reinforces what Soby calls the 'Freudian malaise' which haunts the picture.[16] The father figure is associated both with the law (through the closed book on the table), and with clairvoyance or prophetic vision, through his downcast or closed eyes, which render his gaze inaccessible to the viewer. His affinity with other blind seers such as Homer, Teiresias, or Orpheus resurfaces in 'The Portrait of Guillaume Apollinaire'(1914) and 'The Dream of the Poet' (1914), both featuring a marble or plaster bust of a balding man wearing extremely opaque dark glasses. The hermeticism linked with this paternal 'effigy'[17] finds expression in the cabalistic tracery, graphs, and signs which feature in many of the paintings. The associative links between paternity, secret or encrypted knowledge, and vision/ blindness recur in Plath's many depictions of the obsessively mourned and fanta- sized father figure, including 'The Decline of Oracles', 'Berck-Plage', 'Little Fugue', and 'Daddy'.

For de Chirico, the death and absence of the father installs a compensatory discourse of remembered classicism centred on the authority of Greco-Roman archaeology as transmitted by the Renaissance. His paintings exhibit a highly developed sense of belatedness or secondariness, of the new work as an always nostalgic, mournful interpretation of prior 'classic' exempla. This discourse of remembered, ambivalently idealized 'classicism' is arguably one of the central motifs of Plath's first published volume, *The Colossus*, which displays her expertise in traditional literary form, through intricate variations on traditional stanza structures (such as terza rima) and metres (syllabics, pentameter, folk rhyme). The display of technical proficiency, while doing homage to the authority of the literary canon, is accompanied by tropes of dislocation from any vital or sustaining model of the literary past. The 'colossus' is the emblem of a canonicity congealed into an abstract and monumental *idea* of tradition. At the same time, it is a ruin, an enigmatic collection of fragments tended by a diminutive female latecomer.

In her 1957 review of *The Stones of Troy* by C. A. Trypanis, Plath begins by quoting T. S. Eliot's famous 1923 review of *Ulysses*:[18]

> In using the myth, in manipulating a continuous parallel between contemporaneity and antiquity, Mr. Joyce is pursuing a method which others must pursue after him . . . It is simply a way of controlling, of ordering, of giving a shape and a significance to the immense panorama of futility and anarchy which is contemporary history.[19]

After quoting from Yeats's 'Sailing to Byzantium', Plath ends the review with the comment: 'The weakest poems in *The Stones of Troy* are those where the gap between 'contemporaneity and antiquity' is uncomfortably straddled: where the mythic material remains inorganic and untransformed in the context of the modern poem; where the parallel between old and new is pointed at, rather than realized in the poems' shape and texture'.[20] Plath is measuring poetic value, in New Critical style, by T. S. Eliot's criteria. The 'mythic method', as defined in '*Ulysses*, Order and Myth' (1923), seeks to spatialize traumatic historical change through the cyclical patterns of myth. Despite Plath's tribute to the 'mythic method' of her modernist precursors, the status of the classical past in her own poetry remains resolutely 'inorganic' and academic, gesturing uncomfortably toward its own artificiality. For Plath, as for de Chirico, the legacy of 'antiquity' is at once exemplary and under modernist erasure: ruin, and enigma.

Marianne Martin has discussed the 'theatricality' of de Chirico's art in relation to the active and longstanding involvement of both de Chirico and his brother, Alberto

Savinio, in theatrical production and stage design.[21] She points out that the meta-physical pictures often appear to extend into the spectator's space, the use of architectural perspective producing a shallow, structural scenic effect. The wooden planking which appears in many of De Chirico's metaphysical paintings of 1915–17 undermines naturalism, suggesting a stage, or a ship's deck. The effect is reinforced by the frequency of curtains or curtain-like forms, and by the antinaturalistic lighting of the paintings, with its ubiquitous and exaggerated shadows, often cast by objects or people not depicted in the painting. In her 1956 sonnet, 'Conversation amongst the Ruins', Plath draws on de Chirico's *Interview* (1927), which inserts a stage set into a valley. A male and female figure confront each other amidst cut-away pasteboard fragments of furniture and architecture. In the octet, Plath offers what seems to be a highly conventional gloss on the painting: the catastrophic force of eros has reduced the speaker's 'elegant house' to an 'appalling ruin'. The sestet, however, taps into the unease generated by de Chirico's 'metaphysical' clash of interior and exterior, culture and nature, classicism and modernity. De Chiricoesque anachronism—'fractured pillars' juxtaposed with domestic furniture, the speaker's 'Grecian tunic and psyche-knot' with the male figure's 'coat and tie'—highlights the artificiality but also the psychological fixity of the relation between the two figures. This tableau of oedipalized heterosexuality places the speaker in the shadow of the male figure, 'rooted to his " black look" ', as in Freud's classic paradigm of melancholia, in which the ego takes into itself and identifies with an ideal of the other.[22] At the same time, of course, he is himself incorporated as a hermetic emblem of melancholic obsession, a process echoed in Plath's equally pictorial 'Man in Black'.

De Chirico's 'metaphysical' tactics provided Plath with a spatial and iconographic language within which the temporal dynamic of memory could be explored. Her poetry embeds the figure of the dead father in a web of painterly, art-historical, and literary citation, which dwells on themes of influence, inheritance, and revision. He is linked with the figures of the *oracle* and the *archive*: cryptic repositories of literary and psychic memory through which the poet seeks to validate her own discourse. As mythic origin, the oracle marks the place of a certain institutional or pedagogic authority, and encodes, whether explicitly or implicitly, sexual preroga-tives associated with certain kinds of voicing. At the same time, it is a fictive construct, holding out a tantalizing promise of prophetic truth, completion, or plenitude which can never be verified. Plath's ironic early references to herself as a 'religious devotee of style'[23] or 'neophyte' ('Notes to a Neophyte') imply an eroticized scenario of instruction or discipleship, which shapes much of her writing. An early version of 'On the Decline of Oracles', published in *Poetry* in September 1959, bears an epigraph from de Chirico's manuscripts, referring to his painting *On the Enigma of the Oracle* (1910): 'Inside a ruined temple, the broken statue of a god spoke a mysterious language.' The painting depicts Odysseus consulting the oracle, represented as a ghostly white head behind a curtain. The shrouded, statue-like figure, turned toward the sea, is a literal quotation from the Swiss-German Symbolist painter Arnold Böcklin's *Odysseus and Calypso* (1881–3), a sign of de Chirico's declared reverence for his precursor. Plath's poem identifies the oracular source with the dead father, manipulating a decidedly awkward parallel between her memories of Otto Plath and de Chirico's apprenticeship, described in Soby's book, to Böcklin:

> My father died, and when he died
> He willed his books and shell away.
> The books burned up, sea took the shell,
> But I, I keep the voices he
> Set in my ear, and in my eye
> The sight of those blue, unseen waves
> For which the ghost of Böcklin grieves.
> The peasants feast and multiply.

The daughter relegates to herself the task of tending and preserving a paternal vision or 'voice' which she sees as inaccessible to a world of debased and brutish uncomprehending 'peasants'. His legacy is turned in upon itself; as in the later poem 'Little Fugue', the oracular is threatened with failed or blocked transmission. De Chirico's painting, too, conveys an oppressive sense of obstructed communication. It is bisected by a large brick wall which divides the two protagonists; the curtain which partially screens the oracle is echoed not only by the Odysseus figure's shroud but by the adjacent curtain blowing open at the edge of the painting. It is Odysseus, the ostensible supplicant, who seems cut off, inaccessible, and engrossed in grief. Plath's poem, by inscribing her 'debt' to de Chirico, repeats the circuit of melancholic incorporation of the precursor figure.

Archaeologies: Dismembering/Disremembering

Plath's dialogue with de Chirico turns on their shared apprehension of the cultural past as a piling up of fragmentary signifiers of antiquity or the 'classic', within which an obscure loss is lodged and kept alive, through compulsive repetition. This attitude owes a great deal not only to the Freudian notion of archaeology but also to the Nietzschean revision of classicism in a succession of works, notably *The Birth of Tragedy* (1871) and *Human, All Too Human* (1878). In his *Memoirs*, de Chirico cites Nietzsche's concept of *stimmung* or poetry of atmosphere as the basis of his oneiric 'metaphysical' paintings.[24] For Nietzsche, classicism's elevation of calmness, order, and rationality under the sign of the Apollonian constitutes a reaction-formation against the foundational mysteries of the Dionysiac and Orphic cults. Thomas Mical sees De Chirico's preoccupation with the 'riddle of origins' inscribed within the discourse of classicism as commemorating, in Nietzschean terms, a forgotten sacrificial violence at the foundation of the social contract, and of the classical idea of the polis. He points to the centrality of absent bodies in the built spaces of De Chirico's paintings—as shadows, phantasms, statues, mannequins, or anatomical models—and to the 'repetition of the fragment in place of the whole body'.[25] The fragmented, petrified, or absent body which haunts the architecture of the 'metaphysical' landscapes and still lifes—and which moves between statue, mannequin, and anatomical model—signals, he argues, the occluded status of the body within the space of the classical. This is equally a central concern for Plath, who, in poems including 'The Stones' and 'Daddy', shares de Chirico's fascination with the sacrificial narrative of dismemberment and reconstruction as the obverse of the classicist ideal.

If, as Rubin and others have argued, de Chirico's paintings use perspective to unsettle the viewer, this disturbance of vision is crystallized in the sightlessness of the mannequin. The presence of the mannequin subjects the pictorial space of the painting to Medusan effects, both blinding and petrifying. In 'The Disquieting Muses',[26] the speaker declares her allegiance to a trio of 'dismal-headed/God-mothers', who enlist her in a project of endless, inexplicable mourning. Reading this poem on a BBC radio programme, Plath commented:

All through the poem I have in mind the enigmatic figures in this painting—three terrible, faceless dressmaker's dummies in classical gowns, seated and standing in a weird, clear light that casts the long strong shadows characteristic of de Chirico's early work.[27]

The poem uncovers a treacherously double legacy within the seemingly cozy paraphernalia of a suburban girlhood, with its 'cookies and Ovaltine', piano and dance lessons, and 'made to order stories | Of Mixie Blackshort the heroic bear'. The good mother offers a sentimental idyll, and consequently floats away on 'a green balloon bright with a million | Flowers and bluebirds that never were | Never, never, found anywhere'. She is usurped by her 'disquieting' surrogates, with whom, it is hinted, she is in secret collusion:

> Day now, night now, at head, side, feet,
> They stand their vigil in gowns of stone
> Faces blank as the day I was born,
> Their shadows long in the setting sun
> That never brightens or goes down.
> And this is the kingdom you bore me to,
> Mother, mother. But no frown of mine
> Will betray the company I keep.

The poem can be read as a fable of entry into the symbolic order, in which the advent of the mannequin commemorates a lost primal oneness with the maternal object. The speaker's legacy—the 'kingdom' she inherits—is the bleakly antinatural, modernist landscape of de Chirico's painting of the same name (see Pl. 40), inscribed as the negation of maternal sentiment and indeed of the maternal body. The mannequins, with their segmented bodies marked by visible stitching, are at once forlorn and menacing. They supply an image of mutilated and muted femininity, most obviously in the case of the seated figure, whose clasped arms frame a bulging stomach, hollowed out by a shadowed void. Yet if at one level the mannequins are maternal effigies, at another their abandonment, incompleteness, and inability to stand without support evokes the pathos of the infant at the threshold of the symbolic order. The standing mannequin, seen from behind, faces a cityscape dominated by the imposing fourteenth-century facade of Ferrara's red Castello Estense. The juxtaposition of the mannequins with this fortress suggests a highly ambiguous 'guardianship'; similarly, in the poem, the broken window panes of the father's study in the third stanza suggests the threat the Muses pose to paternal law.

'The Disquieting Muses' is one of the first of Plath's poems structured by a child's perspective, and more particularly by its ambivalence towards the parental figure, a tactic which anticipates the nursery rhyme rhythms of 'Daddy'. Here, too, the visual analogue of de Chirico's painting is suggestive. The bric-a-brac at the mannequins' feet—including a striped stick and a rectangular box ruled into triangles of contrasting colour—resembles alchemical objects or playthings, recalling similar objects arrayed in paintings such as 'The Evil Genius of a King' (1914–15) and 'Still life Torino 1888' (1914–15). In his prose writings, de Chirico insists that the work of art's purpose is 'to come close . . . to the mentality of children', and on the necessity 'to live in the world as in an immense museum of strange things, of curious variegated toys that change their appearance, which we as children sometimes break to see how they are made inside, and, disappointed, discover they are empty'.[28] The poem taps into the 'child mentality' of a nursery rhyme and Gothic fairy tale: the infant christening is blighted by the wicked stepmother. Plath echoes the painting's sense of paralysis through verbal repetition ('Mother, mother'; 'to nod | and nod and nod'; 'you cried and cried'; 'I learned, | I learned, | I learned'), and narrative circularity.

In both poem and painting, entry into the symbolic order is linked with deface-ment. The mannequins are 'mouthless, eyeless, with stitched bald head', and have 'heads like darning eggs', a simile which yokes together the world of female domestic labour with an image of denied or aborted birth. The maternal reflection which confers meaning and identity upon the infant is replaced by an 'eyeless' gaze which petrifies her story before it has begun. One of de Chirico's mannequins is doubly defaced, with a detachable head, placed on the ground beside the blue box on which it sits. In their defacement and muteness the muses are closely allied with Plath's lunar imagery ('The Moon and the Yew Tree', 'Barren Woman', 'Elm', 'Edge'). They recall André Green's description of the 'dead mother' as 'a mother who remains alive but who is, so to speak, psychically dead in the eyes of the young child in her care'. The dead mother precipitates a condition of 'blank mourning', which empties meaning from the world. 'The patient', writes Green, 'has the feeling that a malediction weighs upon him, that there is no end to the mother's dying and that it holds him prisoner.'[29]

One of the central innovations of 'The Disquieting Muses' in the context of the Plath canon is its conception of the unconscious as itself a theatrical space or 'other scene', which constantly returns to a primordial puzzle of origins. The metaphor of the 'stage' equally dominates 'Electra on the Azalea Path' and 'The Colossus'. In the former, the paternal figure belongs to the de Chiricosesque discourse of remembered classicism. His death is an event located in a mysterious interface between dream, memory, and myth:

> Small as a doll in my dress of innocence
> I lay dreaming your epic, image by image.
> Nobody died or withered on that stage.
> Everything took place in a durable whiteness.
> The day I woke, I woke on Churchyard Hill.
> I found your name, I found your bones and all
> Enlisted in a cramped necropolis,
> Your speckled stone askew by an iron fence.

The father is associated with the frozen tableau of an unchanging classical or 'epic' tradition, whose artificiality and inaccessibility is highlighted by his daughter's visit to his grave. The more she attempts to retrieve the lost paternal object through fetishized relics or part-objects (the phallic 'speckled stone', the name carved on it, even the 'bones' themselves), the more it recedes into myth and literature, like the legendary Colossus of Rhodes, which disappeared without trace and may never have existed. This scene of writing has affinities not only with de Chirico's 'metaphysical' paintings but also with the baroque aesthetics of the ruin, of theatricality, and of melancholic contemplation. The speaker 'borrow[s] the stilts of an old tragedy'. The 'artificial red sage' that adorns the neighbouring grave turns the tragic 'blood-theme' of the *Oresteia* into a greasepaint fake: 'the rains dissolve a bloody dye: | The ersatz petals drip, and they drip red.'

The oedipalized scenario of 'Electra on the Azalea Path' relies on a bricolage of psychoanalytic, literary, and biographical texts. As in 'The Colossus', the classical paradigm of Aeschylus's *Electra*, in which the daughter avenges the murder of her father Agamemnon by inciting the murder of her mother Clytemnestra, is conflated with its latter-day psychoanalytic rewriting: the family romance, in which, according to Freud's narrative of female sexual development, the girl-child's formative discovery of her castration leads her to turn her affections away from the mother and toward the father. In 'The Colossus', the protagonist is part priestess of an 'oracle', part archaeological laborer. Like the speaker of 'Electra', she is dwarfed or miniaturized by a compulsively repeated ritual of devotion to paternal remains:

> A blue sky out of the Oresteia
> Arches above us. O father, all by yourself
> You are pithy and historical as the Roman Forum.
> I open my lunch on a hill of black cypress.
> Your fluted bones and acanthine hair are littered
>
> In their old anarchy to the horizon line.

This rhetoric of mourning and objectification is governed by anachronism; the 'blue sky out of the Oresteia' which 'arches above' the protagonists of 'The Colossus' has the flattened, depthless gloss of a stage property, recalling the antinaturalistic lighting of de Chirico's landscapes and still lifes. The discourse of classicism associated with the paternal effigy is shadowed by intimations of a forgotten or obscured violence; the colossus, after all, is both an architectural ruin and a dismembered body which the speaker desperately longs to reconstruct. In 'The Colossus', the speaker's classicism is identified as perverse; she is in love with a paternal law invested in the petrified *membra disjecta* of tradition. Her labor of restitution and repair has become merely fetishistic, an academic study of Greek and Roman architectural styles ('fluted bones', 'acanthine hair'). The cult of the architectural detail, which marks the conversion of the body into stone forms, typifies de Chirico's metaphysical paintings, for example in the pleated robe of the standing mannequin in *The Disquieting Muses*, which resembles a fluted column. Parallel instances in Plath's poetry include the 'pillars, porticoes, rotundas' of 'Barren Woman', the 'flutings' of babies' 'Ionian | death-gowns' in 'Death and Co.', and the 'perfected' woman of 'Edge' ('The illusion of a Greek necessity | flows in the scrolls of her toga').

In casting herself as oracular devotee of an 'epic' literary father, the daughter-in-mourning seems to mark herself as lacking his greatness. Her despairing self-abasement before the remains of a father who cannot be recovered in memory can be seen as a compulsive rehearsal of his imagined or mythic achievements, a ritual of self-humiliation and parodic miniaturization which cuts her down to size. Yet the oedipalized 'Electra' scenario draws attention to its own excessiveness and indeed perversity, signaling a disturbance in the meanings of femininity. 'Tradition' is constituted through a self-conscious mythologizing of the death of the father; it comes to occupy the status of a fetish, a substitutive and compensatory fiction, forestalling a prior loss, which is coded as maternal. As in 'Electra on Azalea Path', melancholic incorporation of the dead father is accompanied by a double movement of symbolic inflation and parodic reduction. The oracle utters only carnivalesque animal noises ('Mule-bray, pig-grunt and bawdy cackles'), which mock the idea of 'Tradition' as a repository of divine authority, as well as the elaborate repressions which constitute the formalist poet-daughter. The discourse of the closed, classical body generates its own negation through the return of a repressed oral materiality.

The reliance of the discourse of classicism on the sublimation of the dismembered body in 'The Colossus' anticipates poems such as 'The Surgeon at 2 a.m.' and 'Daddy'. The latter, much like de Chirico's metaphysical still lifes, is a collage-like assemblage of objects, images, and mediums associated with the father figure, which are manipulated in ritualistic and often hermetic ways. Plath redeploys the image of the colossus as the father's corpse surrealistically spread across the American continent. His permutations include not only the 'marble heavy . . . | Ghastly statue', but also a black shoe, photographic image, and a miniaturized 'model'. His oracular powers are parodied: 'The black telephone's off at the root | The voices just can't worm through'. He becomes a scapegoat, ritually dismembered into metonymic body parts such as foot, toe, head, mustache, blue eye, cleft chin, bones, and heart. As in 'Electra' and 'The Colossus', this assemblage of part-objects merely underlines the irrecoverable status of the original. The rituals of dismemberment and reconstruction which the poem visits upon the father are mirrored in the representation of the daughter, whose 'pretty red heart' is 'bit . . . in two' and who is 'pulled out of the sack' and 'stuck . . . together with glue'. The iconography echoes that of de Chirico's painting 'I'll be There . . . The Glass Dog' (1914). A sculptured female torso with a section removed from its breast to reveal a stylized heart is placed alongside a diagram, chalked on a wall or screen, of a mannequin in male dress, with the seam marks that indicate stitching.

'Daddy' can be seen as the culmination of a dialogue between Plath's and de Chirico's work, which remakes the modernist legacy as a mourning ritual organized around parental objects of frozen or petrified desire. De Chirico brings to this dialogue a revision and critique of classicism based on a sustained reading of

24. 'Chapel meeting' at Green Hall Auditorium, Smith College, 1950, watercolor

25. Woman with folded arms, *c*.1948–50, tempera

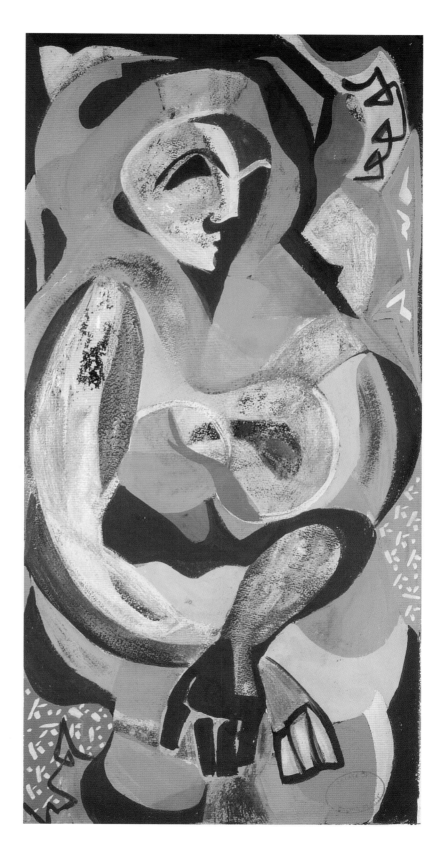

26. Hopkins House, 1951, coloured ink

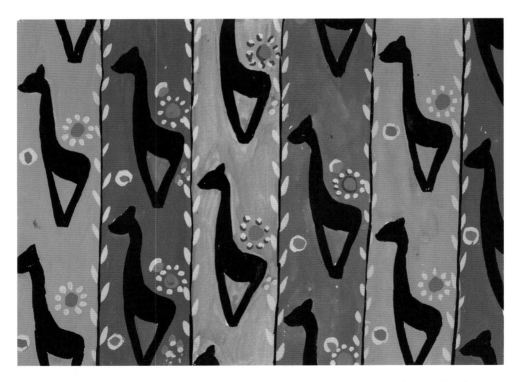

△ **27**. Giraffe pattern with flowers, *c*.1950–1, tempera

▷ **28**. Yellow house, *c*.1950–1, tempera

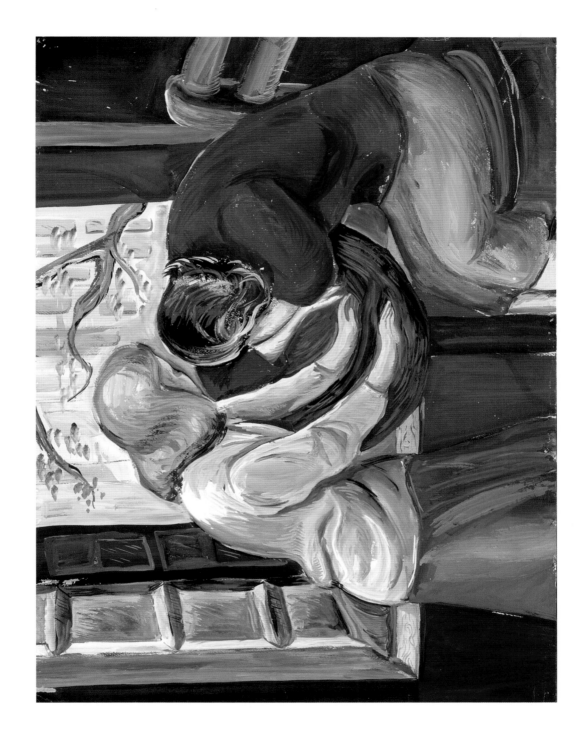

△ **29.** Still life, c.1950–2, oil

▽ **30.** Two women at window, c.1950–1, tempera

△ **31**. Woman with halo, *c*.1950–1, tempera ▷ **32**. Two women reading, *c*.1950–1, tempera

◁　**33**.　Nine female figures, *c.*1950–1, tempera   △　**34**.　Triple-face portrait, *c.*1950–1, tempera

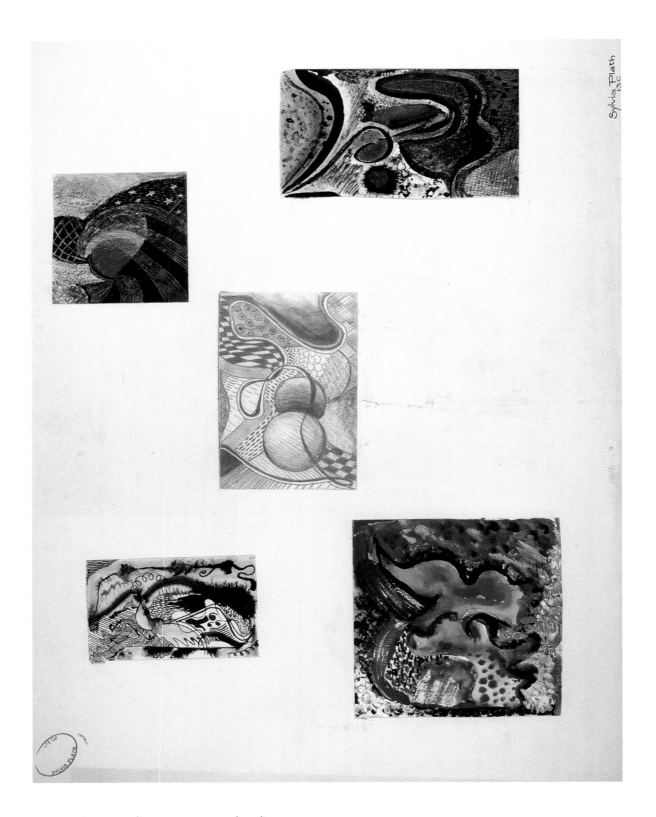

35. Five abstract studies, *c*.1950–1, mixed medium

I don't know whether or not Perry told you, but I am at present sporting a rather fabulous fractured fibula. The fatal event took place on a mountain in Saranac Lake almost two weeks ago. Obviously I was learning how to ski. It was fine until my friend urged me to ride the tow. There was a flash of ecstasy as I stood on the top of the glass hill and saw levels of snowy mountains stretching away into grayness, and the flat, sensuously winding river far below, pale green, reflecting the greenish sky. Then the plunge. Gaily I plummeted down straight (I hadn't learned to steer yet.) There was a sudden brief eternity of actually leaving the ground, cartwheeling (to the tune of "You Belong to Me" blaring from the lodge loudspeaker) and plowing face first into a drift. I got up, grinned, and started to walk away. No good. Bang.

Luckily I was staying with a young doctor and his family next to the tuberculosis sanatorium, so I had all kinds of expert medical treatment. The doctor (who became a writer when he had to leave medical school for a few years with T.b.) even let me read the novel he wrote about his sanatorium experiences— a passionate, James-Joycian study of introspection involving every controversial subject from sex to God to modern art. He's going to try to get it published soon, but I am sure it is too spectacularly intellectual for more than small, elite group-appeal. For one thing, his vocabulary is unbelievable. While undertaking the cure of tb he also undertook the task of learning the dictionary from cover to cover. As a result, I, (who thought I had a pretty good vocabulary!) was forced to search for multitudinous words in Webster per page. Which brings up the question of the artist's purpose as far as communicating with humanity is concerned. (Dr. Lynn is fed well and has a wife, which is a case in point for your theory of the leisure class...)

36. Illustrated letter to Myron Lotz, page 2, January 1953, mixed medium

37. Collage of Cold War images, 1960, mixed medium

38. Woman behind screen, Art scrapbook #4, *c*.1950–1, mixed medium

39. 'The Child's Brain',
    Giorgio de Chirico,
    1914, painting

40. 'The Disquieting Muses',
    Giorgio de Chirico,
    1917, painting

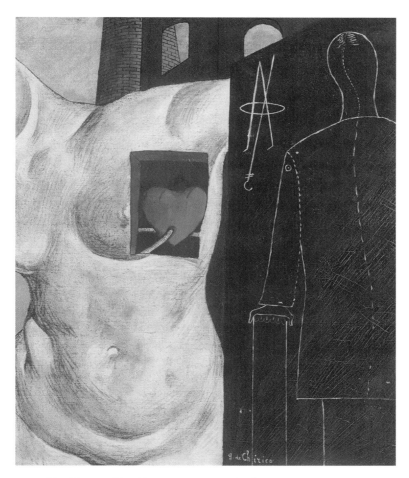

33. 'I'll be There . . . The Glass Dog', Giorgio de Chirico, 1914, painting

Nietzsche, while Plath contributes a reading of Freudian psychoanalysis increasingly alert to its oedipalized sexual politics. The work of both can be described as a 'dream writing' governed by a tropology of spatial enclosure and mortification, and tied to an imaginary construct of 'lost time'. For both, the emphasis on the excavation of the self's psychic 'prehistory' is linked with a broader project of re-membering the body within the genealogies of classicism. De Chirico's modernist example was thus not only crucial to the development of Plath's distinctive icon-ography; it also provided her, paradoxically, with many of the diagnostic tools which enabled her to mount a critique of 'classic' modernism itself as a legacy.

5

Sylvia Plath and the Costume of Femininity

SALLY BAYLEY

From an early age, artist and writer Sylvia Plath was preoccupied by images of female self-construction or what we commonly call 'glamour':[1] the alluring costume of femininity promoted by women's magazines and Hollywood culture. The young Plath was also aware of the role of the domesticated female, and images of the suburban life appear in the creative repertoire of her juvenilia. Later in her career, as a housewife and mother, she began to play with the idea of the unglamorous or entrapped female with sharp irony and contestation, forms of feminine experience that appear in her 1960s *Ariel* poems and her 1961 novel, *The Bell Jar*. Central to this experience is the suburban home with its protagonist, 'the wifey' whose stupefied existence places her among the 'cow people | Trundling their udders home'.[2]

This essay examines Plath's involvement with constructed forms of femininity reflective of the prescribed social and cultural codes of post-World War II America: the processes of female socialization. In particular, I explore the body of commercial and cultural imagery arising from Plath's artwork: the drawings, home-made cards, collages, and paintings that form an important part of her early corpus, from the early 1940s to the early 1950s when she was an undergraduate at Smith College. Tracing Plath's early interest in the acculturated female within this body of work,

I look at how this interest distinctly informs her mature writing—most notably, her *Ariel* collection.

How to Be a Woman

Plath's 1956 poem, 'Two Sisters of Persephone' presents a split model of woman-hood, the woman who remains 'within' the domestic sphere and the woman 'without': 'Two Girls there are: within the house | One sits; the other, without'.[3] The self relegated to the house lacks an audience for her 'mathematical' genius; furthermore, she cannot reproduce. Her counterpart, the sister 'without', is fertile and 'bears' a male heir. Plath's use of metaphor betrays her understanding of a self divided, a female self whose shadow self 'sits' within the house. Here, in this poem, Plath represents the calculating 'mathematical machine' that is the housewife's daily routine, binding her to a larger mainframe that controls a whole generation of women.[4] This divided female self becomes the central narrative of several of Plath's *Ariel* poems such as 'Lesbos' and 'The Tour', where competing forms of femininity serve to upstage one another.

As part of a 'personal odyssey' tour of American college campuses during the mid-fifties, Democratic presidential candidate Adlai Stevenson gave a commence-ment speech in 1955 at Smith College, Massachusetts,[5] where the young Sylvia Plath was graduating. The speech focused on the 'unanimous vocation' of Plath's contemporaries 'to be wives and mothers' who would 'influence' their husbands and children.[6] Stevenson hit upon two central issues of the fifties: firstly, the role of the wife and mother in the service of her husband and children as inculcator of morality and social purpose; and secondly, the fifties' domestic policy of contain-ment of the female.

In his essay 'The Social Structure of the Family' (1949), the American sociologist Talcott Parsons highlights the clearly differentiated sex roles within a marriage. The marriage relationship, he argues, was the strongest dynamic in contemporary society contributing to female segregation. Parsons suggests that women were prepared for their roles as housewives and mothers despite receiving equal treat-ment by their parents. Once married, they were to remain in their allocated roles, thereby serving the dual purpose of shielding their spouses 'from competition with each other in the occupational sphere'.[7] Parsons pinpoints the retreat of the married woman into the shadows of the housewife's role as fundamental to the 'functional importance of the solidarity of the marriage relationship to our kinship system'. In other words, the woman's decision to marry and not pursue a career was a necessary factor in achieving the balance of power required for a successful marriage. Parson's argument ratifies the prevailing notion of the female as the 'lost sex'—what became known as the 'feminine mystique',[8] the 'problem that has no name'—manifested in the 'quiet desperation' of the American housewife locked into the torpor of a suburban existence.[9]

Parson's view of the American family with its differentiated sex roles was the dominant theory in post-war sociology. As Lynn Spiegel states in her introduction to *Welcome to the Dreamhouse: Popular Media and Postwar Suburbs* (2001), the division of public and private spheres reflects an ideology, and as such operates as a means of 'social control and power' and controlling social space.[10] It was considered a natural assumption that the potential of the female for social status be more limited and therefore more predictable. Young girls were not likely to turn into 'bad seeds', for they were 'more apt to be relatively docile' than young boys were.[11] Underlying this precept was a psychology based on the persuasive theories of psychoanalysts Marynia Farnham and her husband, Ferdinand Lundberg. Their treatise, *Modern Woman: The Lost Sex* (1949), condemns the woman who 'seeks a sense of personal value by objective exploit', and threatens her with such 'lunatic omens' as the loss of her emotional capacity, 'orgastic failure', and damage to her husband's 'sexual capacity'.[12] Such myths prevailed and were fed by the mass market of women's magazines. *Ladies Home Journal, Seventeen,*[13] and *Mademoiselle,* magazines that served as Plath's earliest forums for her own publications, were the same forums that aired advice to the young Sylvia on her femininity. Articles such as 'How to Be a Woman' warned that being a woman was a career, an imperative that couldn't be avoided. Brett Harvey notes that such journalism unloosed threats upon the developing female to take up the 'joys' of the domestic 'profession': 'turning out a delicious dinner' or 'converting a few yards of fabric . . . into a new room'.[14]

At the centre of this campaign of persuasion is Lundberg and Farnham's defin-ition of femininity as 'receptiveness and passiveness' and a willingness to accept 'with deep inwardness and readiness' the final goal of her sexual life: 'impregnation'. In other words, even the act of sex was subordinate to the role of mother, and pleasure, according to *Modern Woman*, evades the female unless she would 'in the depths of her mind, desire, deeply and utterly, to be a mother'.[15]

Domestic Role Models

Alongside the message from popular psychology, Plath's particular familial culture and history helped shape the process of her socialization. Patricia Macpherson highlights an ideology of self-fulfilment behind Plath's drive to achieve, an attempt to build a life of achievement over 'the void of unworthiness' inherited from the immigrant status of the Schober family, the family of her mother, Aurelia Plath.[16] In her introduction to *Letters Home,* Aurelia Plath confesses that as a youth she found a 'complete escape' in 'the sugar-coated fiction of the day, wherein the poor and virtuous always triumph', and that Louisa M. Alcott's *Little Women* was a book she had learnt almost by heart.[17] To escape the drudgery of her imposed domestic life, the young Aurelia Plath lived within a 'dream world' of knowledge. She writes of having 'a book tucked under every mattress of the beds it was my chore to make daily', a vicarious means of self-education imitating her own mother's 'cheery' acceptance of educating herself through her daughter.

A handmade greeting card made by Plath for her grandmother during her adolescence supports this notion of the inherited role model of the female martyr. This 'Happy Grandmother's Day'[18] card poses the question: 'Are you always working every minute?', a question clearly directed at the model of domesticity the young Plath witnessed with the Schober family[19] (see Pl. 5). Plath writes, as a mature woman, of her resentment of the female-dominated household in which she grew up:

> The little white house on the corner with a family full of women. So many women, the house stank of them. The grandfather lived and worked at the country club, but the grandmother stayed home and cooked like a grandmother should.[20]

As this journal entry suggests, in later years Plath deeply resented her lack of male role models and, in particular, the intensity of the mother–daughter dyad—a fact that surfaces in poems such as 'Medusa' and the 'Disquieting Muses'.[21] A 1950–1 painting by Plath, 'Two Women at Window', may be indicative of this relationship, as indicated in a letter to Eddie Cohen she wrote during her first year at Smith:

'When you catch your mother, the childhood symbol of security and rightness, crying desolately in the kitchen...it kind of gets you'[22] (see Pl. 30). The painting may be read as a composition of grief in which the figure of the daughter stands helplessly over her distressed mother. Echoing the reciprocity at the heart of their relationship, the daughter in this interpretation bends over her mother as a supplicant of her mother's pain, while her mother folds herself within the out-stretched form of her daughter, a passive recipient of her daughter's sympathy. Sociologists have argued for the greater significance of the mother–daughter relationship in the practice of child-rearing, particularly in the case of daughters,[23] but as the journal entry on the 'little white house' suggests, Plath's resentment is more specifically directed against her familial female role models, who offered her a view of life based upon self-sacrifice and domestic containment.[24]

An image of Plath's grandmother on the front of her home-made card substan-tiates this picture: sitting at the bottom of a flight of stairs dressed in the outfit of a 1950s housewife, her life appears to be ruled by the never-ending cycle of domestic chores. On the inside of the card, Plath has also written 'Happy Mother's Day', and drawn images of herself, her mother, and Warren, her brother. This incorporation of the identities of both her mother and grandmother into one card strongly suggests that Plath had a sense of both women as products of a domestic regime—an arrangement in which any singular identity is denied.

The subtext to this merging female identity, however, is a defiant effort on the part of the adolescent Plath to establish her own identity as a professional. On the back of greeting cards she made as a child and adolescent, she placed a logo, typically a flower head with the image of a coin at the centre, and 'Plath & Plath' (as she collaborated at times with her brother), or 'Plathmark', often dated 1932, the year of her birth. One 1946 greeting card to her mother[25] has a note on the back written by Aurelia, confirming the young Plath's budding interest in the commer-cial potential of her creativity: 'Sylvia saved $10 toward her camp money. Earned a good part of it.'[26] As Barry Shank has noted: 'The greeting card market is the institution where longing for a language of feeling meets the structuring effects of large-scale business organisations driven by for-profit calculation,'[27] a fact which the young Plath, with her imitation logos, seemed, in some sense, quite aware. This early interest in the potential of financial gain from creative works re-emerges in Plath's scrapbooks from her early period at Smith College, where advertisements from the printing industry are collated with the mantra for creativity to make money: 'Plant now the fertile seed of your thought on paper . . . let it germinate and grow, bearing the fruit of your work and aspiration. There's a harvest market ahead for all that is sown well now.'[28]

However, it was the model of what Aurelia Plath in her introduction to *Letters Home* described as reluctant 'submission' to the father figure that governed the Plath household: a traditional pattern of gender role-play with Otto Plath's academic work taking precedence over family life.[29] Plath's 1943 greeting card, a birthday present for her 'Grampy', shows two women dressed in 1940s style aprons, baking; the lines on the front of the card read: 'Both Grammy and mummy | were baking with care | in the hope that Grampy | soon would be there'[30] (see Pl. 4). Plath's card captures a strong sense of the 'Plath house' orientated around the activities of its male members, a fact echoed in several of her journal entries during the first year of her marriage to Hughes, where Plath wrote, for example, of 'planning one of Ted's favourite suppers' during their honeymoon in Benidorm, Spain.[31] Three months before this trip, Plath included a sort of journal tribute to her female role models: to her grandmother, dying of cancer, 'who took care of me all my life while my mother worked', and her mother who continues 'working, teaching, cooking, driving, shovelling snow from blizzards, growing thin in the terror of her slow sorrow'.[32]

The Ready-Made Doll's House

Another 1943 birthday card Plath made for her grandmother begins with the lines: 'The neighbours are gossiping over back fences' and ends with: 'What can it be that they guard like a treasure? The answer's so simple . . . the treasure they guard is their priceless grandmother!'[33] The young Plath, with a strong sense of the post-war consumer culture, listed her grandmother amongst a catalogue of consumer imagery: a refrigerator, oil, the department store escalator, and the family home itself. Her grandmother, as the real 'treasure' of the family home, however, is a far more valuable good. This early birthday card signals Plath's fascination with the image of the American home, a fact substantiated by a series of art scrapbooks at the Lilly Library filled with images of American-style homes, completed during her first year as an undergraduate at Smith college, in 1950–1. Pages and pages of gathered images of advertisements of ranch house homes, images taken from *Better Homes and Gardens* and other contemporary home magazines testify to Plath's fascination with the home environment. One such advertisement reads: 'We wanted a house that would be different, with a broad entrance that would make the house warm and welcoming,'[34] or 'The Shimonek House is built entirely with native materials—pink sandstone and cedar.'[35] In one image, two children play cards on the porch of a suburban home; in another, a young woman reads in a stylish interior, while a similar figure stands within her fashionably outfitted kitchen as an accessory to the décor: culturally idealized domestic spaces containing idealized forms of femininity.[36] One page, filled with images of 'Ready-Made' homes, includes a turquoise blue bedroom interior, with two sinister-looking dolls sitting on a twin bed, as forms of accessories to this space. The doll as a miniaturized and 'ready-made' form of the domesticated female anticipates Plath's biting satire of what Betty Friedan termed 'the happy housewife heroine' in her 1962 poem 'The Applicant' with its 'ready-made' form of wife, with her 'rubber breasts or rubber crotch'.[37]

A 1954 campaign run by *McCalls* propagated the mantra for the ideal post-war American family whose byword was 'togetherness'. This Campaign of Togetherness situated the husband as 'designated leader and hero' battling on the corporate frontline in order that his family could afford those consumer goods deemed necessary for the good life. An advertisement for prefabricated homes from the same year echoes this sentiment: 'When Jim comes home our family seems to draw us closer together.'[38] In a 1955 interview for *Better Homes & Gardens*, Mrs. Dale Carnegie took up the rhetoric of togetherness, by appropriating a metaphor of the American home: 'Lets face it girls. That wonderful guy in your house—and in mine—is building your house . . . split-level houses fine for the family, but there is simply no room for split-level-thinking or doing—when Mr and Mrs set their sights on a happy home.'[39] The 'split-level' metaphor chosen by Mrs. Carnegie seems to highlight, painfully accurately, precisely the sort of 'split' or double self of women trapped, in what the heroine of *The Bell Jar*, Esther Greenwood, experiences as the 'mutually exclusive' cul-de-sac of female socialization.[40]

Plath's interest in the family home reflects the post-war fascination with the American suburban home as the most essential commodity: the rapid growth of the 'ready-made' suburbs, heralded by the Levittown community, 17,000 houses built for 82,000 residents in 1951,[41] and described in *The Bell Jar* as the 'escape proof cage' where the housewife exists among 'lawn sprinklers and station-wagons and tennis rackets and dogs and babies'.[42] More than one of Plath's art scrapbooks from Smith includes exterior images of the American suburbs, including a series of small black and white photographs of suburban homes[43] whose signature motif, the white picket fence, Esther Greenwood confronts as she is driven back through the 'white, shining, identical clapboard houses'.[44] One of two similar paintings Plath completed during her time as a Smith undergraduate (1950–2), 'Yellow House' (see Pl. 28), highlights her preoccupation with the suburban theme and the placid homogeneity of the American middle-class suburb. This home, painted a garish yellow, recalls the yellow of Esther's sickness upon her return to the suburbs; the flat, two-dimensional appearance of the painting suggests the restricted view of the world from the suburbs.

When Esther retreats to the suburbs, as a citizen of the United States, she assumes her private life will be offered the safe cradle of its 'motherly breath'. Such a setting is also featured in a four-fold birthday card Plath made for her grandfather and signed, 'For Grampy, From All of Us', where the Plath and Schober family appear in a bucolic setting as the model American family, embracing what Eisenhower called 'the American way' of life. Plath's depiction of the 'gossiping neighbours' in her 1943 birthday card also pre-empts the image of Dodo Conway, Esther's neighbour in *The Bell Jar* who seemingly embraces the whole 'sprawling paraphernalia' of suburban motherhood and domesticity. Dodo's house, however, does not conform to the socially prescribed 'community' style of 'adjoining lawns, and friendly, waist-high hedges'.[45] In 1950s suburban America the notion of privacy, analogous to the notion of democracy, carries its own organizational restrictions. Dodo Conway lives a life that does not subscribe to the norm: she has seven kids instead of two to four, and her house is painted brown and grey instead of the 'white clapboard' of the rest of the neighbourhood. In Esther's neighbourhood, this is regarded as 'unsociable'.[46] These seemingly minor infringements of the suburban code are enough to undermine her privacy and community respect. She is an anomaly and therefore the 'talk of the neighbourhood'.[47]

Images of domesticity as well as the undesirability of that state saturate Plath's work. Two of her paintings she made as an undergraduate at Smith College portray these spaces. One tempera painting entitled 'Two Women Reading'[48] resembles an advertisement for the blissful condition of the domestic life, and as such, can be read as a satire of that lifestyle.[49] The women are perched on the canvas like figurines: pert, inert, and serene. The landscape that encloses them is highly cultivated: an immaculate lawn and a villa redolent of an image from an edition of *Better Homes & Gardens*. A series of perpendicular lines criss-cross the canvas creating a series of flat, geometrical shapes, heightening the artificiality of the scene. Domestic props surround the women: a picnic and an elegant vase whose colours are echoed in the surrounding landscape are reminiscent of a Matisse interior (see Pl. 33). Although situated outside the home, these women are still enclosed by the props of the domestic world, a fact that echoes the domestic policy of containment of post-war America.[50] In *The Bell Jar*, Plath's heroine writes herself into a novel in which she imagines herself 'sitting on the breezeway, surrounded by two white clapboard walls, a mock orange bush and a clump of birches and a box hedge, small as a doll in a doll's house'.[51] Esther cannot finish her novel, as her mind itself is made miniature by her suburban containment.

The Constructions of Glamour

In a famous diary entry from 13 November 1949, the young Sylvia Plath writes of having been 'too thoroughly conditioned to the conventional surroundings of this community...I am already partly lost. I am a great deal too fond of pretty clothes...my vanity desires luxuries which I can never have.'[52] Plath's diary entry, written at age seventeen, is an important one in terms of its testimony to the homogenizing process of female socialization. Yet it also reflects what was, for Plath, a lifelong interest in feminine fashion as a form of theatre, as her two cut-out dolls and series of outfits housed at the Lilly Library testify[53] (see Pl. 15). The entry is revealing for its association of 'convention', 'clothes', and 'community', a message relayed in the popular women's magazines.

A regular feature of *The Ladies Home Journal* during the 1950s, for example, was the column entitled 'The Sub-Deb', aimed specifically at teenage female readers for the purpose of initiation into the cultural notion of 'successful' womanhood. A July 1949 'Sub-Deb' column by Maureen Daly offers its young female readers advice on the most crucial of feminine attributes, her appearance: 'Decide right now that no special magic is going to make you look different overnight—you have to do the waist-bending exercises, hair-brushing and clothes-choosing all by yourself!' The column takes a more serious turn with its injunction to its young readers to discipline themselves to study 'the teen-fashion section of a good magazine' as if it were 'a school textbook', and to then place themselves at the centre of 'the experiment' as if this imaginative self-projection were 'the picture in real life'.[54] Plath's drawing entitled 'Heather-Bird Eyebrows',[55] which began as a character sketch for what would become her 1952 short story (see p. 66), 'Initiation', is based upon her invitation to join a high school sorority. The drawing depicts a graceful young woman in evening dress with her hand raised in a dismissive gesture. We learn from the notes surrounding the drawing that the young protagonist, although keen to know 'what goes on among these carefully beautiful girls with their mysterious chatter about their dates', refuses entry into the sorority club. Instead, she chooses to align herself with the processes of her imagination and self-reflec- tion, signified by the man she meets on the bus who mentions the flight of the heather-birds, and by the presence of the 'little old man' she observes on a park bench, absorbed in watching the rituals of the sorority club initiations. The latter is clearly an early embodiment of the audience-critic of Plath's imaginative and creative processes, a role later taken up by her husband, Ted Hughes. 'Initation' thus demonstrates both Plath's interest in the process of induction into the feminine codes of her peer group, but also her contestation of this implied conformity. Furthermore, these social codes and practises provided her with vital fodder for the more important process of writing.

Images of glamour frequently erupt throughout Plath's senior high school history notes, where, for example, pencil sketches of forties starlets disrupt the more 'serious' diachronic narrative of male history—what Plath called her 'car- tooning'.[56] One such sketch drawn onto 'The Influence of the War on American Life' school notes[57] features a full-length drawing of a glamour girl dressed in a late forties style bodice and flared skirt. Her right arm and hand reaches out towards the centre of the page, while her figure in its diaphanous skirt draws the reader's attention away from the narrative of war. Alongside Plath's list of pedagogical self-instructions to 'read the text' of the First World War, and to 'master' its terms, Plath's starlet is presented as a sort of Ava Gardner persona. Her shapely figure, taking up the entire length of a page, appears to have been called in to distract the

Topic III The Influence of the War on American Life

Day 1.
    1. Read the chapter, pp. 692 to 710.
    2. Explain the terms, pp. 710
    3. Answer the questions pp. 711
B. Things to be done by all pupils working for additional credit.
    1. Select from the readings, pp. 710.
    2. Prepare one of the topics, pp. 710.
    3. Read from Hicks, Hamm, Faulkner and Kepner.

Topic IV Our Part in the Peace

Day 1.
    1. Read the text, pp. 712 to 721.
    2. What was President Wilson's purpose in going to Paris?
    3. Tell of our prestige in Europe.
    4. Explain the position in which Mr. Wilson found himself in Paris.
    5. Read from the reference books in the library and bring to class a complete account of the peace conference of January 18, 1919.
    6. Why did Mr. Wilson insist that his plan for a League of Nations should be considered first? How did the other members feel about it? What concessions did Wilson make to France to get the League?
    7. Give the substance of the 26 articles of the League. (See pamphlet.)
    8. Describe the machinery of the League. (Faulkner and Kepner pp. 718 to 721.
    9. Quote Article X.
    10. Why was the Covenant of the League made an integral part of the peace treaty?

Day 2.
    1. Read the text, pp. 721 to 733.
    2. Be able to give the chief points in the completed peace treaty as it was presented to Germany.
    3. Study the new map of Europe and note all changes that were made. (Show Europe in 1914 and Europe in 1919.)
    4. What parts of the League were severely criticized by our Congress?
    5. What action did Wilson take to gain support of the treaty? What result?
    6. How did Wilson answer these criticisms?
    7. What resolutions were offered by Lodge? What results?
    8. Explain why the treaty was not ratified?
    9. What is your opinion of our failure to ratify the treaty and to enter the League of Nations?
    10. Read the summary, pp. 731 and 732 with great care.

Day 3.
    1. Master each term, pp. 732.
    2. Answer each question, pp. 733.
    3. Review the entire chapter.
    4. Be able to write on the topic: "Our Part in the Peace."

B. Things to be done by all pupils working for additional credit.
    1. Construct two maps of Europe, one showing 1914 and the other 1919.
    2. Read from the references, p. 732.
    3. Select a topic for study from pp. 733.
    4. Report on: "Interesting Men of the Wilson Era."
    5. Take one side of the debate: Resolved: That the United States should have entered the League of Nations.
Day 4. A review of Unit VII
Day 5. A test on Unit VII

34. 'The Influence of War on American Life', *c.*1949–50, pencil on school text

troops from the horrors and tedium of the military experience: an alluring and enchanting siren whose idealized form enters into the 'master' narrative of war as a potentially usurping 'mistress' from the realm of popular culture.

While Plath was a top student of American history, these synchronic eruptions suggest a doodling, dreaming young Plath whose attention was often far from the narrated (and predominantly male events) of her classroom history lesson. Plath's feminization of the 'facts' of the historical discourse subverts the high mindedness of its message, offering a gentle lampooning of what might often appear to be a series of arbitrarily selected facts.[58] A clear example of this subversion appears next to Plath's notes on 'How Our Country Acquired Distant Possessions and Put Democratic Government to the Test'. Next to the course's statement of purpose is a sketch of a forties bouffant-haired glamour female with long eyelashes; in her left ear appears a dangling earring. Similarly, on the back of a series of notes on the facets of the American government, the 'Judicial Department', a pen-ink thumbnail sketch of a fashionable young woman is seen wearing an elegant hat. Her closed eyes are indicative, perhaps, of Plath's own distracted state from the facts of the classroom. Similarly, on notes entitled 'The Advance to the Pacific', a thumbnail sketch of a young woman wearing a hat with the head of a flower suspended over her appears, while in notes for the 'State Government', a pencil sketch portrait of a classmate is featured, with a great deal of attention given to the spring of curls covering her forehead. Plath's fantasy females certainly upset, and indeed question, what seems to be the rhetoric of high-minded nationalism and imperialism that permeates this decidedly male model of pedagogy and historical emphasis. An essay she wrote for her senior year history test, in fact, succinctly expresses her own feelings about imperialism and its relation to modern economics and warfare:

> The causes of modern wars in general may be classified under the following headings: navalism, militarism, imperialism, economic imperialism, secret alliances, newspaper propaganda, nationalism, neo-mercantilism. (This latter occurs when a nation furthers its private investments abroad and then promises to defend the rights of its private investors.) All these causes listed above promote the jealousy, greed and dangerous over-patriotic fervor conducive to modern warfare.[59]

A series of these glamorous belles also run throughout Plath's Smith College class notes, images drawn from the women's magazines to which she was now submitting stories and poetry. In June 1952, for example, she wrote to her mother complaining that *Mademoiselle* has no policy of accepting illustrated stories.[60] Clear outlets for these 'illustrated stories' are her college notebooks, where *Mademoiselle*-style women repeatedly appear. As with the 'Initiation' piece, behind these enticing belles often lurks the genesis of a story. In Plath's 'Notebook for Intellectual History of Europe', pen-ink sketches of women appear, typically dressed in evening gowns, suggesting the gown Esther wears on her infamous date with Constantine in *The Bell Jar*. In one instance, a young woman appears in an evening dress holding a cigarette in her hand, presenting a sort of Marlene Dietrich character who patrols the borders of her notes, offering a kind of 'double' or alternative discourse—one of narrative creativity—to the 'intellectual' content of Plath's notes.[61]

This sort of 'doubled' discourse seems to come to a head in a striking example found in Plath's notes on 'Medieval Literature'—notes mostly on Chaucer.[62] Here Plath again offered up a series of doodles of young women, in this case, mostly pen-ink headshots, with the same wide and exaggerated eyes. On the final page of this notebook, Plath wrote, as a note to herself, a series of questions entitled, 'Why does a man propose to a woman?' Her answers include, in a series of 'alternative' notes to the Chaucer material: 'escape from loneliness', 'hunts for mother everywhere', 'illusions—asserts masculinity', 'escape (as one takes dope) in romantic affair', 'to seem like typical competent young man seeking creative companionship'. Beneath these notes on male propositions, Plath writes an instruction: 'Read Roman de la Rose, Piers Plowman'. Placed alongside the literature notes themselves, Plath's annotations on the male traditions of romance, of which Chaucer's *Troilus and Criseyde* is a prime example, offer up a more practical and contemporary take on the conventions of romance: a version of a Sub-Deb column. In this sense, the head shots of glamorous women that surround these notes appear as a form of 'line-up' of potential female partners who may, or may not, accept the male proposition. Thus Plath's 'cartooning' and alternative note-taking manages to convert and subvert Chaucerian material into the sort of narrative found in a column from one of her beloved women's magazines.

As Gary M. Leonard comments in his essay 'Sylvia Plath and Mademoiselle Magazine' (1992), the magazine culture of the 1950s perpetuated a code of femininity whose essence was the commodification of the female form.[63] Central to the code was the advertising industry whose slogans filled the pages of magazines such as *Mademoiselle*, which Plath herself viewed as a crucial forum for her writing. Plath's internship as a guest editor for *Mademoiselle* suggests that the platform of the women's magazine was a place she felt she must embrace. In a letter to her mother, Plath writes of the ecstatic experience of devouring one of her stories published in *Mademoiselle*: 'took the car alone for a blissful two hours . . . with a bag of cherries and peaches and the Magazine',[64] a letter that underlines the consumptive process of reading popular women's magazines.

Leonard points to a self-help article from the 1953 edition of *Mademoiselle* that Plath was partly responsible for producing. The article is typical of the type of agony aunt advice handed out to young women in the guise of psychoanalysis—advice that invariably involved some form of feminine masquerade: 'Start with the surface, because that's what shows, then work your way down to the big basics. Consider that venerable saying: You're as young as you feel. Substitute: you feel as vital as you look.'[65] The emphasis is purely upon the female potential for visual transformation: the process of 'substituting' one form of self for another. The advice given implies that psychological problems can be remedied by the ability of the female to transform her physical self. Indeed, her physical self is both her redemption and her cure.

Romantic Conventions and Self-Invention

Plath's art scrapbooks are a testimony to her interest in the cultural commodification of the female as object of visual consumption, the role of the female in what Baudrillard has identified as 'the commodity system',[66] the process of hard sell of feminine attributes Plath parodied in 'The Applicant'.[67] Yet they also speak to the overall process of consumer consumption aided by the female image, which depends upon a delectable self-presentation, what Erica Jong in her poem 'The Objective Woman' terms the 'firmessence' of her 'ultralucence'.[68] A statement from an advertisement[69] in one of Plath's art scrapbooks confirms this belief: 'Take a tip from the women who have always used fashion as a weapon for their personal victories', while an advertisement for lipstick[70] includes a drawing of a woman holding a red lipstick up to her already red lips. Next to this image a faceless female mannequin steps out between pastel pink curtains; a metonymic form of a 'packaged' Christmas greeting; she carries a bouquet of flowers instead of a face, and a 'Merry Xmas' sign above her head. Her 'use-value', according to the commodity system of advertising, is determined by a tautology in which the subject is defined by the object and vice versa.[71] On the opposite page Plath assembled an image of a maroon-pink car with a registration plate of '1942', while the advertisement declares that 'goods sell a lot easier than they used to', before providing the reason for this as the 'feminine appeal in product design'.[72] Plath's art scrapbooks from 1950–1 are filled with examples of carefully culled images of women marketing the 'power' of the 'dream', images in which the female as a cultural product sells market goods.

What Plath catalogues in these scrapbook images is the clear association of market forces, the hard sell of feminine glamour: desirable young women sell products. Another art scrapbook collage portrays the figure of a woman emerging mannequin-like from behind a diaphanous veil; cinematic in its lure, the piece holds both the woman, and her viewer, captive (see Pl. 38). Like a Botticelli Venus, the female emerges into view as the object of male romantic desire. Caught by the male gaze (the gaze of the camera), she is both subject and object—the complete romantic commodity. Surrounded by heart-shaped rose petals, this screen siren costumes herself in the vestments of romance, while on the opposite page, another female face frozen in time and space reinforces the allure of the 'eternal feminine'. The aesthetic is one of film noir, redolent of Barbara Stanwyck as Phyllis Dietrichson in the 1944 film noir classic, *Double Indemnity*, a film Plath saw.[73] Like the film noir heroine/killer, Plath's female figure leads the male gaze towards visual and emotional entrapment.

However, as is mostly the case with the Plathian *oeuvre*, we find evidence of Plath's parody of the cultural conventions of romance. A 1952 valentine card depicts a swooning female reclined across a heart-covered chaise-long, clearly under the heady influence of romance—and love sickness. Valentine hearts circle her head, and she holds a single rose clutched in her limp hand, with the other hand at her forehead. Her eyes are closed and her expression is desolate. The line across the top of the card reads 'I Shall Fall into Decline', while the inside continues:[74] 'If you won't be my Valentine,' Here, Plath as a young woman is both the subject and object of romance. 'Caught' within the visual narrative of the card, she chooses to satirize both herself and the convention that has her acting out of what she perceives to be ludicrous social role-play. It is quite clear from this image that Plath is aware of the system of social production in which the young female in her feminine costume plays the part of an object of consumption, laid out upon her couch.

A pre-1956 poem,[75] 'Cinderella' depicts a young girl's flight of fantasy towards the eternally desired fairy-tale romance. Within a social context this is very much the fairy-tale ending promised young girls by the chief proponent of the fairy-tale romance, Walt Disney. As Susan Douglas comments, Disney was the epitome of fifties America with its 'generosity of spirit, its trusting innocence, its good-natured, harmless fun'. As Douglas explains, however, beneath the sugary sprinkle of the Disney screen lurked a stereotype of the female that belied its innocent appeal.[76]

A series of four tempera paintings completed as a young teen indicates the influence of the Disney aesthetic on the young Plath. These paintings depicting nursery rhyme and fairy-tale characters, including Snow White and Red Riding Hood, reflect the saccharine commercial and emotional palette of Disney.[77] In one instance, Snow White,[78] a typically idealized Disney 'good girl', stands framed within a portico bound in by limits of the painting's composition; in the distance is a series of hills (see Pl. 6). The composition suggests a young girl penned in by the limits of fairy-tale convention where the hills, as the boundaries of her world, signify the narrow horizon of her fairy-tale desire—the culturally prescribed fairy-tale ending.

As Marina Warner suggests, Disney animations consistently presented the heroine as a paragon of girlish goodness, a typical Disney film maintaining a high degree of 'disequilibrium between good and evil': the virtuous girl and the wicked older woman.[79] Only a very good, selfless girl, could find herself awake with her prince by her side, or fit her foot into that one golden slipper. Thus Plath writes in 'Cinderella' of the young girl 'in scarlet heels | Her green eyes slant, hair flaring in a fan of silver as the rondo slows';[80] the one moment of sheer fantasy achieved by virtue of her apprenticeship to the fairy-tale convention.

Plath carries female stereotypes into her 1961 novel *The Bell Jar* where, as Lynda K. Bundtzen notes in her essay, 'Women in The Bell Jar: Two Allegories' (1989), we meet the bifurcate version of womanhood in the form of the naive, regulated Betsy, a model of womanhood that will lead Esther, like Betsy, towards the 'model' homemaker of B. H. Wragge's advertisements.[81] On the other side of Betsy is the sexy, sophisticated Doreen. Belying the roles of both women are female archetypes:

the choice between a Cinderella or her ugly step-sisters, the fairy-tale heroine or her antagonist. Doreen, in a social situation, will become the painted woman, attracting men like flies, the eternal femme fatale. Betsy, on the other hand, preserves the sweet innocence of a Snow White or Sleeping Beauty. This is the model of womanhood disdained by the speaker of 'The Disquieting Muses', the innocent Shirley Temple mould of the post-war starlet whose 'twinkle-dress' symbolizes her virtue.[82]

Plath was well aware of how her own image could be manipulated by cultural symbols of glamour. In a 1954 letter to one of her boyfriends, Gordon Lameyer, she writes of her decision to convert that year to a 'brown-haired personality', as opposed to the platinum blonde 'personality' with which she began her career at Smith.[83] This new personality, 'serious, industrious, unextracurricular', will wear 'Bermudas, knee socks and loafers instead of racy red heels, parachute skirts and an aura of chanel'. Plath's concern for a need to cultivate a more practical, less 'gilded' version of self—the scholarly self described in 'Two Sisters of Persephone'—is reflected in an instruction to herself to 'dress down', to drop the glamour-doll look. This deliberate instruction to undo glamour is a theme that will continue to emerge in poems such as 'Sow' (1957), where a strong sense of a deconstructed self, 'impounded from public stare', seeps into the description of this 'Brobdingnag bulk'.[84] Indeed, Plath's 'Sow'[85] can be read as a statement of the right of the female to exist, in private, without the demands of glamour. And so the demand for another version of femininity begins to arise.

Anti-Glamour and the Domestic Horror Show

In keeping with the 'split-level' version of womanhood, Plath betrays a strong fascination with the other side of glamour, a sort of anti-glamour she associates with the female kept 'within' the house of 'Two Sisters of Persephone'.[86] A draft of an unpublished poem, 'Kitchen Interlude',[87] explores what will become the full-blown theme of her later *Ariel* poem 'Lesbos': the 'horror show' of the domestic life. In 'Kitchen Interlude' the air is 'thick and sickening', the speaker is 'doped and thick' on domestic drudgery as she is in 'Lesbos'.[88] 'Lesbos' is a clear example of how the domestic space defines the occupant. The kitchen, the domestic matrix, implodes with fraught tension as the speaker describes her space in images evocative of a low-budget horror film:

> the fluorescent light wincing on and off like a terrible migraine,
> Coy paper strips for doors . . .
> An old pole for the lighting.[89]

As in the earlier poem, where we find the same effect of lighting, 'the bright candor of the sun' creates 'squares of light across the floor'. In 'Lesbos', allusions to lighting and colour reinforce the sense of a set, a contrived *mis en scène*, in which the speaker observes herself, objectified. In 'Kitchen Interlude', time runs away 'like scattered grains of salt', creating a sense of what the speaker in 'Night Dances' calls 'nowhere'.[90]

In Plath's poem, 'The Tour',[91] this 'nowhere' becomes another domestic horror show brought on by the invasion of the family home by the unexpected visit of an elderly aunt. Contrary to the normative socialization of the American housewife, the speaker is not prepared for social interaction, and appears on the domestic threshold in unappealing garb. Plath's speaker invites her visitor into her sanctum, and then proceeds to destroy the idealized reality of the homelife by conjuring a series of absurd, nightmarish scenes in which the speaker herself plays chief terrorizer. At the heart of this domestic nightmare is the vision of the unglamorous housewife, a ghoulish female with 'no hair', dressed in 'slippers and housedress with no lipstick'.[92] This is the inversion of the idealized home of Mrs. Carnegie, a home 'burnt out', a home in which glamour and domesticity have slipped into a 'a bit of mess'.[93]

Plath's 1954 letter to Gordon Lameyer, recounting the practice of 'playing parts', is filled with tropes of theatrical self-construction, 'the actor behind' the 'camou-flaging mask', the 'varied roles' ascribed to the female: 'the urbane and seductive party-goer; the eggs-and-bacon-and-coffee girl in a housecoat who can also exist on olives, Roquefort and daiquiris while clad in black velvet, and make a switch to a tanned saltwater and sunworshipping pagan'—all roles Plath cast for herself.[94] These 'parts and facets of personality' emerge in their most bitterly ironic form in the late *Ariel* poem 'Lady Lazarus',[95] where the avenging femme fatale of anti-glamour finally seizes the central role from her double self. The speaker's demands to be 'unpeeled' can also be read as an exhortation of removal from the wrappings of an entire culture, a ritualistic 'unperforming' of the constructs of glamour with all its 'facets' and 'parts'. In the same letter to Lameyer, Plath posits whether, after all this playing of parts, one should 'release the lady or the tiger'. In her final years, it would seem that Plath released both parts in the form of 'Lady Lazarus', a poem whose central narrative is a self who 'unperforms' the norms and mores of her culture by a ritual of self-defacement and debasement ('My face | a featureless fine Jew linen').[96] Plath's letter draws attention to the source of this performative self—a culture saturated in the visual, where multiple selves may appear 'diametrically opposed to one another'.[97]

The canny narrator of *The Bell Jar* posits Esther Greenwood's experience of breakdown as a sort of horror show in which a self fully cognisant of her processes watches herself spiral downward towards suicide. Esther narrates her experience of breakdown as a process of acute defamiliarization, in which she encounters herself through a series of foreign or unknown selves: on one occasion, a 'sick Indian' staring back at her from the mirror.[98] When asked what she 'would like to be' for a photo-shoot in Jay Cee's office, Esther flounders; in response to Jay Cee's attempt to construct her as a poet, Esther disintegrates, unable to assimilate the accessory of the paper rose Jay Cee offers her, into any notion of herself.[99] Esther's crisis is the inability to perfect what Plath, in her letter to Lameyer, calls 'the protective and camouflaging mask' of the socialized self.

The feminine 'look' that Jay Cee attempts to construct through Esther reflects a wider cultural interest in self as product, self-on-view and *as* view. Plath's Smith College art scrapbooks, made during a period of her life later assimilated into material for *The Bell Jar,* are a testament to her absorption in a culture of viewing. Cinematic images abound: in one instance, an advertisement for 'Dorsay' perfume foregrounds a black and white figure of a young mannequin with huge heavily made-up eyes; in another, a female appears with an accentuated right eye, her head lit up with strong lightning. Next to her a Miro-esque eye appears with a black pupil set against a blue sky,[100] the eye itself as a form of landscape, but functioning, also, as a metonym for an entire culture locked into acts of visual consumption.

In her *Journals* Plath records seeing the Luis Buñuel and Salvador Dali film *Un Chien Andalou* (1929).[101] The central motif of the film comes in the opening sequence where the camera focuses on the character of Luis Buñuel stropping his razor. Stepping onto the balcony, he gazes at the moon. This celestial orb is instantly replaced with a woman and, enlarging rapidly, her left eye. The bare blade then descends on her unprotected pupil, a graphic incident. Plath describes this opening sequence in a series of nervous iterations of the appearance of the girl's face on screen in relation to the moon and the razor. In her notes on *Un Chien Andalou*, Plath records the relation between the male character, the face of the female, and the moon, a tripartite relationship that leads to the final shot of the razor sequence, described by Plath as 'close up of gore'.[102] In this relationship of images, the moon, as emblem of a clichéd romantic view, substitutes the female view, a fact suggested by the flitting back and forth of the camera between razor, moon, and the face of the female (Simonne Mareuil), before Buñuel's character slices across her eye and her view is, literally, cut through. Plath's notes on this 'shock film' are clearly concerned with the process of female viewing and the delimitation of that view by the positioning male auteur. It is the narrative of substitution that seems to concern Plath: the moon replacing the female face and, in turn, the female face replaced by the face of the male butcher, a sadistic rendering of the fairy-tale narrative in which rescue is substituted for butchery, the face of the female for pure 'gore'.

Plath's notes on this film form a sort of bizarre retelling of her 1945 pencil sketch, 'The Mermaid and Moon',[103] in which the figure of a forties starlet appears as a mermaid gazing at the moon. This mermaid, a precursor of the fifties 'doll', lifts her right hand upward toward the star as if in a wistful request for rescue. The presence of the male rescuer is suggested in the form of the castle that constitutes the background of the sketch: the fairy-tale prince whose appearance promises to transform and rescue the cul-de-sac narrative of the mermaid doll. This sketch can also be read as a prototype for the 1958 poem 'Lorelei', Plath's rendering of the German version of the folk tale inherited from her mother, who used to sing a version of the tale to her.[104] The 'plaintive cry' of her mother's song is perfectly captured in Plath's reaching mermaid, in that both poem and sketch share the same gothic aesthetic: 'The massive castle turrets | Doubling themselves in a glass | All stillness'.[105] The hemmed-in existence of the Rhine maiden—the 'nightmare' conjured by 'borders of hebetude', the 'ledge' of 'high windows'—is another rendering of the domestic nightmare of Plath's 1962 poem 'Eavesdropper' whose landscape is a construct of dark borders: hedges, curtains, and windows through which the captive female speaker is consumed by a male.[106] In *The Bell Jar,* Plath's final comment on constructions of glamour, the trappings of suburban life, and the entrapments of American film culture appears to be parodied. In the bottom of her pocket, Esther Greenwood retrieves a 'smudgy photograph' of a dead starlet and matches it up to a snapshot image of herself. There is a perfect 'match': Esther and the starlet are synonymous, 'mouth for mouth, nose for nose', one part equable to the other.[107] In a culture engaged in visual exchange, one female is very much like another, and the face of a dead starlet as transferable as any other commodity.

The Woman Behind the Mask

Esther's catalogue of commodities is a comment on the reliance and function of social masks. In her poem, 'Pro Femina' Carolyn Kizer speaks of the unique female capacity for constructing masks:

> Our masks, always in peril of smearing or cracking,
> In need of continuous check in the mirror or silverware,
> Keep us in thrall to ourselves, concerned with our surfaces.[108]

As Plath writes in her *Journals*, 'Masks are the order of the day, and the least I can do is cultivate the illusion that I am gay, serene, not hollow and afraid.'[109] The theme of social masquerade runs throughout Plath's *oeuvre* but is apparent in two of Plath's senior high school paintings, 'Woman in Green at Table' and 'Woman with Folded Arms'[110] (see Pl. 19). Both paintings offer imitations of Picasso's monumental primitive females, whose faces, drawn from African masks, are models imitated by Plath's contemporary William de Kooning in his 'Woman' series of paintings completed during the 1940s–50s. On the De Kooning canvas the femmes fatales of the post-war movie screen—Marilyn Monroe, Jayne Mansfield, Bette Davis—are reduced to ferocious monsters, an aesthetic that takes revenge on the saccharine sweetness of the Disney heroine or the squeaky clean brand of femininity endorsed by actress Doris Day.

Like the women of Picasso's *Demoiselles D'Avignon*, Plath's 'Woman in Green' is faceless: without identity or purpose. The proportions of her body defy the neat proportions of a feminine silhouette; her arms are elongated and her huge hands clutch at a blue rock. Her exaggerated pendulous breasts dominate the canvas.

Similarly, 'Woman with Folded Arms' presents a primitive version of the female subject whose arms loom large over hands like pigs trotters. The painting's mango-orange earth tones are far removed from the pink and blue Technicolor of the Disney screen.

As her college art notebooks testify, Plath's interest in the primitive aesthetic developed during her art history classes at Smith College. They are filled with commentary on Rousseau's jungle scapes, Picasso's African figures and masks, the colours and forms of Van Gogh and Matisse.[111] In her notes on Picasso's sketches, 'La Mere' and 'Old Man at Table', she comments on the tendency towards 'expressionistic distortion, surrealistic expression of psychological'—an aspect of Picasso's work that clearly draws her interest. Writing in her journals in February 1958, she records a 'terrible primitive drawing dream', the result of an art class she had audited with a Smith instructor, Mrs. Van der Poel, in which Plath describes a series of distorted images 'jutting forth' like 'African masks & doll masks on Mrs. Van der Poel's screen'.[112] In the context of her art classes, Plath's dream reads as a personalized synthesis of the primitive aesthetic, a sort of gothic horror show of the imaginative potential of distortion and exaggeration.

The culmination of this aesthetic of distortion is her October 1962 poem 'Lady Lazarus', in which a female protagonist performs a personalized horror show, a form of emotional and psychological self-deconstruction. The show is primal and barbaric, a cruel deconstruction of the fifties sex symbol; and so, rather than seducing us, 'the nose, the eye ... the full set of teeth' become agents of horror.[113] What is served up is a monstrous inversion of the Hollywood screen siren, a cultural side to the homogenized glamour of mid-century America. Coming at the end of her career, 'Lady Lazarus' is the darker relative of the two selves presented in 'Two Sisters of Persephone' (1956), or the 'two' of 'In Plaster' (1961); the self 'kept in the dark'.[114] This later poem suggests that the 'duet of shade and light' played out in the domestic stalemate of 'Two Sisters' is an unsustainable cultural paradigm; as the speaker of 'In Plaster' expounds, two selves cannot both be 'superior'. And so 'Lady Lazarus' offers a solution: a deconstruction of the 'painted face[s]'[115] of the popular culture industry. This is the end of the cultural show: the series of roles that have, until now, served the feminine masquerade.[116] What comes 'smiling' through in Sylvia Plath's late portrayal of the feminine costume is a parodic performer whose existence depends, not upon cultural constructions, but upon her own talent and nerve.

6

Sylvia Plath's Visual Poetics

FAN JINGHUA

Prolonged engagement with visual arts is one of the strongest sources for Sylvia Plath's writing. Plath's artworks range from pencil and ink sketches, to detailed paintings and collages of print images, in different styles of expression and in varied materials and media. Until the age of 20, she envisioned both writing and visual art as viable options for her career. Although the large bulk of Plath's artistic works proves the potentiality of a promising artist in her, I will not argue for the recognition of her double identity as a painter-poet. Instead, I will try to delineate and demonstrate the influence of visual art and its sensibility upon her poetics from the perspective of visual art techniques and her own visual art practices. My argument is that Plath's poetics is developed out of the interaction between the visual and the verbal, and there is a visual art principle working throughout her poetic creation.

Visual art had always been an abiding influence upon Plath's poetics, as can be seen in both her structuring of imagery in her poetic compositions and her appropriation of themes and visions from various visual artworks. Plath's consciousness of visual elements in poetry not only finds expression in the random thoughts recorded in her journals, but also in more orderly course essays. While visual arts practice may not be a pre-requisite for writing pictorial poems, Plath's adeptness in various art forms and sensitivity to different elements in visual arts obviously prompted and facilitated her integration of visual art techniques into her poetry. A study of her writing in relation with visual arts, therefore, may further reveal the underpinnings of her visual poetics.

Settling the Terms

One basic function of language is to describe a visual scene or object which is absent to the reader. In ancient Greek, a rhetorical exercise called ekphrasis (pl. ekphraseis) is designed to train students to describe such scenes or objects and bring them vividly before the reader's eyes. Visual artworks are the most available objects for ekphrastic practice, and as ekphrasis develops into a literary genre, an ekphrastic piece is ordinarily understood in the narrowest sense as a poem addressing a painting. In the current critical parlance, ekphrasis is generally defined as the verbal representation of a visual representation, in which the objects of the visual representation usually refer to plastic artworks such as paintings and sculptures.

Poetry and painting are two different modes of representation, with two different sign systems. Underlying the two art forms, however, is a common principle rooted in the mimetic aesthetics in the West, as is epitomized in Horace's dictum *ut pictura poesis* ('as is painting so is poetry'). While Horace does not elaborate on the techniques involved in the implied principle, one may assume the same principal element of compositional design, which can be exemplified by Homer's description of Achilles' shield in *Iliad*,[1] the most famous classical piece of ekphrasis. In that passage, the descriptive order of the scenes in the narration corresponds with the spatial order of the patterns in the imaginary shield. This method of description, which will be encompassed in the term ekphrastic principle in this essay, is fundamental in the comparative study of the compositional design between painting and poetry.

As a genre develops from a practical technique, ekphrasis predicates certain methods and themes. The reason to introduce ekphrasis into the study of Plath's visual poetics is that this concept can accommodate not only her compositional method in scenic poems and her art poems addressing specific paintings, but also her visual art practice. Ekphrasis in this essay will thus refer to both compositional techniques applicable to visual and verbal arts and a thematically oriented literary genre. Specifically, for elucidating Plath's visual poetics, this essay will demonstrate how she develops and applies ekphrastic principle in three sequential phrases of her poetry.

For the purpose of my analysis herein, the periodization of Plath's writing will be mainly related to her engagement with visual arts. The early phase in her writing career refers to the years up to summer 1957, before she returned to Smith as a teacher. In this phase, she was active in both media, producing varied genres of artworks while studying in Smith College, or illustrating her prose writing while studying in Cambridge or traveling in Paris and Spain. The second phase of Plath's writing, the two years of her return to America, ending in December 1959, were essential to her professional maturity, not only because of the art poems she composed in 1958, but also because of the after-effect of these poems on her writing during her residence in Yaddo in fall 1959. When she went to settle down in England, her writing career will be referred to as the late phase of her poetry, in which her ekphrastic poetics gradually takes in multiple perspectives, and more cinematographic and dynamic elements.

In the early phase, Plath is read as a technically conscious painter-poet struggling with the structuring of imagery in poetry and the planar design in her artworks. In the second phase of the art poems, she incorporates a temporal dimension into the ekphraseis so that the transcription of paintings is fused with personal voice and vision. In the late phase poems, in which Plath builds more and more on discrete images to transcend mimetic similitude, the ekphrastic principle is an internalized method, and almost every image in her poetry can be understood as a node pointing to visual entities that link to each other or dynamically interact.

Compositional Design and Thematic Fusion Across Media

Sylvia Plath's early experiment with visual art elements is found in three strands of poems. The first strand displays more concerns with the basic formal aspects of the poetry, especially in her efforts to make use of color schemes, sound effects, and line breaks to achieve visuality in the poems. In a 1950 poem 'Gold Leaves Shiver',[2] short lines in stanzas with varied number of lines, and successively indented one-word lines, are used to convey the rhythm and visual illusion of falling leaves. In a journal entry written in 1951, Plath explains that she chooses certain words for her poems on the basis of 'the visual appearance and sound of words' as these words may function like 'the color and texture in a painting'.[3] This entry best exemplifies her early understanding of the relation between the poem and the painting. Although what she tries to find appears to be a direct simple relation between the elements in verbal arts and those in the visual arts, it shows her conscious effort to find a principle that can work for both modes of artistic expression.

In many of her pastels and temperas, bright colors are used in sharp contrast to each other with almost no neutral tones and perspectival depth. In the temperas 'Two Women Reading' and 'Nine Female Figures' made for her Smith arts classes, geometrical fragmentations of the painting planar, coupled with the color scheme, create a visual rhythm in the compositional design (see Pls. 33 and 34). While these paintings may suggest the influence of masters like Matisse, Degas, or even Mondrian, it is the formal design and color scheme that is significant in these artworks, as is the case in most of her early poems.

In her poems, Plath also tries to apply the color scheme of paintings. In 'Midsummer Mobile'[4] she not only directly alludes to specific visual artists or artwork motifs, but also tries to configure the reader into a viewer of a painting. The first line, 'Begin by dipping your brush into clear light', performs both structural and thematic functions, enforcing the poem-as-painting concept. She prescribes 'Dufy-blue' for the sky, encourages the viewer to 'outdo Seurat', and resorts to the 'mellow palette of Matisse' so that the 'singularly designed' composition can be 'like a rare Calder mobile in your mind'. Her strenuous efforts to become what she calls 'a word-artist'[5] sometimes appear to be overdone, as can be seen in the strained lines: 'fleck schooner flanks with sun and set | A tremolo of turquoise quivering in | The tessellated wave'. These phrases are quite pompous in terms of lucidity, concision, and accessibility. Difficult as they are to read aloud, they do create a complicated if not exquisite verbal mosaic for the eyes.

This poem also shows Plath's conscious effort to position the reader in the way that the frame of a painting functions to encase an *objet d'art*. The frame of a painting, as Arnheim notes, 'not only limit[s] the range of visual objects intended to constitute the work . . . [it] also define[s] the reality status of works of art as distinguished from the setting of daily life.'[6] Plath's method of structuring the picture in this poem is primarily to give a frame-like enclosure to the poems. The frame, no matter in the form of semantic or formal enclosure, can highlight the perception of visuality in the represented scene. The poem 'April Aubade'[7] is a good example of this approach. This poem starts with an imperative: 'Worship this world of watercolor mood | in glass pagodas hung with veils of green', thus transforming the April scene into an encased, exquisite *objet d'art*. Just as the coda, or ending couplet of the poem tries to summarize, the poet hopes that the viewing–reading experience can produce a particular illusion.

Plath's conscious experiment with traditional forms can also be seen as her efforts to maximize the visual textuality of poetic composition, especially when this experiment is inspired by paintings. The 1953 poem 'To Eva Descending the Stair',[8] apparently inspired by Duchamp's cubistic painting *Nude Descending a Staircase*, makes use of villanelle form. With the first lines: 'Clocks cry: stillness is a lie, my dear; | The wheels revolve, the universe keeps running', and repetitions of certain sounds and lines, including 'Proud you halt upon the spiral stair', Plath in this villanelle attempts to reproduce the illusion of stasis and motion of the painting. Prescriptive forms, therefore, through the rhyme schemes and meters, may help to weave different poetic elements into one organic whole. This also points to the New Criticism metaphor of poetic composition as a well-woven tapestry, a then-prevailing wisdom which instructs her in the composition of her early poems.

The thematic flatness in these poems, however, shows that Plath's formal concern is not yet induced or incorporated into the vision. The method of framing, for example, will be developed and incorporated into later scenic poems, when she learns how to put spatial and temporal dimensions into her ekphraseis. Compared with her poems in this phase, thematic concern appears to be more important in her portraiture. Among her paintings with a semi-interior or closed space, the portraits are remarkably more somber than landscapes with figures. Although geometric tension is still fundamental in the compositional design, the use of darker colors implies a psychological import not usually found in the 1958 art poems. In her 1951 'Self-portrait in Pastel', for example, she represents herself with a disquieting reddish face and an unbending look into the viewer, affirming the self-awareness also found in both her journals and poetry (see Pl. 24). The gaze in the poem 'On Looking into the Eyes of a Demon Lover'[9] can be explored to exemplify its uncanny similarity to those in not only this self-portrait, but also an earlier one she made in pencil, and an abstract portrait that fuses three faces into one (see Pl. 35). The speaker looks into 'the eyes of a demon lover', who turns out to be herself. The 'two pupils' are 'moons of black' that 'transform to cripples | all who look', but the speaker claims that she may seek her 'image | in the scorching glass', for 'what fire could damage | a witch's face?' The rhetoric question finds its affirmative echo in the last stanza, in which the speaker announces that 'in that furnace' she finds 'radiant Venus | reflected there'. The projection of this dauntless self in poetry can be read as a visual representation of her famous 'I am I' and 'the girl who wanted to be God' declaration of adolescent independence in her 1949 diary, which subsequently presents her alternating perceptions of both the beautiful and flawed image she sees when looking into the mirror.

Self-portraiture as metaphorized into a mirror, in fact, is a particularly important motif in Plath's poems. To look into the mirror is to position herself as both a subject and an object, as is in the case of self-portraiture. The objects in both self-portraiture and mirror-looking are reflections of the gazing subject. In many of Plath's poems, the speaker's self can be understood as either the gazing subject or the gazed object. Yet the change of the speaker's position in her body of poetry follows a general trajectory from a gazer to the gazed, which responds to the shifting from the rich color scheme in early poems to the colorless sculptural stasis in later poems. Parallel to this shift is the gradual weakening of the controlling power of the gazer's 'I'/eye. The self in Plath's early poetic phase epitomizes in the omnipotent 'I'/eye in 'Soliloquy of the Solipsist',[10] in which the eye–I has the absolute power over the world it sees.

The supreme power of the solipsist 'I'/eye, however, is weakened in later poems like 'Barren Women',[11] where the disappointed speaker imagines herself to be the mother of 'several bald-eyed Apollos'. Here, the reciprocal reflection between the subject and the object breaks down, as the subject 'I' is denied the reflection from the 'bald eye' of the object. This poem inevitably recalls the 1963 poem 'Child',[12] in which the speaker 'want[s] to fill [the child's clear eye] with color' (see pp. 140–1). The motif of painter's gaze is again brought into the poem, while the speaker's own mind ('this dark | Ceiling without a star') may be compared to a piece of unusable canvas. If the speaker's fear is reflected through her fascination of looking at her own reflection in the mirror in 'Mirror' and 'Childless Woman', the woman in 'Edge',[13] one of the two very last poems, is 'perfected' partly because her eyes are no longer of any use to the extent that they are not to be brought into the poem, just like the 'sheeted' mirror in 'Contusion'.[14]

When portraying other figures, the personal psyche of Plath as painter is projected into a social context. One painting in tempera, 'Two Women at Window', portrays two women by a window, where one woman appears to be comforting the other, who has streaks of white hair (see Pl. 30). The painting apparently represents a difficult situation of everyday life such as stress or bereavement, as well as the helplessness of those who view it from the outside. Yet the fact that Plath made this painting during her first year at Smith, while feeling under intense pressure to perform and writing in her journal of feeling depressed, possibly lends to its interpretation as a veiled self-portraiture, similar to the mirror-viewing experience she noted earlier.

In a high-school painting in tempera, 'Three Figures', a golden aura surrounds the contours of what appears to be a father, a mother, and a child (see Pl. 13). The father figure, wearing a mournful expression similar to those found in pictures of Christ on the cross, is positioned to hold the child and mother, where he is clad in Christ-red and the child in Mary-blue. The design of this painting immediately suggests both the Holy Trinity pyramid and the composition in a pieta. The hand of the father is disproportionately prominent in the foreground, accentuating his protection of the family, and in the biblical sense, the family of man at large whose burdens he accepts as his own. The three members carry the same facial expression and features, and both the strokes and the features resemble those found in Munch's works. The child-like figure, however, does not have youthful features, and appears disturbingly like the mother, which may be also suggestive of the painter's matrophobia. The fear of becoming her mother finds a fuller expression in Plath's later life, hinting at the possibility that she will fall into a predicament similar to that of her childhood, where memories of her family toubles became prominent in many texts.

While these comparisons may reveal some coterminous characteristics between Plath's early poetry and paintings, the unequal development of her artistic expressions forestalls any extended generalization. What can be safely argued can only be based on the observable formal aspects, that when applied in her poetry may be largely the result of study in the milieu of New Criticism. After being raised in the prevalent theoretical environment of New Criticism, it is no doubt that Plath was quite aware of textual visuality or verbal icon in poetry. As a matter of fact, among the books she heavily annotates in her personal library are *The Well Wrought Urn* and *Understanding Poetry*. The former of these two most popular New Criticism canons derives its title from Keats's 'Ode on a Grecian Urn', the most famous of romantic ekphraseis. New Criticism's fastidious analysis of formal aspects of poetry prepares her for the coming maturity in poetic pictorialism, but Plath's recourse to verbal extravagance in the early phase of her writing career can only make up for the lack of thematic depth before she is able to integrate her own style and voice into the verse fabric.

Perspectival Deepening and the Art Poems

Normally in the earlier phase of Plath's poetry, in order to achieve the illusion of reading a poem as viewing a painting, a framed or an isolated image is vividly described. Technically, the incorporation is realized by enlarging the spatial and temporal dimensions in the poems, making the otherwise static landscape move. Plath's basic way is to make the frame appear to be moving, as if the viewer and the landscape are moved away from each other, so that an illusion of a deepening perspective is created. This proves to be a genuine way to move away from rigidly applying the planar composition and color scheme design from her artworks, and it shows Plath's new understanding of how to appropriate visual art techniques into poetry. When she successfully incorporates her personal life into the purely descriptive poems, a fresh phase in her poetry begins.

In this strand of poems, Plath's way of representing the scene is often to capture an image first, and then gradually bring in the peripheral views. As isolated images are embedded into a broader background, they become constituents of the overall composition of a picture, and their function is increasingly subjected to their relation with the adjacent images. When the full view of the described landscape is presented from the standpoint of a viewer, who can be identified as the spectator-poet, the viewing experience of the landscape is not only spatially and temporally consistent with the reading experience, but also contains an internal motion that increasingly engages the viewer into the context.

The best example to illustrate Plath's technical change from compositional design to perspectival deepening is 'Winter Landscape, with Rooks'.[15] Obviously,

Plath is aware of the significance of this poem. In a journal entry written on 20 February 1956, she records that this is a 'Good Poem' in that 'it moves, and is athletic: a psychic landscape'.[16] No matter how she uses the word 'moves', she obviously evaluates this poem in terms of the energy in it. The term 'psychic' implies a conscious departure from the New Criticism poetics of objectivity and impersonality. In transcribing the bleak winter landscape, great care is taken to maintain the compositional balance of the color and volume of the images. The primary colors are black, white, and orange, referring respectively to the sinister pond, the single and incongruous swan, and the descending sun. Each of the three objects performs one particular function to maintain the balance between different tensions. The 'single swan' and its 'white reflection' construct a symmetrical image, balancing the 'hauling down' power of the black pond, while the 'cyclops-eye' sun 'descend[ing] above the fen' raises the focus of attention above and beyond the horizon:

> The austere sun descends above the fen,
> an orange cyclops-eye, scorning to look
> longer on this landscape of chagrin;

The color contrast between the orange sun and the black-and-white pond scene not only changes the compositional balance, but also sets the viewer further back and partly sets off the tension between the black pond and the white swan. The fen composes the major part of the 'landscape of chagrin', and it has become, with the collaboration of the 'clouded mind', the opposing power to the poetic subject 'I' who observes the scene from the perspective of the rook. As a result, the whole scene is inbuilt with three rings of a spectator–spectacle whirlpool. The innermost ring consists of the swan and the pond, the middle one of the sun and the fen–pond, and the outermost one of the rook and the fen–landscape with the sun.

The rook crows are deliberately not explicitly described until near the ending of the poem. There is an increasing push-away of the focus of the gaze, until the persona is identified with the 'brooding' rooks and shares the same perspective with them. The rooks are present in the perceived scene, and this indicates that the observing subject 'I' actually sees them. Therefore, the rooks become both a perceiving subject and a perceived object, holding the authorial power of the poet while functioning as an emblem for the persona's self-referentiality. In the final stanza the speaker states that 'Last summer's reeds' are now 'engraved in ice', the same state of 'your image in my eye', and wonders whether the 'heart's waste' may become green, positioned as a possible thwarting of the 'bleak place'. When Plath thus refers to the landscape in this poem as 'psychic', she obviously does not see herself as a detached objective spectator. In this poem, the emotional involvement with the scene as well as the 'you' becomes the defining factor in changing the represented landscape into a mindscape, while the relationship of color to mood becomes part of this transformation.

The technique of perspectival deepening finds variations to achieve different objectives in different poems. The 1959 'Watercolor of Grantchester Meadows', perhaps the only one being referred to as 'ekphrastic' in the current scholarly literature,[17] appears to be portrayed in a quite conventional way in terms of its spatial order of composition. The watercolor plane is cut, probably diagonally, by the Granta into two parts, and the reading of the poem implies a viewing-painting order. The first stanza describes the meadow to one side of the river, and the second stanza portrays the river scene; the third stanza appears to be a distant level view, while the last stanza shifts into a high angle view in order to focus on the owl that 'shall stoop from his turret' to prey on the rat. In this poem, the compositional order can be seen as a reversal of the perspectival deepening, so that the last image of the predatory owl is highlighted to shroud the 'benign | Arcadian' landscape with a menacing atmosphere. The final push-away seems to still the scene, at a right distance so that the perspective of the painter-poet is broadened just enough to see the owl and the rat.

The suddenness of the owl's attack in 'Watercolor of Grantchester Meadows' is changed into the quick flash of the 'panorama of smoke and slaughter' of Brughel's painting *The Triumph of Death* in the second part of 'Two Views of a Cadaver Room',[18] written in 1959. The poet chooses here to enlarge and elaborate on the two lovers who are 'blind to the carrion army'. In the final couplet, she moves the detail of the picture away from the viewer-reader, so that the whole picture is put into the perspective of 'the lower right hand corner', the final words of the poem. In the 1959 'Man in Black'[19] and 1961 'Blackberrying',[20] however, it is not the deepening of the perspective that changes the perceiver's visual field. Instead, the poet chooses to describe the scene in relation to the fixed vanishing point. By focusing on the vanishing point, the scene is charged with a coercive centripetal force. In the former, it is the man in black that 'rivet[s]' all the elements together, while in the latter, it is the 'thing to come' that functions as 'the last hook' for the speaker-persona to hold on to.

Although perspectival deepening appears to be a compositional technique, it subtly superimposes a personalized vision upon the otherwise objective representation of a scene. When an image is initially 'framed' and then positioned into a broader view, it is both re-contextualized and privileged, while the perceiver with a full view of the represented scene is provided with two or more perspectives, as in cubism. As a result, paradoxically, the broadened visual field both reinforces the authority of the perceiver in the aesthetic/critical viewing experience, and makes the reader-viewer identify with the poem's final twist of overtone that changes the landscape into a mindscape. In this sense, the ekphrastic technique is integrated into the content, and this is essentially the objective of both Plath's ekphrastic efforts and my analysis.

One of her first groups of mature poems is the art poems mainly written in 1958. These can be called ekphrastic poems to the truest and narrowest sense, as they speak directly to artworks and try to represent them both technically and thematically. To borrow Lessing's argument that poetry is essentially temporal while painting is spatial, an ekphrastic poem places the stringent demand on the poet to convert the spatiality in a visual artwork into the temporality in a poem. The challenge of this genre lies not merely in the thematic reproduction of what can be visually perceived in a pictorial plane, but also in the recreation of the illusion of a picture through linguistic features unique to poetry.

In March 1958, Plath composed eight art poems, two on de Chirico's paintings, two on Henri Rousseau's, and four on Paul Klee's etchings and paintings. As her journal entry of 29 March 1958 indicates,[21] the eight art poems obviously include, besides the five art poems placed in the 1958 section of *Collected Poems*, 'The Disquieting Muses', 'On the Decline of Oracles', and 'Snakecharmer', which are placed in the year 1957. These art poems may prove to be more significant than currently acknowledged in terms of both her writing career and her poetics. Plath made a claim that these poems would 'qualify [her] to be The Poetess of America',[22] a claim which has never been seriously investigated. Although sounding a little grandiose, these poems do 'open up new material and a new voice' as she had 'discovered [her] deepest source of inspiration',[23] and they were 'poems breaking open [her] real experience of life in the last five years'.[24] This experience had been 'untouchable' and it obviously refers especially to the years after her suicide attempt in 1953 and her subsequent treatment. It seems that writing poetry which appropriated the visions of the painters became a way of 'breaking open' her experience. Essentially, ekphrasis involves two different modes of representational signs, and obviously visual arts and verbal arts appeal to different aesthetic perceptions. To respond to artworks, for Plath, is not only to provoke her imagination and maximize the representational capacity of words, but also to induce her to look inward and provide a way to tackle her hitherto untouched experience.

Plath experiments with different ways to approach the modernist artworks that inspired these poems, but 'The Disquieting Muses'[25] is perhaps the most representative art poem in terms of both formal and thematic concerns. Many critics have elaborated on it and acknowledged its merits and importance in establishing her personal voice. In this poem, she incorporates her personal history in transcribing the de Chirico painting, but the most remarkable technique is her method of replacing the spatial dimension in the pictorial plane with the temporal dimension of her personal life history. She perspicaciously chooses to focus on the apparently static quality of 'disquietingness' to verbalize the atmosphere, which she perceives to be typical in the Chirico city, as illustrated by 'the statue, recumbent, of Ariadne, deserted, asleep, in the center of empty, mysteriously-shadowed squares'.[26] This quality of 'disquietingness' would find echoes in later poems, such as 1961 'Barren Woman', in which an empty museum becomes analogous to a barren woman that 'echo[es] to the least footfall'.[27] The physical space is given a psychological import, just as her psychic landscape may have implied.

'The Disquieting Muses' frames a period of time, during which the contention between the mother and the 'godmothers' forms the fundamental static movement. The protagonist's growth is chronologized into an implicit drama between the 'godmothers' and the mother, and the protagonist appears to be put behind a screen. This corresponds to the visual effect in the picture plane, with the dominant stagnant thickness of color and the hovering emptiness and silence over the space of the square. The shadow is shown to have 'stretched' and it stops 'stretching' at the end of the poem ('Their shadows long in the setting sun | That never brightens or goes down'). When the time shifts to the present at its end, this is equated with 'the day [she] was born', and it seems that the present is also stopped and stagnated. Thus, the dynamics of the drama is 'sealed' under the stillness of temporal flow.

The formal arrangement of the poem both functions as a kind of framing and recreates the stasis of the painting. The poem starts with the 'christening' of the persona and at the end it again evokes 'the day [she] was born'. The temporal span is stilled in the conclusion that 'This is the kingdom [the mother] bore [her] to', and the spatial implication of 'kingdom' points back to the painting of a 'mysteriously-shadowed square' and the power-filled space in contrast with the power-free fissure. The visual setting becomes not merely a stage ready for Plath but also the *mis en scène* that entices her to 'project' her concerns.

Two reasons may be attributed to the success Plath anticipated about the eight art poems. On the one hand, Plath is determined to be a 'word-artist', and in American modern poetry up to her days, there had been very few pictorial poems written by women poets. On the whole, these poems exhibit her mastery in the techniques of both visual arts and poetry. On the other hand, while the modernist masters such as W. H. Auden have produced poems based on visual arts, like Keats's, their poems are mostly 'objective' verbal artifacts. Plath's claim that the art poems would make her 'The Poetess of America' apparently rests on the fact that her poems integrate artistic excellence with her emotional engagement and personal voice. The art poems mark a new phrase in Plath's writing career. After the art poems, the personal voice, usually in the first person speaker, gets into her poetry, with successful early mature pieces like 'Full Fathom Five', 'Mussel Hunter at Rock Harbor', 'Lorelei', and, of course, the poem 'Colossus'.

Internalized Visual Thinking from the Ekphrastic to the Dynamic

The use of frame, compositional design with color scheme, and perspectival deepening are three primary visual art techniques Plath uses in her poems until her creation of the eight art poems. The incorporation of personal history into the ekphrastic pieces contributes to the success of these poems, like the technique of perspectival deepening which helps change a natural scene into a psychic one. These two techniques, however, are applicable mostly in poems about visual arts or highly visual scenes. The weakness found in most of the art poems may be attributed to the lack of 'lyrical' power and tension, despite Plath's assertion that they are 'lyrical . . . and thunderous poems'.[28] Nevertheless, through these poems,

Plath proves her ability to translate a static scene or an artwork into a dynamic poem.

After the art poems, Plath rarely writes poems speaking to specific artworks. Although no specific visual artworks can be identified from descriptive passages in her late works, her post-1958 poems may still provoke associations with visual artworks, in terms of image-formation, thematic borrowing, or compositional construction. In some sense, it is this unidentifiability that shows Plath's internalized way of visual thinking as a working principle behind her writing. The poem 'Heavy Women' may suffice to demonstrate how this works. The heavy women are initially equated with Venus 'pedestaled on a half-shell | Shawled in blond hair and the salt | Scrim of a sea breeze'. These lines immediately remind us of Botticelli's *The Birth of Venus*, while Venus's facial expression may be seen as a combination with that of Venus in another of his masterpieces, *Primavera*. It may also be argued that the infants attending Venus are derived from Zephyrus in *The Birth of Venus* or Eros in *Primavera*, although they can also be the 'pink-buttocked' holy infants in the arms of 'blue' Mary in Raphael's Madonna paintings. Yet the overall composition of this poem shows great similarity with that of *The Birth of Venus*, while the thorn trees may be, again, evolved from those in *Primavera*. This comparison, however, may appear to be far-fetched and based solely on her personal associations, but it is the provocation of association with visual artworks that may be argued to be the manifestation of the internalized visual thinking.

When the poet does not allude or refer to any specific visual artwork or motif, but still calls forth strong visuality, the principle of visual thinking is set to work. Both the image and the laconic lines in 'Edge', for example, may remind the reader of a Greek sculpture or sarcophagus: 'The illusion of a Greek necessity | Flows in the scrolls of her toga' may provoke both visual and thematic association with a sculpture. The illusion of the flow can be understood as a still motion, which is superimposed onto the image of the coiled child folded back into a body, itself a visual image of still motion compared with rose petals closing in the stiffened night garden. The superimpositions compositionally and thematically demonstrate the life-in-death and the resurrection cycle implied in the poem. The poet goes beyond the limitations of ekphrasis in these poems in terms of technique and themes, using multiple or shifting perspectives, and the freedom to incorporate visual art techniques and motifs greatly enriches them.

Freed from specific artworks, Plath implements different visual art techniques into her poems and creates a visuality of high tension through an accelerated motion of images. The compositional design is not rigidly observed, and high-lighted images are often presented in such a way that they appear to be dispropor-tionate with each other. For example, in the relation between the tulips, the sun, and the speaker in Plath's 1961 'Tulips', these flowers loom overpoweringly larger in representation and perception than in reality. They appear to be more subjectively represented, like the subjective shot in film. Indeed, cinematographic techniques gradually take on more bearing in Plath's later poems.

The enlarged image can be seen in poems written as early as 1959 such as 'The Beekeeper's Daughter',[29] which starts with a series of close-up images that appear to be smothering the speaker, just as in the tulips do:

> A garden of mouthings. Purple, scarlet-speckled, black
> The great corollas dilate, peeling back their silks.
> Their musk encroaches, circle after circle,
> A well of scents almost too dense to breathe in.

Perceptibly, the power of these lines lies in the immediate reciprocity and tension between personal engagement and objective verbalization. What differentiates the pictoriality in these lines from that in her earlier art poems is that the description here is subjectified and charged with a personal vision. In poems such as 1959 'Medallion' and 'Mushrooms', the speaker presents herself as a contemplative gazer instead of a distant observer. The perceiver is intimately identified with the perceived.

This identification appears to be a development of Plath's visual thinking, and in this process the isolated image in the earlier poems become self-contained verbal pictures. These pictures take on a greater weight; they not only hold a visual 'stopping power' as focal points, but also provide a starting point for the reflective musing in the poem. As she projects her vision upon these images and describes them in her own discursive language, these images become recognizably idiosyn-cratic and emblematic.

If there is a so-called myth-formation in Plath's poetry, it is these emblematic images that construct the mythical world. An emblem can be defined as 'a memorable combination of texts and images into a composite picture', but it may refer broadly to any verbal picture that can be isolated from a text or co-text to perform 'the dual functions of representation and interpretation'.[30] These composite pictures or emblematic verbal icons may immediately bring forth tangible visual images in the reader's mind. Emblematic icons, which are abundant in Plath's later poems, may include the references and allusions to recognizable visual artworks or visual art motifs. They can come as references to actual visual artworks or common emblems. For example, the Colossus ('The Colossus') and pietas ('Winter Trees') may immediately evoke visual associations with specific motifs, which imply generally agreed-on images and significance. Or they can come as icons with minimal description. For instance, 'a white Nike' and 'bald-eyed Apollos' ('Barren Woman') and 'White Nike' ('The Other'), 'Mary-blue' ('Heavy Women') and 'blue Mary' ('Widow'), and 'Blake's [etchings]' ('Death & Co.') may refer to particular visual art motifs, with subjectified or superimposed interpretations. These emblems not only contain meaning in themselves as minimized representations but also enrich the meaning of the poems through intertextuality. They can be viewed as semi-decontextualized vehicles or units of meaning, and may function as nodal links to recreate a new context for the represented images in the poems and put a third dimension into the thematic planarity of them.

In terms of visual art motifs, the emblematic pictures can also be veiled descriptions indicative of or inspired by visual artworks. Van Gogh's paintings, especially the paintings with stars and cypresses such as 'Starry Night', 'Starlight Sky over the Rhone', and 'Road with Cypresses and Star' apparently inspired several of Plath's poems, including 'Stars over the Dordogne' and 'The Moon and the Yew Tree'. One journal entry on 1956 New Year's Eve, when Plath was traveling with Sassoon in France, may be used to support the assertion. She described the evening sky outside the train window as follows:

> Stars now too against the sky, turning in spirals, growing to look like Van-Gogh stars, and the strange black trees, wind-blown, tortuous, twisted, idiosyncratic pen sketches against the sky: cypresses. And quarries, steep like a cubist painting in block and slanting roof-lines and rectangular whitish shacks, bleached in the light, with geometric shadows.[31]

This passage re-illustrates that Plath habitually refers to and compares with visual art techniques in her description to re-enforce the representational capacity, and also demonstrates that she consciously recycles and builds her own repertoire of images. The serenity in the description seems to find ways into 'Star over the Dordogne', and the turbulence revealed in the image of these cypresses is quite analogous to the disturbing 'Gothickry' of the yew in 'The Moon and the Yew Tree' and even 'Little Fugue'.

The use of frame in earlier poems may be still seen, but Plath also uses multiple frames in some poems, just as multiple frames in the form of segmentation of one picture plane are also seen in one of her paintings, 'Nine Female Figures'. In her later poems, the frames are used to enact a visual narrative. Every stanza in 'Elm' can be seen as a scene taken by a camera lens, while the scenes presented in 'Apprehensions' form a polyptych, with each of the four stanza representing one panel. The color schemes in each of the four panels in white, gray, red, and black contrast and complement each other. The technique of juxtaposition refers back to her early collage works and predicates her later poetics of juxtaposition of images. Some poem sequences such as 'Berck-Plage' may also be read as paintings in one series.

Perspectival deepening in her early poems is realized by pushing the frame of a scene away from the viewer, and the motion is transformed into a kind of temporality in some of the art poems. This technique is further developed into a section of cinematic narrative in the form of a sequence of continuous images. Typical examples may be 'Blackberrying' and 'Getting There'. The former poem can be seen as one long sequence shot taken by a panning camera moving toward the end of the lane, while the latter the long shot is montaged with inserted images by association.

I have tried to demonstrate the development of Plath's visual poetics from the early stasis to the later dynamics. Her art poems present features of a planar transcription of visual scene with a temporal dimension, while her landscape poems often adopt a perspectival deepening to bring out an illusion of physical movement on the reader's perception. When the static mode of representation is combined with techniques that eventually allow for both the perceiver's reflection on and identification with the perceived, as the one-frame representation changes to a dual-perspective representation, the physical distance between the perceiver and the perceived is increasingly shortened. Plath's later poems demonstrate an internalized principle of visual thinking, when she is freed from any dependence on specific visual art techniques or artworks. The ease to incorporate visual art motifs or allude to artworks greatly increases the power of her later work, as if the early poems are planar and closed while the later ones are multidimensional and open on every emblematic image. While Plath's subject matter and the image patterns she used may remain relatively consistent throughout the different phases, her methods of (re-)presenting the subject matter and arranging the images were being constantly revised.

Afterword
The Sister Arts of Sylvia Plath

SUSAN GUBAR

Published posthumously in *Ariel* (1963), the verse Plath composed during the last few years of her life has established her international reputation as a brilliant mythmaker of herself and of modern womanhood. Plath's frequently read, anthologized, and taught poems—'The Disquieting Muses', 'The Colossus', 'You're', 'Daddy', 'Nick and the Candlestick', and 'Lady Lazarus'—explore the pains and the pleasures of being a daughter, a wife, and a mother, as do the resonant sequence of poems that have come to be called the Bee sequence. At the age of thirty and in the wake of the breakup of her marriage with Ted Hughes, Plath knew she was producing her best work, which was created in and burned at a white heat. Passionate figures like 'Lady Lazarus' and the daughter of 'Daddy' soon consumed the contemporary imagination. In phrases ringing with fury, a revengeful 'Lady Lazarus' taunts, 'I rise with my red hair | And I eat men like air' and the murderous daughter of 'Daddy' warns, 'If I've killed one man, I've killed two . . . Daddy, daddy, you bastard. I'm through'.

But what laid the groundwork for this astonishing outpouring of innovative dramatic monologues, curiously repetitive rhymes, and stark, often shockingly macabre imagery? It is not often that one is given a window into the youthful creativity of a major author, but this volume offers admirers of Plath's brilliant verse access to the adolescent sources and subjects of her inspiration. Surprisingly, the sources and subjects of this most literary of writers revolve around visual matters. In particular they can be traced in the drawings and paintings she produced during her teenage years. In *Eye Rhymes*, then, Sylvia Plath joins the ranks of twentieth-century women artists who used visual and verbal forms to elaborate upon that curious web of intersecting injunctions we have come to call femininity, women artists who have inhabited every conceivable geo-political locale.

Primarily a painter, Frieda Kahlo presented herself on one canvas with shorn hair, wearing an oversized man's suit, under an ironic banner of words from a popular song: 'Mira que si te quise, fue pro el pelo, | Ahora que estás pelona, ya no te quiero' ('Look, if I loved you, it was your hair. Now that you are bald, I don't love you any more'). Primarily a writer, Margaret Atwood drew watercolors of bird-women, dead brides, and gowned insects related to the fairy tales and myths upon which her fiction and verse frequently elaborated. Plath's artistry also calls to mind the astonishing work of Charlotte Salomon, whose pictorial autobiography, *Charlotte: Life or Theater?*, consists of hundreds of brightly colored gouaches overlaid with transparencies on which she wrote her thoughts about a troublingly self-destructive family history and the impending societal catastrophe that would eventually land her in Auschwitz. More recently, Faith Ringgold has penned narratives about women's artistry in the Harlem Renaissance on a series of storytelling quilts. More like Atwood than Kahlo, Salomon, or Ringgold, Sylvia Plath eventually relinquished visual art to focus almost exclusively on securing her literary reputation.

Taken together, the scholars in *Eye Rhymes* consider the repercussions of a fact Kathleen Connors establishes biographically, that Sylvia Plath vacillated about whether to pursue visual arts or writing as an undergraduate major in college and as a profession. Clearly influenced by and indeed in some instances consciously modeling her visual as well as her literary productions upon the experimental canvases of de Chirico, Rousseau, Gauguin, Klee, Picasso, and Hopper, Plath won early honors for pictures that earned them exhibition. In various ways, the essays included in *Eye Rhymes* trace the continuity between Plath's early visual productions and her later literary compositions. As their authors note, the Horatian dictum— '*ut pictura poesis*' ('as is painting so is poetry')—can work in a complex number of ways to clarify how Plath's pictorial techniques and themes resurface similarly or differently in her verse.

Even before Plath's artworks were collected and published in this volume, they inspired many people to visit the archives in which they were housed. One such visitor, the poet Catherine Bowman, viewed Plath's personal effects, cut-outs, and drawings at the Lilly Library, and they inspired her to produce a remarkable series of poems entitled *The Plath Cabinet*. Bowman asks a question that animates the contributors in this book as well as its editors and readers: how did the mature Plath approach the sister arts of drawing and poetry, and in particular the artwork presented in print for the first time here? Creatively addressing Horace's maxim, Bowman intimates that Plath's poetry does not simply grow out of the visual work. The late verse, Bowman suggests, repeatedly struggles with and against the pictorial images Plath produced at an earlier stage in her development. By consulting *The Plath Cabinet*, we can perceive in the drawings, cut-outs, and portraits of Plath's juvenilia a sort of idolatry of the feminine that was later refigured into an iconoclastic attack in the greatest of Plath's poems. Because she attends to documents from Plath's childhood and adolescence, Bowman draws attention to the idolatry, moving us inside the divided mind that would turn against itself through a violent rejection of feminine ideals and then through self-violence. The early pictures, from this vantage, set up a series of attitudes and poses that provided the fuel for acts of demotion in the later poems.

Several poems in *The Plath Cabinet* signal their common form through a repeated title, modified by a singular date. For example, Bowman writes a number of poems entitled 'Things to Do'. Representative and here in its entirety is 'Things to Do, 1946':

> Learn about posture, see Great Lakes, get lowest
> marks ever (shh! don't tell anyone), work
> on World War II notebooks, go through torture
> of having hair washed, start a whistling group,
> paint an arched-back mermaid, proclaim desire
> to be God, make yellow-butter cake with two layers,
> learn how Nature protects her animals.

Putting aside for a moment the clear allusion to one illustration in this volume—the 1945 'Mermaid and Moon' (composed when Plath was 12)—what are we to make of the title of this poem? Bowman considers the rhetoric of perfectionism, of working hard every day to produce better posture, hair, layer cakes, as well as knowledge about nature (the Great Lakes) and culture (World War II). For a girl willing and able to discipline herself to the requirements of self-improvement and patiently tick off each item on her personal 'to-do' list, practice makes perfect. Should a girl want to become God—an ambition Plath did 'proclaim' privately when seventeen years of age—stringent measures are necessary, requiring culinary and cosmetological as well as pedagogic routines.

Pointedly about the rhetoric of betterment in the diaries and letters, Bowman's poem can also be read as ekphrasis (the verbal description of a visual work of art). From this perspective, how does Bowman's 'Things to Do, 1946' illuminate 'Mermaid and Moon'? The Lorelei with her back arched, half-human and half-fish, does not seem to accord with the neat lesson that 'Nature protects her animals'. On the contrary, immobilized on her ice floe, a patently unnatural aberration can only gaze at an unapproachable castle, star, or moon, or reach for the mirror by her left arm to stare at her own face. Like the Little Mermaid, the Siren, or the Lamia, but also like the lost woman in Mathew Arnold's 'The Forsaken Merman' (a poem read to the young Plath by her mother), 'she will not come though you call all day'; instead she will remain an outsider: most obviously because she has no legs or feet to stand on, but also because she is a transgenic organism, a stranded and singular anomaly divorced from both nature (the sea, the moon, the star) and culture (the walled-about castle).

With the ice patch floating less on a moat, more on an open channel, the mermaid seems adrift in currents that could easily sweep her out to destruction. Plath's Lorelei recalls Heine's famous lyric, especially its opening line: '*Ich weiss nicht was soll es bedeuten*' ('I don't know what to make of it'). The tragic state of being in which the perplexed Lorelei finds herself occurred after she threw herself into the sea because of despair at a faithless lover; often her singing destroys men. Seduced and abandoned, she inhabits a ghostly life-after-death, and her art retaliates against beloveds who reject her, as does that of 'Lady Lazarus' and the daughter of 'Daddy'.

Unlike the famous threats and curses of those personae, though, what remains unnerving about the atmosphere of Plath's early 'Mermaid and Moon' is precisely the tone or attitude Bowman captures in her short poem, namely its speaker's naïve and disturbing affection for and investment in an image so damaging to the psyche of a would-be artist. Here is a trope that could be said to diagnose the sickening situation of creative women—told they are closer to nature than culture, thought to be freaks, warned that female aesthetic ambition destroys the male of the species, earning women only narcissistic isolation. Yet the 'femme fatale' is tenderly recycled by a youthful Plath who seems enamored with the role. The mermaid's hair is voluminously thick and nicely coiffed (indeed, curiously unspoiled by moisture!), the torso modestly serpentine, the face in profile picture-perfect, the hands delicate. Being in love with the role means being enthralled by death, or so Plath's 1958 poem 'Lorelei' suggests: the 'ice-hearted calling' and silence of the sister-singers lodged on 'pitched reefs of nightmare' cause the speaker's thoughts to drift toward annihilation: 'Stone, stone, ferry me down there'.

In terms of 'Things to Do', if producing 'an arched-back mermaid' is what is required, a steely Plath will undertake it, no matter how detrimental such a task might be to her own health and welfare. Interpreting the picture from the perspective of Bowman's poem, it seems to say, as Plath does in 'Lesbos', 'I should sit on a rock off Cornwall and comb my hair'. According to Bowman, the subjugated young Plath believed that one must learn the requisite postures and positions, get the lowest marks, go through tortuous hair treatments as a payment for—or as part of the process of—becoming God, a presumptuous female creator. Of course such an attitude of voluntary, even voluptuous compliance with a stock and perniciously gendered template might be expected of any 12-year-old girl on the brink of puberty, especially one inducted into what now seem the retrograde sexual ideologies of the Cold War.

But how much of Plath's subsequent poetry rages against or flaunts precisely this infatuation? Put otherwise, Bowman's 'Things to Do, 1946' lets us interpret Plath's 'Mermaid and Moon' as part of a girlhood collusion with feminine submission against which Plath scandalously fought later in her life with words she likened to 'Axes | After whose stroke the wood rings' ('Words'). Sparked by Ted Hughes' abandonment, the incendiary and now canonical lines of 'Lady Lazarus' ('I rise with my red hair | And I eat men like air') or the daughter of 'Daddy' ('If I've killed one man, I've killed two— . . . Daddy, daddy, you bastard, I'm through') elaborate upon the mature realization that practice may make perfect, but 'perfection is terrible' ('The Munich Mannequins'). Indeed, when 'The woman is perfected', in the poem 'Edge', 'Her dead | Body wears the smile of accomplishment'.

To deal with Plath's youthful ambivalence about the acquiescence feminization requires, Bowman devotes a number of poems in *The Plath Cabinet* to Plath's 'Paper Dolls'. One prose poem subtitled 'Yellow Lightbulb Party Dress' moves from an amorous nocturnal scene to a figure 'encased in shellac':

> A cage of secrets. At the neck, a black thread to be plugged in. Let's tap-dance in time to the on-off switch. Her legs together, one knee slightly bent. Transparent yolk and transparent trim. Four buttons. Pushed-up breasts. A circuitry of liquid—gauzy cords of six imaginary ingredients. World host to many worlds. This madness called love.

Again by positing Plath's girlhood complicity with a debilitating engendering against which she would later contend, Bowman helps us interpret a plate reproduced in *Eye Rhymes*, in this case the fashion plates featured in 'Stella and Blonde Cut-out Dolls and Outfits'—nicely named since cut-out clothes will allow a cut-out 'Stella' to 'cut out'—go out, and have some fun.

At the opening of Bowman's poem, romance radiates from the glamour of the fashionable outfits Plath designed in 1945, when she was 12: transparent fabrics evoke firefly light and champagne, free-flowing skirts shadowy dancing, pushed-up breasts stars over an Adirondack lake, ornate trim musical notes. But Bowman's euphoria over 'This madness called love' clinches or buckles with an 'except': 'except for the tight belt at the waist'. At this point, the poet directs us to look at the imprisonment of the female form 'encased in shellac', buttoned and yoked in a 'cage of secrets' that recalls the scales on the torso and fins, hermetically sealing the recumbent mermaid. The bodiless and headless cut-out clothes bespeak anxieties about female embodiment, as does the mermaid. But in this verse about the living doll, Bowman emphasizes the imprisoning armature of culture's clothing, rather than an unnatural nature. In the brittle carapace of costume, Bowman goes on to suggest surrealistically, Plath modeled herself—'legs together, one knee slightly bent'—on a light bulb. Turned on or off, she plugged herself into a circuitry of desire that would burn her up, as it does in 'Elm' when, 'Scorched to the root', her 'red filaments burn and stand, a hand of wire'; and as it does, too, in 'Fever 103', when she has 'been flickering, off, on, off, on. | The sheets grow heavy as a lecher's kiss'; and again in 'The Hanging Man', where she sizzles within 'A world of bald white days in a shadeless socket'.

Headless and sometimes armless, the two-dimensional cut-out costumes readily made for 'Stella' turn her into the mannequin or applicant or opus that Plath conjured in so many poems about plastered women or about herself as 'flat, ridiculous, a cut-paper shadow' ('Tulips'). In the 1959 'Poem for a Birthday', for instance, Plath exclaims, 'I inhabit | The wax image of myself, a doll's body. | Sickness begins here'. If one juxtaposes the elegant cut-outs—with their fur flounces, slinky fabrics, décolletage, sumptuous and colorful designs—with 'Are You Always Working?' (another illustration in this book and from the same period), Plath's early awareness of the disparity between the romance of courtship and the reality of domestic drudgery surfaces. For the cartoon-like drawing, with its remarkable sense of perspective, reads like the 'After' image of the 'Before' Stella, now at the foot of the stairs, smudged and exhausted by her incessant housework, while a cat with nine lives trails further dirt through the house. With her hair caught up in a bandana headscarf, a scrub brush clenched in her left hand, pail and mop at the ready, this domestic drudge reaches up her right hand, perhaps to wipe away the tears on her face. Before or after, a woman's work is never done, the items on her personal to-do list never ticked off.

The two self-portraits reproduced in this volume—the first produced by Plath at 17 years of age, the second at 19 years of age—remarkably extend the youthful artist's engagement with the issues of femininity and embodiment. Because in both Plath presents herself tight-lipped, I will use the first poem in Catherine Bowman's collection, 'Sylvia's Mouths', to approach them:

> That mouth made to do violence on,
> the straight mouth, mouth's instant flare,
> cave-mouth, mouth skewered on a groan,
> Mother, you are the one mouth,
> all-mouth licks, frog-mouth, fish-mouth.
> I fly through the candle's mouth, the straight mouth,
> mouth opens clean as a cat's. Mouth-hole or eye-hole,
> I draw on the old mouth, mouth full of pearls,
> his mouth's raw wounds, cupped quick to mouth,
> mouth-plugs, mouth hole crying their location,
> gold mouths cry, gleaming with mouths of the corpses.
> A garden of mouthings, I am all mouth.

Less an organ signifying speech and agency, the mouth emanates vulnerability and suffering here, while the repetition of the word 'mouth' itself functions as a kind of unanswered cry.

A swarm of allusions to Plath's poems controls this verse. One thinks of Plath's mouth, infamously kissing and then biting Hughes, of course. But also 'a garden of mouthings' in 'The Beekeeper's Daughter'; the dead wife with her 'Mouth full of pearls' in 'Paralytic'; the 'mouth-plugs' of 'Medusa'; the 'late mouths' of 'Poppies in October'; the 'naked mouth, red and awkward' of the grave in 'Berck-Plage'; the 'O-mouth' of the moon in 'The Rival'; the 'mouth just bloodied' in 'Poppies in July', as well as the baby's mouth opening 'clean as a cat's' in 'Morning Song'. What to make of this mouthing off—this 'I am all mouth', a line from Plath's 'Poem for a Birthday'—in terms of the two self-portraits with their determinedly closed mouths?

In both the self-portraits, Plath presents an attractive but wary picture of herself with her lips clamped shut, as if illustrating a much later line from 'Berck-Plage': 'I am not a smile'. In neither of these self-portraits does she resemble 'Dame Kindness', complacently asking nothing of life ('Kindness'), or the perfected and dead woman of 'Edge', who 'wears the smile of accomplishment'. Yet the shift from pencil to colorful pastel testifies to her growing sense of irony as well as bafflement and mounting resentment. In the pencil version, the long flowing hair and the thickly brushed eyebrows soften the intense gaze of an alluring face that seeks to cast its spell on the viewer. She calls to mind seductive and glamorous movie celebrities like Lana Turner or Veronica Lake, or the 'Betty Grable' signature Plath affixed to a *Varsity* clipping of herself in a halter-top swimsuit. With her sidelong glance, she seems as unreal as any adolescent girl's silly self-idealization.

How much more doubtful is the pastel version with its down-tilted head illuminated, as if by a candle whose 'yellows hearten' ('Nick and the Candlestick'). Here the thicker upper lip closes down on the lower lip with a sullen refusal to lick, open, speak, or sigh. Plath has drawn a mantle V on her chest, just blue and pink stripes that hint at an academic hood or a superwoman's victory logo. To scholars of her later work, it might recall 'the new virgins' dreaming 'of a duel they will win inevitably' or the white hive as 'snug as a virgin' in the opening of the Bee poems, or her major female precursor, Virginia Woolf, or less obliquely Plath's subsequent determination to flaunt the weirdly conventional colors of gender, to replace pastel pinks and blues with the sinister reds and blacks of her poetic palette. It is, of course, simply a T-shirt or a sweater: she's no fashion plate, no 'Stella' here. Nor can one imagine some Stanley Kowalski manhandling her.

That her upper body shows and that it looks ready for action distinguishes the pastel from the penciled version. Sporting not flowing actress tresses but a short bob, in the pastel she gazes distrustfully out at the viewer, like a circumspect pugilist sizing up her viewer-antagonist. Somewhat like a boxer's, her nose looks battered or bruised. One might just chalk this up to amateur technique. But together with the cross-hatching brush strokes behind her, the second self-portrait—with the T-shirt's cuffs rolled up—evokes a person readying herself for the struggle it will take to present herself as she feels herself to be. 'I draw on the old mouth', Bowman writes, explaining how Plath in many of her poems put on a face to meet the faces of the peanut-crunching crowd that would become her audience. In both self-portraits, the drawn 'mouth's instant flare' seems to say to the viewer, 'I am in control' ('Stings') or 'I didn't call you. | I didn't call you at all' ('Medusa') or 'I do not speak' ('Lesbos'). Both forecast and brood over 'The courage of the shut mouth' in the poem 'The Courage of Shutting-Up'. The self-portraits warn us, then, that no matter how autobiographical the work, Plath remains unknown and unknowable.

Yet eventually, even when she spoke about not speaking, Plath chose the courage of composing and reciting poems 'written out loud' and 'written for the ear, not the eye', as she explained to Douglas Cleverdon in a BBC program. She elected to voice the stuttering 'I', 'I', 'I' on the tongue, decided not to pursue the silent figures of pencil, charcoal, watercolor, pastel, or oil. Unlike the separately enclosed women, many without mouths, in her brightly painted 'Nine Female Figures' or the harlequin-lipped woman in 'Triple-Face Portrait', she was to be preeminently a poet, a speaker whose lips opened to hiss and croon, cry and decry the 'garden of mouthings' that made and unmade her. The curvilinear forms of 'Nine Female Figures' box up individual faces and body parts or plaster them on billboards in an urban setting, while the often triangular shapes of 'Triple-Face Portrait' carve the woman's head into a sutured assemblage of a mask with sightless eyes, a decoratively lipsticked and fastened mouth. Commanded by being so constituted, the picture-perfect female figures of the mute juvenilia contrast with but illuminate the designing women plying their graphic calls and callings in the verse.

Approached by way of W. J. T. Mitchell's speculations, in his provocatively titled book *What Do Pictures Want?*, Plath's poetic *oeuvre* can be understand as a repudiation of her early visual images, but a repudiation fully cognizant of their stubborn staying power. These pictures wanted too much. While Mitchell believes that visual images make demands on the viewer, the pictures produced by a youthful Plath wanted too much from their creator: her pictures put young women in forms and conventions that demand a human sacrifice and therefore of course her own silencing. The greatness of the late poems pivots on a demand to be heard about a recognition pertaining to her youthful images; namely that, in W. J. T. Mitchell's phrasing, the power of pictorial idols 'resides in their obdurate indestructibility, which only gains strength from the sense of futility that accompanies the vain attempt to destroy them' (27). That those idols are feminine accords with the insights of theorists from Joan Rivière and John Berger to Laura Mulvey, all of whom (albeit in various ways) document the historic connection between women surveyed *as* images, men as surveyors *of* images. Whereas Plath's visual images reinforce a femininity constructed to be looked at, the poems are spoken by a looker, a searing and sneering seer, who rails against the abjection of reification. Even when Plath's speakers must feel their way in the dark—'I simply cannot see where there is to get to'—they testify to the cold 'light of the mind' ('The Moon and the Yew Tree').

Unquestionably Plath made the right decision when she relinquished her ambition in the sister art of painting so as to dedicate herself to her poetic gift. But the verse cannot be fully appreciated without some knowledge of the drawings, cutouts, and portraits. In a 2004 introduction to *Ariel*, with the poems now ordered as Plath had intended them to be, Frieda Hughes protested against critics who 'dissected, analysed, reinterpreted, reinvented, fictionalized, and in some cases completely fabricated' her mother. *Eye Rhymes* serves as a corrective to such distortions by providing evidence of Plath's early aesthetic evolution. Frieda Hughes wanted her mother's life, not her death, to be celebrated, and the previously unacknowledged talents of her early life are commemorated in *Eye Rhymes*, which will afford material for any number of insights into the poet, including those I have attributed to Catherine Bowman.

The sinister and yet seductive sisterhood of women that first surfaced in Plath's drawings, cut-outs, and portraits imbued her later verse with a ferocity about the condition Helena Michie has called 'sororophobia'. She was indeed 'all mouth' for women in her generation and also in subsequent generations, readers struggling not only with our fatal erotic attractions but also our jealousy of and competition with each other. Mouthy, she spoke about our intense admiration and detestation of ourselves, and thus for us. Until her untimely death, she had her eyes wide open, as she does in both these self-portraits, and we are indebted to this volume for letting us see how she first saw herself with her lips tightly shut.

While I was approaching Plath's verse in relation to Catherine Bowman's forthcoming work, it struck me how unnervingly Plath's poems reverberate during a time that might seem to have hurtled women forward, and therefore at a great remove from and beyond the circumstances that confined her. Bowman's texts show again that the brilliance of Sylvia Plath's verse sent her echoing phrases traveling off from the center, as she determined they would. Plath assiduously studied what she had been handed and she dealt her pretty blades of words to revile the pack she had been dealt. Her early adoration of and later revulsion against the feminine explain the ambivalence with which Bowman approaches a predecessor as obsessed with the desire to speak as with the desire to shut up or be shut up. About Plath's role as a formidable muse for later women poets, one can do no better than to supplement one of Bowman's fragmented quotes with Plath's completed sentence, maybe inflecting it with the sort of awe and anger one hears in rap lyrics or hip hop or in the unapologetically feisty 'spoken word' poetry that derives from the third-wave of feminism: 'Mother, you are the one mouth | I would be tongue to'.

ENDNOTES

Chapter 1: Living Color: The Interactive Arts of Sylvia Plath

1. UJ, p. 211.
2. Ibid., p. 359.
3. Ibid., p. 520.
4. Sylvia Plath Collection (Correspondence), Mortimer Rare Book Room, Smith College
5. *sic*: 'dlightful', 'wright', 'of', 'to'.
6. *Poets of New England*, ii. no. 108, 'Electra-fying: Sylvia Plath and the Myth of the Omnipresent/Absent Father', part 2, 1986.
7. JP, p. 25.
8. LH preface, PMII, Box 9, fol. 3.
9. Letter from Aurelia Plath, 8 and 9 April 1939, PMII Box 1, Correspondence, fol. ?.
10. PMII, Box 14, Miscellaneous, Artwork, fol. 2.
11. 2 June 1945, PMII, Box 7, Diaries and calendars, fol. 1.
12. JP, p. 26.
13. 17 July 1945, PMII, Box 7, Diaries and calendars, fol. 1; PMIII, Small format works, Drawings, fol. 1.
14. PMIII, Medium format works, Drawings, fol. 2. I am indebted to 'Smithie' Katie Peebles, Iu scholar of Folklore and English literature, for pointing out some of the special qualities of this bird.
15. 'Hear the crickets chirping | In the dewy grass. | Bright little fireflies | Twinkle as they pass' ('Poem', *Boston Herald*, 10 Aug 1941). 1962 BBC interview with Peter Orr from *The Poet Speaks: Interviews with Contemporary Poets Conducted by Hilary Morrish, Peter Orr, John Press, and Ian Scott-Kilvery*, (London: Routledge, 1966).

16. UJ, p. 58.

17. Ibid., p. 35.

18. Letter to Cohen age 17 about *Alice in Wonderland*, 11 August 1950, PMII, Box 1, Correspondence.

19. PMII, Memorabilia, High school scrapbook, Oversize no. 3, fol. 3.

20. Daily camp journal back cover, PMII, Box 7, Diaries and Calendars, fol. 2.

21. JP, p. 52.

22. 21 June 1947, PMII, Diaries and calendars, Box 7, fol. 3.

23. 10 Jan 1947, ibid.

24. 17 Jan 1947, ibid.

25. 7 May 1947, ibid.

26. 28 Jan 1947, ibid.

27. PMIII, Small format works, Drawings, fol. 7.

28. *The Wellesleyan* high school yearbook, p. 78, PMII, Box 10, High school memorabilia, fol. 4.

29. Ibid., p. 19.

30. 3 June 1945, PMII, Box 7, Diaries and calendars, fol. 1.

31. 7 July 1946, ibid., fol. 2.

32. PMII, Box 14, Miscellaneous, Artwork, fol. 2.

33. High school scrapbook, PMII, Memorobilia, Oversize no. 3, fol. 6.

34. Ibid.

35. PMIII, Medium format works, Tempera paintings and prints, fol. 9.

36. PMIII, Small format works, Watercolors, fol. 3.

37. PMIII, Medium format works, Temperas, fol. 3.

38. PMIII, Large format works, Pastels and charcoals, fol. 5.

39. Sylvia Plath Collection (Artwork—Oversize), Mortimer Rare Book Room, Smith College.

40. PMIII, Medium format works, Temperas, fol. 3.

41. Sylvia Plath Collection (Artwork—Oversize), Mortimer Rare Book Room, Smith College.

42. PMIII, Medium format works, Temperas, fol. 3.

43. Ibid.

44. Letter to Ann Davidow, ALS, 5 March 1951, Sylvia Plath Collection (Correspondence), Mortimer Rare Book Room, Smith College.

45. UJ, pp. 34–5

46. PMII, Box 8, Writings—Prose—Fiction, verso 'Den of Lions' last page, fol. 11.

47. PMIII, Large format works, Temperas, fol. 6.

48. PMII, Box 1, Correspondence.

49. Ibid.

50. Ibid.

51. Ibid.

52. Ibid.

53. LH, pp. 67–8.

54. Letter to Ann Davidow, ALS, 5 March 1951, Sylvia Plath Collection (Correspondence), Mortimer Rare Book Room, Smith College.

55. PMIII Small format works, Temperas, fol. 9.

56. PMII, Box 8, Writings—Prose—Fiction, fol. 10.
57. Edward Butscher, *Sylvia Plath: Method and Madness* (New York: Seabury Press, 1976), 87.
58. PMIII Large format works, Temperas, fol. 4.
59. Ibid., fol. 6.
60. Ibid.
61. UJ, pp. 54–6.
62. 15 Nov. 1951, PMII, Box 8, Writings—Prose—Fiction, fol. 17.
63. UJ, pp. 59–60.
64. Sylvia Plath Collection (Artwork), Mortimer Rare Book Room, Smith College. For more on this collage, see Robin Peel, *Writing Back: Sylvia Plath and Cold War Politics* (Madison, NJ: Fairleigh Dickinson University Press; London: Associated University Presses, 2002), pp. 57–61, and Jacqueline Rose, *The Haunting of Sylvia Plath* (London: Virago Press, 1991), 9–10.
65. 7 Dec 1961, LH, p. 438.
66. PMIII, Large format works, Temperas, fol. 6.
67. Ibid., fol. 4.
68. Dana Sperry and Dan Reidy gave me helpful insights on the methodology of this painting.
69. I am indebted to Liese Hilgeman for pointing out the split movement between upper and lower body of the woman with a halo.
70. Smith College Archives.
71. PMIII, Large format works, Pastels and charcoals, fol. 5.
72. Plath's nickname was 'Sivvy'.
73. I am grateful for Liese Hilgeman's comments on the two moods exhibited in Plath's face in this portrait.
74. PMIII, Large format works, Temperas, fol. 6.
75. *sic*: 'wile'.
76. The scrapbook is not in the Lilly or Mortimer archives.
77. 9 Jan 1945, PMII, Box 7, Diaries and calendars, fol. 1.
78. 23 April 1945, ibid.
79. 'Childhood Fears', PMII, Box 10, High school memorabilia, fol. 1.
80. Wanda Hazel Gág, *Growing Pains* (New York: Coward-McCann, 1940).
81. 17 May 1947, PMII, Diaries and calendars, Box 7, fol. 3.
82. No date.
83. 17 Sept 1946.
84. PMII, Box 8, Writings—Prose—Fiction, fol. 17.
85. 9 Sept 1947, PMII, Correspondence, Box 1.
86. PMII, Box 10, Writings—Prose—Nonfiction, fol. 1.
87. Ibid., fol. 8.
88. PMII, Box 8, Writings—Poetry, fol. 1.
89. 'Photo of Plath in Wellesley Garden': Helle Collection of Plath Family Photographs (item 38), Mortimer Rare Book Room, Smith College.
90. 18 June 1945, Box 7, PMII, Diaries and calendars, Box 7, fol. 1.
91. Fall 1946, ibid., fol. 2.
92. 18 July 1946, ibid.

93. 13 Nov 1949, ibid., fol. 4.

94. PMII, Box 10, High School memorbilia, fol. 1.

95. 10 Feb 1947, PMII, Box 7, Diaries and calendars, fol. 3.

96. PMII, Box 8, Writings—Prose—Fiction, fol. 12. For more on this story see Linda Wagner-Martin, *Sylvia Plath: A Literary Life* (New York: Palgrave Macmillan, 1999), p. 52.

97. 17 June 1947, PMII, Box 7, Diaries and calendars, fol. 3.

98. PMIII, Medium format works, Pastels, fol. 2.

99. 'I thot I could not be hurt', quote from LH, p. 34.

100. LH, p. 36, 'darker recesses of the self', says Aurelia.

101. For more on this poem, see the third chapter of Diane Middlebrook's *Her Husband: Hughes and Plath—A Marriage* (New York: Viking Press, 2003), p. 31.

102. PMII, Box 10, High school memorabilia, fol. 6.

103. 11 Sept 1947, PMII, Box 7, Diaries and calendars, fol. 3.

104. 20–1 Oct 1947, ibid.

105. 23 Oct 1947, ibid.

106. 11 Aug 1950, PMII, Box 1, Correspondence.

107. PMII, High school scrapbook, Oversize no. 3, fol. 7.

108. Sylvia Plath Collection (Prose—'Initiation'), Mortimer Rare Book Room, Smith College.

109. PMII, High school scrapbook, Oversize no. 3, fol. 1.

110. *Wild Steelhead & Salmon*, 5(2) (winter 1999), p. 55, http://www.earth-moon.org/th_intv_steelhead.html.

111. 'The Christmas Heart' and 'I Lied for Love', PMII, Box 8, Writings—Prose—Fiction, fol. 3.

112. Ibid.: 'Sarah', fol. 16; 'Allison', fol. 10; 'Grammercy Park', fol. 12; 'Dialogue', fol. 11, 'The Attic View', fol. 10.

113. Ibid., fol. 10.

114. Ibid., fol. 11.

115. Ibid., Box 7a, Writings—Poetry, fol. 10.

116. Ibid.

117. 10 Feb 1947, PMII, Box 7, Diaries and calendars, fol. 3.

118. PMII, Box 7a, Writings—Poetry, fol. 9.

119. PMII, Box 14, Miscellaneous, Artwork, fol. 13.

120. 27 Aug 1945, PMII, Box 7, Diaries and calendars, fol 2.

121. PMII, Box 9, Writings—Prose—Nonfiction, fol. 2.

122. 'Sylvia Plath Tours the Stores and Forecasts May Week Fashions', *Varsity*, 26 May 1956.

123. PMII, Box 12, Smith College memorabilia, fol. 8.

124. PMII, Box 10, Writings—Prose, fol. 8.

125. Dated 25 March 1953, ibid., Box 10, fol. 7.

126. PMII, Smith College memorabilia, Box 12, fol. 7.

127. UJ, p. 97.

128. Sandra M. Gibert and Susan Gubar, *The Madwoman in the Attic: The Woman Writer and the Nineteenth-Century Literary Imagination* (New Haven, CT: Yale University Press, 1980).

129. PMII, Box 8, Writings—Prose—Fiction, fol. 17.

130. UJ, p. 72; 'Nancy', 'Big Sid', PMIII, Small format works, Drawings, fol. 7; Johnny S, PMIII, Large format works, Pastels and charcoals, fol.5; 'Mother', PMII, Box 14, Mixed medium drawings, fol. 2.

131. 'As a Baby-Sitter Sees It', *Christian Science Monitor*, 6-7 November 1951.

132. CP, pp. 174–5.

133. *The New Yorker*, 27 (6 March 1971).

134. LH, p. 83.

135. Letter to Davidow, ALS, 5 March 1951, Sylvia Plath Collection (Correspondence), Mortimer Rare Book Room, Smith College.

136. PMII, Box 7a, Writings—Poetry, fol. 9.

137. 26 Jan 1953, UJ, p. 168.

138. 21 Feb 1953, PMII, Box 3, Correspondence.

139. PMII, Box 3, Correspondence.

140. January 1953, PMIV, Correspondence.

141. 5 May 1953, UJ, p. 181.

142. 25 Dec 1953, Lameyer MS.

143. Plath made a reference to Dickinson's influence on her poetry in 30 April 1953 letter to her mother, where she included the poems 'Admonition', 'Parallax', and 'Verbal Calisthenics'. While *Letters Home* (110) includes an edited quote from this letter—'Tell me what you think of the poems . . . any resemblance to Emily Dickinson is purely intentional'—this entire reference to Dickinson was cut from the top of the archived letter—a rare form of editing, even for Aurelia, who regularly corrected spelling and grammar, and standardized punctuation of Plath's letters. To remove text, she usually blacked out lines.

144. PMII, Box 8, Writings—Poetry, fol. 5.

145. 13 June 1953, PMIV, Correspondence.

146. PMII, Smith College Scrapbook, Oversize no. 8, fol. 23.

147. *Falcon Yard* covered her early years of marriage, and *Double Take/Double Exposure* her final year of marriage.

148. PMII, Box 8, Writings—Prose—Nonfiction, fol. 7.

149. PMII, Box 8, Writings—Prose—Fiction, fol. 19.

150. 19 Feb 1956, UJ, p. 199.

151. 20 April 1954, PMII, Box 4, Correspondence.

152. 13 March and 14 April 1954, Lameyer MS.

153. January 1955, LH, p. 151.

154. PMII, Box 19, High school memorabilia, fol. 3.

155. 27 Sept 1953, Lameyer MS.

156. 12 Jan 1956, Lameyer MS.

157. 20 Jan 1956, UJ, p. 209.

158. 21 Jan 1956, Lameyer MS.

159. UJ, p. 297.

160. 25 March 1956, PMII, Box 6, Correspondence.

161. 25 Aug 1956, ibid.

162. 18 Oct 1955, Lameyer MS.

163. Sylvia Plath Collection (Artwork), Mortimer Rare Book Room, Smith College.

164. 5 Nov 1957, Box 6, Correspondence.

165. 4 Feb 1958, UJ, p. 324.

166. 18 April 1958 interview; Side A of 'The Voice of the Poet', Random House Audio recordings (1999).

167. LH, p. 346.

168. 29 July 1957, UJ, p. 293.

169. Ibid.

170. 3 July 1957, UJ, p. 401.

171. 29 July 1957, ibid., p. 287.

172. Basil Ivan Rokoczi, *The Painted Caravan: A Penetration into the Secrets of the Tarot Cards* (The Hague, Holland: L. J. C. Boucher, 1954).

173. 2 Oct 1956, PMII, Correspondence, Box 6.

174. UJ, p. 335. For more on Plath's colors, and their relation to Grave's 'Triple Moon-goddess', see Judith Kroll, *Chapters in a Mythology: The Poetry of Sylvia Plath* (HarperCollins, New York, 1978), pp. 41, 292

175. Ibid., p. 325.

176. Ibid., p. 379.

177. Ibid., p. 327.

178. Ibid.

179. 19 Feb. 1958, UJ, p. 469.

180. CP, pp. 158–60.

181. UJ, p. 582.

182. Ibid., p. 583.

183. Ibid., p. 233.

184. Sandra M. Gilbert, 'In Yeats's House. The Death and Resurrection of Sylvia Plath', in Linda Wagner-Martin (ed.), *Critical Essays of Sylvia Plath* (Boston: G. K. Hall, 1984).

185. Tracy Brain, *The Other Sylvia Plath* (New York: Longman, 2001), 141–3, 169n.

186. Steven Axelrod, *Sylvia Plath: The Wound and the Cure of Words* (Baltimore: Johns Hopkins University Press, 1990), p. 110.

187. UJ, p. 269.

188. LH, p. 305.

189. UJ, p. 315.

190. 4 Sept 1958; 11 March 1959, 'Nine Letters to Lynne Lawner', *Antaeus* 28 (winter 1978), 31–51.

191. UJ, p. 485.

192. Ibid., p. 494.

193. Ibid., pp. 337–8.

194. Ibid., p. 287.

195. Virginia Woolf, *A Room of One's Own* (Richmond: Hogarth Press, 1929), p. 49.

196. 11 March 1956, UJ, p. 234.

197. Ibid., p. 275.

198. Sylvia Plath Collection (Books), Mortimer Rare Book Room, Smith College.

199. Virginia Woolf, *The Waves* (London: Hogarth Press, 1931), pp. 82–3.

200. Ibid., p. 297.

201. UJ, p. 286.

202. Rose, *The Haunting of Sylvia Plath* p. 5.

203. Gilbert, 'In Yeats's House', p. 266.

204. H.D., *Tribute to the Angels* (London/New York: Oxford University Press, 1945), p. 105.

205. See 'Mrs. Bennett and Mrs. Brown' (Richmond: Hogarth Press, 1924); *New York Herald Tribune*, 23 and 30 August 1925.

206. Lynn Gordon Hughes, 'Olive Higgins Prouty', available at http://www.uua.org/uuhs/duub/articles/olivehigginsprouty.html

207. Ibid.

208. LH, p. 354.

209. UJ, p. 510.

210. 13 October 1959.

211. 21 October 1959.

212. 'Explorations', 19 Oct 1959; 'Mosaics' 12 Oct 1959, PMII, Clippings—Writings, Oversize no. 10.

213. 5 May 1959, PMII, Clippings—Writings, Oversize no. 10.

214. UJ, p. 307.

215. Ibid., p. 508.

216. 4 March 1957, ibid., p. 276.

217. 'Poppies in October' first draft. Sylvia Plath Collection (Poetry), Mortimer Rare Book Room, Smith College.

218. 'Edge', 'Kindness', 'Child', and 'Balloons' were not chosen by Plath for *Ariel*.

219. CP, p. 285.

220. Ibid., pp. 74–6.

221. Ibid., p. 271.

Chapter 2: Plath at War

1. The picture is part of Plath's report on World War I, entitled 'A War to End Wars', which she prepared for Social Studies 1 in her eighth-grade year. This and other reports are held among Plath's school papers in the Mortimer Rare Book Room, Smith College. I am grateful to Karen Kukil, Associate Curator of Rare Books at Smith, for calling these materials to my attention.

2. On the uncertainty surrounding Otto Plath's birthplace and nationality, see the note by his wife, Aurelia Plath, LH, p. 8.

3. William M. Tuttle, *Daddy's Gone to War: The Second World War in the Lives of American Children* (London/New York: Oxford University Press, 1995), p. 232.

4. UJ, p. 49.

5. 'A War to End Wars' is an extensive report, including nineteen separate sections dealing with many aspects of World War I, especially but not only topics in military and political history. One section includes the poems 'In Flanders Fields' by John McRae and 'America's

Answer' by R.W. Lillard. The last page gives the lyrics to 'Pack up Your Troubles in Your Old Kit Bag' and includes Plath's picture of a soldier and a girl by a lake and another picture of two soldiers—one with a bloody head bandage, smoking a cigarette, and another smiling.

6. Uta Gosmann describes 'Daddy' as a 'fusion of personal and collective elements' of memory; this and other Plath poems are '"personal" only insofar as they depict a subject's confrontation with her inner otherness' ('Sylvia Plath's Poetics of Memory', in Maria Holmgren Troy and Elisabeth Wennö (eds.), *Memory, Haunting, Discourse* (Karlstad, Sweden: Karlstad University Press, 2005), p. 44).

7. Marianna Torgovnick, *The War Complex: World War II in Our Time* (Chicago: University of Chicago Press, 2005), p. 10.

8. Ibid., p. 11.

9. Ibid., p. 9.

10. Cynthia Enloe, *Does Khaki Become You? The Militarization of Women's Lives* (London: Pluto Press, 1983).

11. UJ, p. 466.

12. Ibid., p. 485.

13. For the effect of her education on the development of Plath's political views in the context of Cold War America, see Robin Peel, *Writing Back: Sylvia Plath and Cold War Politics* (Madison, NJ: Farleigh Dickinson University Press; London: Associated University Presses, 2002); *idem*, 'The Idealogical Apprenticeship of Sylvia Plath', *Journal of Modern Literature*, 274:4 (summer 2004), pp. 59–72.

14. Letter, 13 April 1947.

15. Letter, 24 Sept 1948.

16. UJ, p. 41.

17. Ibid., p. 42.

18. Ibid., p. 195.

19. Ibid., p. 212. On this episode and on the creative exchange between Plath and Hughes generally, see Diane Middlebrook, *Her Husband: Hughes and Plath—A Marriage* (New York: Viking, 2003), pp. 18–22. On Plath's masculine identification, see Michael Davidson, *'Guys Like Us': Citing Masculinity in Cold War Poetics* (Chicago: University of Chicago Press, 2003).

20. Jacqueline Rose, *Why War? Psychoanalysis, Politics and the Return to Melanie Klein* (Blackwell, 1993), p. 16.

21. Jacqueline Rose, *The Haunting of Sylvia Plath* (London: Virago Press, 1992).

22. Ibid., p. 141.

23. Rose, *Why War?*, p. 238.

24. CP, pp. 222–4.

25. Rose, *The Haunting of Sylvia Plath*, p. 233.

26. CP, pp. 235–6.

27. Drawing on the work of Julia Kristeva, Klaus Theweleit, and Jacqueline Rose, Susan Schweik develops a similar analysis of Elizabeth Bishop's wartime poem 'Roosters'. She writes:

'"Roosters" works . . . within a distinct tradition of women's lyrics which use war as metaphor for conflicts in the home or bedroom or psyche (looking backward to Dickinson, forward to [Jane] Cooper and Plath); but here, as elsewhere in that tradition, the war is also more than metaphor, not only mask. There is no difference between war and not-war, public and private, for metaphor to fuse into identity' (Susan Schweik, *A Gulf So Deeply Cut: American Women Poets and the Second World War* (Madison: University of Wiseansin Press, 1991), p. 234).

Chapter 3: Plath, Hughes, and Three Caryatids

1. Sylvia Plath, 'The Arts in America: Collage of a Collegian', unpublished MS, p. 2, PMII, Box 9, Writings—Prose—Nonfiction, fol. 1.
2. For illustrative articles on the caryatids, see the Perseus website and links at http://www.perseus.tufts.edu/cgi-bin/ptext?doc=Perseus%3Atext%3A1999.04.0004&query=entry%3D%231427&layout=&loc=karystians.
3. Roberta K. Tarbell, *Hugo Robus (1885–1964)* (Washington, DC: Smithsonian Institute, 1980), p. 210.
4. LH, p. 171, 2 February 1955. Emphasis is DM's.
5. *Chequer* accepted two of her poems in November (LH, 7 November 1955, p. 194): 'Epitaph in Three Parts' (CP, pp. 337–8) and '"Three Caryatids without a Portico", by Hugo Robus: A Study in Sculptural Dimensions'.
6. '"Three Caryatids without a Portico", by Hugo Robus: A Study in Sculptural Dimensions' is reprinted in Keith Sagar, *The Laughter of Foxes* (Liverpool: Liverpool University Press, 2000), p. 49. The other poem published in the same issue of *Chequer* was 'Epitaph in Three Parts', which Ted Hughes included in his edition of Plath's *Collected Poems* as the last example of 'Juvenilia'.
7. Daniel Huws, review of *Chequer*, in *Broadsheet* (issues not designated) quoted in Sagar, *Laughter of Foxes*, p. 48.
8. LH, p. 237, 2 February 1956.
9. Readers had to wait fifty years for *St Botolph's Review*, No. 2, edited by David Andrews Ross and Daniel Weissbort (two of the original editors of the journal), published 2006.
10. UJ, p. 211, 26 February 1956.
11. Miranda Seymour, *Robert Graves, Life on the Edge* (London: Doubleday, 1995), pp. 349, 352–4. Graves's lectures were later published as *The Crowning Privilege: The Clark Lectures, 1954–5* (London: Cassell, 1955; New York: Doubleday, 1956).
12. Huws, quoted in Sagar, *Laughter of Foxes*, p. 48.
13. Robert Graves, *The White Goddess* (London: Faber, 1961), p. 11.
14. Noted by Anne Skea, 'Starting the Journey' and 'The Path of the Hanged Man—Mem', in her website commentary *Poetry and Magic* (http://www.zeta.org.au/~annskea/Poet-Mag.htm), which provides extensive discussion of the symbolisms of these poems in the total context of BL.
15. I am indebted to Annie Finch for this evaluation of Plath's meter. 'The form alludes to sapphics, with the short final line to each stanza and with the meter of the first two lines

primarily trochaic and dacytlic. But the poem is definitely not sapphics. After the first two lines the meter is resolutely iambic, two iambic tetrameters followed by an iambic trimeter in each stanza. (If it were sapphics, the meter would continue to be dactylic and trochaic, the stanzas would be four lines long instead of three, and most importantly each final line would consist of a dactyl-trochee. Given the theme of the poem, maybe it wouldn't be going too far to suggest that the tercet of daunted caryatids refers on some level to these sapphic-like tercets themselves—they could have supported the "classic sister" of the true sapphic form, if the gods had only granted them such a trial. Of course, Plath would have had few models for actual sapphics in English—only a stray poem by Swinburne, Hardy, Pound existed until a few decades ago. It's an intriguing question whether the true sapphic form might have represented for her a kind of unattainable power when she wrote this poem.' E-mail from Annie Finch, 23 September 2001.

16. Symbolisms referred to in this paragraph: 'Three Women' (CP, pp. 176–87). 'White Nike' in 'Barren Woman' (ibid., p. 157) and 'The Other' (ibid., p. 202); 'Statue' in 'Morning Song' (ibid., p. 157) and 'Barren Woman'; 'Museum' in 'Morning Song' and 'Barren Woman'; 'Marble' in 'Barren Woman', 'The Rival' (ibid., p. 166), and 'The Other'; 'Stone' in 'The Rival'; 'Perfected' in 'Edge' (ibid., p. 273).

Chapter 4: Conversation amongst the Ruins: Plath and de Chirico

1. UJ, p. 359.
2. James Thrall Soby, *Giorgio de Chirico* (New York: Museum of Modern Art, 1955), pp. 248, 110, 166.
3. The only study which attends in any detail to Plath's relationship to de Chirico is Sally Greene's article, 'The Pull of the Oracle: Personalized Mythologies in Plath and De Chirico', *Mosaic*, 25(1) (1992), 107–20. See also Christina Britzolakis, *Sylvia Plath and the Theatre of Mourning* (Oxford: Oxford University Press, 1999), pp. 59–65.
4. Between March 20 and March 28, Plath produced eight poems based on paintings, following a request by the magazine *ARTnews* for a poem on some aspect of art. See Anne Stevenson, *Bitter Fame: A Life of Sylvia Plath* (London: Viking, 1989), p. 123.
5. Ted Hughes, 'Notes on Poems, 1956–63', in CP, p. 275.
6. See Annette Lavers, 'The World as Icon: On Sylvia Plath's Themes', in Charles Newman (ed.), *The Art of Sylvia Plath: A Symposium* (Bloomington, IN: Indiana University Press, 1970), pp. 100–35.
7. UJ, p. 211.
8. Cited by Soby, *Giorgio de Chirico*, p. 48.
9. See William Rubin, 'De Chirico and Modernism', in *idem* (ed.), *De Chirico* (New York: Tate Gallery/Museum of Modern Art, 1982), pp. 55–80.
10. See Robert Rosenblum, 'De Chirico's Long American Shadow', *Art in America*, July 1, 1996. Amongst the paintings influenced by De Chirico, of particular interest in relation to Plath's work, is Louis Guglielmi's *Terror in Brooklyn* (1941), which features a trio of mourning women trapped in a bell jar in a perspectivally distorted urban landscape.

11. Rubin, 'De Chirico and Modernism', p. 59.

12. 'Soby', ibid., p. 75.

13. Sigmund Freud, *Civilization and its Discontents*, trans. David McLintock (Harmondsworth: Penguin, 2002), p. 7.

14. Cited by Soby, *Giorgio de Chirico*, p. 136.

15. Hal Foster, *Compulsive Beauty* (Cambridge, MA: MIT Press, 1993), p. 68.

16. Soby, *Giorgio de Chirico*, p. 75.

17. Soby Ibid.

18. Sylvia Plath, 'The Stones of Troy', *Gemini* 2 (1957), 98–103.

19. T. S. Eliot, '*Ulysses*, Order and Myth' (1923), in *Selected Prose*, ed. Frank Kermode (London: Faber and Faber, 1975), 177.

20. Plath, 'Stones of Troy', 103.

21. Marianne W. Martin, 'On de Chirico's Theater', in Rubin (ed.), *De Chirico*, pp. 81–100. Other forms of theatrical influence discussed by Martin include the *fin de siècle* dream play, the shadow theatre, and early trick and mystery films. For a discussion of the phantasmagoric and protocinematic aspects of Plath's poetry, see Britzolakis, *Sylvia Plath*, pp. 135–46, 199–205.

22. Sigmund Freud, 'Mourning and Melancholia', in *On Metapsychology*, Penguin Freud Library (Harmondsworth: Penguin, 1991), pp. 245–68.

23. LH, p. 314.

24. See, for example, Giorgio de Chirico, *The Memoirs of Giorgio de Chirico*, trans. Margaret Crosland (London: Peter Owen, 1971), p. 55: 'the true novelty discovered by this philosopher....is a strange and profound poetry, infinitely mysterious and solitary, which is based on the Stimmung (I use this very effective German word which could be translated as atmosphere in the moral sense), the *Stimmung*, I repeat of an autumn afternoon, when the sky is clear and the shadows are longer than in summer, for the sun is beginning to be lower.'

25. Thomas Mical, 'The Origins of Architecture, after De Chirico', *Art History* 26(1) (February 2003), 82.

26. CP, p. 75.

27. 'Notes', ibid., p. 276.

28. De Chirico, 'Parisian Manuscripts' (1911–15), repr. in Soby, *Giorgio de Chirico*, pp. 245, 246.

29. André Green, 'The Dead Mother', in *On Private Madness* (London; Hogarth, 1986), pp. 142–3.

Chapter 5: Sylvia Plath and the Costume of Femininity

1. For a definition of glamour see Stephen Gundle, 'Mapping the Origins of Glamour: Giovanni Boldini, Paris and the Belle Epoque', *Journal of European Studies*, 29 (1999), p. 269.

2. 'Eavesdropper' (CP, p. 261).

3. Ibid., p. 31.

4. Ibid.

5. Adlai Stevenson, 'A Purpose for Modern Woman', excerpted from a Commencement Address, Smith College, 1955, in *Women's Home Companion* (September 1955). This speech begins with the statement: 'I think there is much you can do about our crisis in the humble role of housewife.'

6. Nancy Hunter Steiner, *A Closer Look at Ariel: A Memory of Sylvia Plath* (New York: Popular Library, 1973), pp. 108–9.

7. Talcott Parsons, 'The Social Structure of the Family' (1949), in *The Family: Its Function and Destiny*, ed. Ruth Nanda Ashen (New York: Harper and Bros., 1949), p. 193.

8. A term coined by Betty Friedan in her 1963 eponymous feminist text.

9. Betty Friedan, *The Feminine Mystique* (New York: Norton, 1963), p. 15.

10. Lynn Spiegel, *Welcome to the Dreamhouse: Popular Media and Postwar Suburbs* (London/ Durham, NC: Duke University Press, 2001), p. 9.

11. Talcott Parsons, 'Age and Sex in the Social Structure of the United States', in *Essays in Sociological Theory* (rev. edn., London: Free Press of Glencoe Collier, 1954), 90.

12. Marynia Farnham and Ferdinana Lundberg, *The Modern Woman: The Lost Sex* (New York: Harper and Bros., 1947), pp. 142, 271.

13. Plath's High school year book entry, reads, 'Sylvia Plath: warm smile . . . future writer . . . those rejection slips from *Seventeen* . . .'(*The Wellsleyan* (1950), PMII, High School memorabilia, Box 10, fol. 4).

14. Brett Harvey, *The Fifties: A Women's Oral History* (New York: Harper Collins, 1993), p. 73.

15. Ibid., p. 90.

16. Pat MacPherson, *The Puzzle of Sylvia Plath* (Canterbury: University of Kent Press, 1983), p. 1.

17. LH, p. 5.

18. PMII, Box 14, Miscellaneous, Artworks, *c*.1943–6 fol.1. The inside of the card reads: 'Are your children fighting/All their time away?/Well— at least they stop to say/A very happy Grandmother's Day!' The fact that Plath depicts herself with plaits/braids in this card suggests it pre-dates 1947.

19. Sylvia's grandparents came to live with the Plaths in summer 1932 and 1933, and when both Warren and Otto Plath were ill, in winter 1938–9, Sylvia's grandparents took care of her (LH, pp. 13, 22). Sylvia also went to her grandparents when her mother was working on Otto's writing, and during summer 1936. That year, when the Plath family bought a house on Johnson Avenue, near the Schober's on Point Shirley, the two families began living as an extended family (Wagner-Martin, *Sylvia Plath* (London: Cardinal, 1990), pp. 22–3). Following Otto Plath's death in 1940, the Schober family moved in with the Plaths, in keeping with a promise made to Aurelia should Otto not recover (Wagner-Martin, *Sylvia Plath*, p. 31, *Letters Home*, p. 24).

20. UJ, p. 430. This entry is taken from 'Notes on Interviews with RB', Ruth Beuscher, Plath's therapist, who offered Plath what she called 'a supervision in life & emotions & what to do with both' (UJ, p. 428). During these sessions Plath explored, in particular, her 'hate' for her mother and 'all mother figures' (UJ, p. 435).

21. The role of the mother as primary nurturer is a result of what Diane Wille terms in her 1995 article for *A Journal of Research* 'social cultural mandates'. These cultural mandates, according to Wille, 'influence the mother's and father's role expectations for themselves and their spouse'. (See Diane E. Wille, 'The 1990's: Gender Differences in Parenting Roles', *Sex Roles:*

A Journal of Research (December 1995), 803). Plath's resentment of this model of socialization surfaces in poems such as 'Medusa' and 'The Disquieting Muses' (CP, pp. 224–6; 74–6).

22. PMIII, Large format works Paintings, fol. 4. Letter to Eddie Cohen, *c.*1950–1, UJ, 19.

23. See article by Wille, above, as an example of this line of argument.

24. In the same journal entry, Plath writes that 'Life', for her mother, 'was hell. She had to work. Work and be a mother too, a man and a woman in one sweet ulcerous ball. She pinched. She scraped. Wore the same old coat. But the children had new school clothes and shoes that fit. Piano lessons, viola lessons, French horn lessons' (UJ, p. 430). It is the necessity of her mother's self-sacrifice that seems to embitter the mature Plath.

25. Entitled 'To Mother', PMII, Box 14, Miscellaneous, Artwork, fol. 1.

26. Repeated journal entries and letters testify to Plath's strong economical sense and eye for fashion, and so writing to Gordon Lameyer, 9 January 1955, for example, she 'brags' of her ability to 'replenish' her entire wardrobe on a $50 budget (Card to Gordon Lameyer, 9 Jan 1955, Lameyer MS, fol. 1955, Lilly Library.)

27. Barry Shank, *A Token of My Affection: Greeting Cards and American Business Culture* (New York: Columbia University Press, 2004), p. 5

28. PMII, Art Scrapbook #4, Oversize no. 7.

29. LH, pp. 12–13.

30. PMII, Box 14, Miscellaneous, Artwork, fol. 1.

31. UJ, p. 243.

32. Ibid., p. 236.

33. PMII, Box 14, Miscellaneous, Artwork, fol. 1.

34. PMII, Art Scrapbook #4, Oversize no. 7.

35. Ibid., p. 12.

36. Ibid., pp. 17, 19, 20.

37. Friedan, *The Feminine Mystique*, p. 63.

38. David Halberstam, *The Fifties* (New York: Villard Books, 1993), p. 591.

39. Ibid.

40. TBJ, p. 90.

41. Halberstam, *The Fifties*, pp. 132–7.

42. TBJ, p. 109.

43. PMII, Art Scrapbook #4, Oversize no. 7.

44. TBJ, p. 109.

45. Ibid., 112.

46. Ibid.

47. Ibid.

48. Plath rarely gave titles to her artwork. This title and any others that appear in this essay are taken from titles given by curator Kathleen Connors for the 2002 exhibition 'Eye Rhymes: Visual Arts and Manuscripts of Sylvia Plath' at Indiana University, Bloomington.

49. PMIII, Large format works, Paintings, fol. 4.

50. See Elaine Tyler May, *Homeward Bound: American Families in the Cold War Era* (New York: Basic Books, 1988).

51. TBJ, p. 116.

52. 13 November 1949, PMII, Box 7, Diaries and calendars, fol. 4.

53. PMII, Box 14, fol. 3. The dolls and outfits are dated 1945.

54. Linda W. Wagner, 'Plath's "Ladies Home Journal" Syndrome', *Journal of American Culture*, 7(1/2) (1984), p. 34.

55. 'Heather-Bird Eyebrows', 1952, drawing accompanying notes on short story, 'Initiation' (Artwork), Mortimer Rare Book Room, Smith College.

56. On the back of her Yale Prom Card Plath draws images of herself and Dick Norton, her Prom partner, and writes, 'there you go cartooning again'. PMII High school scrapbook, Oversize no. 3, fol. 24.

57. Gamaliol Bradford Senior High School, Wellesley Hills, Mass., United States History 31, Unit VI, PMII, Box 10, High school memorabilia, fol. 2.

58. The debate over what makes good historical pedagogy is an ongoing, reflected in a debate staged in William Croon's 'Teaching American History', *The American Scholar* (1 Jan 1998).

59. PMII, Box 10, High school memorabilia, fol. 1.

60. PMII, Box 1, Correspondence 1952, fol. 2.

61. 'Notes on Intellectual History of Europe', PMII, Box 10.

62. 'Notes of Medieval Literature Unit', PMII, Box 10, fol. 7.

63. Gary M. Leonard, ' "The Woman is Perfected. The Dead Body Wears the Smile of Accomplishment": Sylvia Plath and Mademoiselle Magazine', *College Literature*, 20(2) (1992), p. 64.

64. LH, p. 790.

65. Qusted in Leonard, 'Sylvia Plath and Mademoiselle Magazine', 66.

66. See Jean Baudrillard, *For A Critique of the Political Economy of the Sign*, trans. Charles Levin (St. Louis: Telos, 1972, 1981).

67. CP, pp. 221–2.

68. Erica Jong, *Fruits and Vegetables* (New York: Hot, Rinehart, and Winstone, 1971), p. 49.

69. From an advertisement of Julius Kayser and Co., 'Westvaco Inspirations for Printers Number 136' (PMII, Art Scrapbook #1, Oversize no. 4).

70. Germaine Monteil Cosmetique, Prepared by Menken Advertising Inc. PMII, Art Scrapbook #3, Oversize no. 6.

71. See Baudrillard, *For A Critique of the Political Economy of the Sign*.

72. From an advertisement for 'Westvaco Printers, Number 135, prepared by Geyer Cornell and Newell'. Many of the advertisements found in this scrapbook are taken from print culture. PMII, Art Scrapbook #4, Oversize no. 7.

73. Plath was part of what Stanley Kauffmann has called 'The Film Generation': 'the first generation that has matured in a culture in which film has been of accepted serious relevance' (Stanley Kauffmann, 'The Film Generation: Celebration and Concern', in William H. Hammel (ed.), *The Popular Arts in America: A Reader* (New York: Harcourt, Brace, Jovanovich, 1972), p.45. Kaufmann cites 1935 as the beginning of this 'Film Generation'. Plath records seeing *Double Indemnity* in a 20 October 1944 diary entry. PMII, Diaries and Calendars, Box 7, Miscellaneous, Artwork, fol.1.

74. PMII, Box 14, Miscellaneous, Artwork, fol.1.

75. According to Hughes' ordering of Plath's poems, Plath's juvenilia is dated pre-1956.

76. Susan Douglas *Where the Girls Are: Growing up Female with the Mass Media* (New York: Random House, 1994), p. 27.

77. Marked 'Junior High' on the back by Aurelia Plath, PMIII, Small format works, Drawings, fol. 3.

78. The Disney film *Snow White* was released in 1937 when Plath was 5 years old.

79. Marina Warner, *From Beast to Blonde: On Fairytales and Their Tellers* (London: Vintage, 1995), p. 207.

80. CP, p. 303.

81. Lynda K. Bundtzen, 'Women in the Bell Jar. Two Allegories', in Harold Bloom (ed.), *Sylvia Plath: Modern Critical Views* (New York: Chelsea House Publishers, 1989), p. 126.

82. CP, p. 75.

83. 10 January 1954, Lameyer MS.

84. Plath often associated domestic existence with the existence of cows; in a letter to her mother, dated 12 October 1962, following her separation from Ted Hughes, she writes of hating 'this cow life', where 'cow' refers not only to rural Devon, but also her life as a housewife and mother. This idea is carried into her *Ariel* poem 'Morning Song', where the speaker describes herself stumbling from bed 'floral and cow-heavy' (CP, p. 157).

85. CP, pp. 60–1.

86. Ibid., p. 31.

87. PMII, Box 8, Writings—Poetry, fol. 1.

88. CP, p. 228.

89. Ibid., pp. 227–8.

90. Ibid., p. 250.

91. Ibid., pp. 237–8.

92. Ibid.

93. Ibid.

94. PMII, Box 14, fol. 1, Subject title, 'Life in General & Particular', 10 January 1954, Lameyer MS. In her journals, Plath quite often comments on her desire to sunbathe and bleach her hair in order to achieve her blonde 'look'; for example, writing from Marblehead, summer 1951, she writes: 'Both of us [Plath and Marcia Brown] were deeply tan and our hair was bleached from the sun' (UJ, p. 73).

95. CP, pp. 242–4.

96. Ibid., 245.

97. Ibid.

98. TBJ, p. 108.

99. Ibid., p. 97.

100. PMII, Art Scrapbook # 4, Oversize no. 7.

101. UJ, pp. 56–7.

102. Ibid.

103. PMIII, Small format works, Drawings fol. 1.

104. In his 'Notes on Poems 1956–63' Ted Hughes records that on 3 July 1958 'SP and TH had a session with the ouija oracle'. Hughes notes that on July 4th Plath received a message from the Classical God of Nature, Pan, instructing her to write 'on the poem-subject "Lorelei"'

because this was her 'own kin'. Plath's 'Lorelei' is a version of the 'plaintive German song mother used to play and sing to us' (CP, p. 287). In the 1953 film *Gentlemen Prefer Blondes* the character played by Marilyn Monroe is Lorelei Lee.

105. CP, p. 94.
106. Ibid., pp. 260–1.
107. TBJ, pp. 97–8.
108. Carolyn Kizer, *Mermaids in the Basement: Poems for Women* (Port Townsend, WA: Copper Canyon Press, 1986), p. 42.
109. UJ, p. 63.
110. PMIII, Medium format works, fol. 3. These two paintings most likely date from Plath's senior high school art classes.
111. Plath's 1955 'Notebook for Museum Art Matter', for example, is filled with pages of notes taken on a visit to the Museum of Modern Art, New York City, a visit she records in a June 1953 letter, written during her period as guest editor to *Elle* (PMII, Box 12, Smith College Memorabilia), fol.1.
112. UJ, pp. 332–3.
113. CP, p. 244.
114. Ibid., pp. 158–9.
115. Ibid.
116. The idea of femininity as a form of masquerade stems back to a 1929 essay by psychoanalyst Joan Riviére, 'Womanliness as Masquerade'. Riviere argued that 'genuine womanliness' was 'synonymous with masquerade' and was in fact a device to avoid the display of her masculinity (Stephen Heath, 'Joan Riviere and the Masquerade', in Victor Burgin, James Donald, and Cora Kaplan (eds.), *Formations of Fantasy* (New York / London: Methyen, 1986), pp. 45–59).

Chapter 6: Plath's Visual Poetics

1. *Iliad*, 18.483–608.
2. LH, p. 51.
3. UJ, p. 88.
4. CP, p. 324.
5. UJ, p. 276.
6. Rudolf Arnheim, *The Power of the Center: A Study of Composition in the Visual Arts* (Berkeley / Los Angeles: University of California Press, 1982), p. 52.
7. CP, p. 312.
8. Ibid., p. 303.
9. Ibid., p. 325.
10. Ibid., p. 37.
11. Ibid., p. 157.
12. Ibid., p. 265.
13. Ibid., p. 272.

14. Ibid., p. 271.
15. Ibid., pp. 21–2.
16. UJ, p. 205.
17. Tim Kendall, *Sylvia Plath: A Critical Study* (London: Faber, 2001), p. 29.
18. CP, p. 114.
19. Ibid., pp. 119–20.
20. Ibid., pp. 168–9.
21. UJ, p. 359.
22. Ibid., p. 360.
23. LH, p. 336.
24. UJ, p. 356.
25. CP, p. 75.
26. UJ, p. 359.
27. CP, p. 157.
28. UJ, p. 356.
29. CP, p. 118.
30. A. Preminger and T. V. F. Brogan (eds.), *The New Princeton Encyclopedia of Poetry and Poetics* (New york: MJF Books, 1993), pp. 326.
31. UJ, p. 548.

BIBLIOGRAPHY

Arnheim, Rudolf, *The Power of the Center: A Study of Composition in the Visual Arts* (Berkeley/Los Angeles: University of California Press, 1982)

Axelrod, Steven G., *Sylvia Plath: The Wound and the Cure of Words* (Baltimore: Johns Hopkins University Press, 1990)

Baudrillard, Jean, *For A Critique of the Political Economy of the Sign*, trans. Charles Levin (St. Louis: Telos, 1972, 1981)

Brain, Tracy, *The Other Sylvia Plath* (New York: Longman, 2001)

Britzolakis, Christina, *Sylvia Plath and the Theatre of Mourning* (Oxford: Oxford University Press, 1999)

Bundtzen. Lynda K., 'Women in the Bell Jar', in Harold Bloom (ed.), *Sylvia Plath: Modern Critical Views* (New York: Chelsea House, 1989), pp. 121–31

Butscher, Edward, *Sylvia Plath: Method and Madness* (New York: Seabury Press, 1976)

D., H., *Tribute to the Angels* (London/New York: Oxford University Press, 1945)

Davidson, Michael, *'Guys Like Us': Citing Masculinity in Cold War Poetics* (Chicago: University of Chicago Press, 2003)

De Chirico, Giorgio, *The Memoirs of Giorgio de Chirico*, trans. Margaret Crosland (London: Peter Owen, 1971)

Douglas, Susan, *Where the Girls Are: Growing Up Female with the Mass Media* (New York: Random House, 1994)

Eliot, T. S., '*Ulysses*, Order and Myth' (1923), in *Selected Prose*, ed. Frank Kermode (London: Faber and Faber, 1975)

Enloe, Cynthia, *Does Khaki Become You? The Militarization of Women's Lives* (London: Pluto Press, 1983)

Farnham, Marynia, and Lundberg, Ferdinand, *The Modern Woman: The Lost Sex* (New York: Harper and Bros., 1947)

Foster, Hal, *Compulsive Beauty* (Cambridge, MA: MIT Press, 1993)

Freud, Sigmund, 'Mourning and Melancholia', in *On Metapsychology*, Penguin Freud Library (Harmondsworth: Penguin, 1991), pp. 245–68

—— *Civilization and Its Discontents*, trans. David McLintock (Harmondsworth: Penguin, 2002)

Friedan, Betty, *The Feminine Mystique* (New York: Norton, 1963)

Gág, Wanda Hazel, *Growing Pains* (New York: Coward-McCann, 1940)

Gilbert, Sandra M., 'In Yeats' House: The Death and Resurrection of Sylvia Plath', in Linda Wagner-Martin (ed.), *Critical Essays of Sylvia Plath* (Boston: G. K. Hall, 1984)

—— and Gubar, Susan, *Madwoman in the Attic: The Woman Writer and the Nineteenth Century Literary Imagination* (New Haven, CT: Yale University Press, 1979)

Gosmann, Uta, 'Sylvia Plath's Poetics of Memory', in Maria Holmgren Troy and Elisabeth Wennö (eds.), *Memory, Haunting, Discourse* (Karlstad, Sweden: Karlstad University Press, 2005), pp. 33–44

Graves, Robert, *The Crowning Privilege: The Clark Lectures, 1954–5* (London: Cassell, 1955; New York: Doubleday, 1956)

—— *The White Goddess* (London: Faber, 1961)

Green, André, 'The Dead Mother', in *On Private Madness* (London: Hogarth, 1986), pp. 142–3

Greene, Sally, 'The Pull of the Oracle: Personalized Mythologies in Plath and de Chirico', *Mosaic*, 25(1) (1992), 107–20.

Gundle, Stephen, 'Mapping the Origins of Glamour: Giovanni Boldini, Paris and the Belle Epoque', *Journal of European Studies*, 29 (1999), 269–95

Halberstam, David, *The Fifties* (New York: Villard Books, 1993)

Harvey, Brett, *The Fifties: A Women's Oral History* (New York: Harper Collins, 1993)

Heath, Stephen, 'Joan Riviere and the Masquerade', in Victor Burgin, James Donald, and Cora Kaplan (eds.), *Formations of Fantasy* (New York/London: Methuen, 1986)

Hughes, Ted, *Birthday Letters* (New York: Farrar, Straus and Giroux, 1998)

Jong, Erica, *Fruits and Vegetables* (New York: Holt, Rinehart and Winstone, 1971)

Kauffmann, Stanley, 'The Film Generation: Celebration and Concern', in William H. Hammel (ed.), *Popular Arts in America: A Reader* (New York: Harcourt, Brace, Jovanovich, 1972)

Kendall, Tim, *Sylvia Plath: A Critical Study* (London: Faber, 2001)

Kizer, Carolyn, *Mermaids in the Basement: Poems for Women* (Port Townsend, WA: Copper Canon Press, 1986)

Lavers, Annette, 'The World as Icon: On Sylvia Plath's Themes', in Charles Newman (ed.), *The Art of Sylvia Plath: A Symposium* (Bloomington, IN: Indiana University Press, 1970), pp. 100–35

Leonard, Gary M. ' "The Woman is Perfected. The Dead Body Wears the Smile of Accomplishment"; Sylvia Plath and Mademoiselle Magazine', *College Literature*, 20(2) (1992): 60–79

Macpherson, Pat, *The Puzzle of Sylvia Plath* (Canterbury: University of Kent, 1983)

Martin, Marianne W., 'On de Chirico's Theater', in William Rubin (ed.), *De Chirico*, (New York: Tate Gallery/Museum of Modern Art, 1982), pp. 81–100

May, Elaine Tyler, *Homeward Bound: American Families in the Cold War Era* (New York: Basic Books, 1988)

Mical, Thomas, 'The Origins of Architecture, after De Chirico', *Art History*, 26(1) (February 2003)

Middlebrook, Diane, *Her Husband: Hughes and Plath—A Marriage* (New York: Viking, 2003)

Parsons, Talcott, 'The Social Structure of the Family' (1949), in *The Family: Its Function and Destiny*, ed. Ruth Nanda Anshen (New York: Harper and Bros., 1949), 173–201

—— 'Age and Sex in the Social Structure of the United States', in *Essays in Sociological Theory* (rev. edn., London: Glencoe Collier Press, 1954), pp. 89–103

Peel, Robin, *Writing Back: Sylvia Plath and Cold War Politics* (Madison, NJ: Farleigh Dickinson University Press; London: Associated University Presses, 2002)

—— 'The Idealogical Apprenticeship of Sylvia Plath', *Journal of Modern Literature*, 27:4 (summer 2004), pp. 59–72

Plath, Sylvia, 'The Stones of Troy', *Gemini* 2 (1957), pp. 98–103.

—— *The Bell Jar* (London: Heinemann, 1963)

—— *Letters Home: Correspondence 1950–1963*, ed. Aurelia Schober Plath (New York: Harper and Row, 1975)

—— *Johnny Panic and the Bible of Dreams,* and other prose writings (London: Faber, 1977)

—— *The Collected Poems*, ed. Ted Hughes (New York: Harper and Row, 1981)

—— *The Unabridged Journals of Sylvia Plath*, ed. Karen V. Kukil (New York: Anchor Books, 2000)

Preminger, A., and Brogan, T. V. F. (eds.), *The New Princeton Encyclopedia of Poetry and Poetics* (New York: MJF Books, 1993)

Rokoczi, Basil Ivan, *The Painted Caravan: A Penetration into the Secrets of the Tarot Cards* (The Hague, Holland: L. J. C. Boucher, 1954)

Rose, Jacqueline, *The Haunting of Sylvia Plath* (London: Virago Press (UK), 1991)

—— *Why War? Psychoanalysis, Politics, and the Return to Melanie Klein* (Blackwell, 1993)

Rosenblum, Robert, 'De Chirico's Long American Shadow', *Art in America*, July 1, 1996

Rubin, William, 'De Chirico and Modernism', in *idem* (ed.), *De Chirico* (New York: Tate Gallery / Museum of Modern Art, 1982), pp. 55–80

Sagar, Keith, *The Laughter of Foxes* (Liverpool: Liverpool University Press, 2000)

Schweik, Susan, *A Gulf So Deeply Cut: American Women Poets and the Second World War* (Madison: University of Wisconsin Press, 1991)

Seymour, Miranda, *Robert Graves, Life on the Edge* (London: Doubleday, 1995)

Shank, Barry, *A Token of My Affection: Greeting Cards and American Business Culture* (New York: Columbia University Press, 2004)

Skea, Anne, 'Starting the Journey' and 'The Path and the Hanged Man—Mem', *Poetry and Magic* [online articles] (2004). <http://www.zeta.org.au/~annskea/PoetMag.htm> accessed 4 March 2001

Soby, James Thrall, *Giorgio de Chirico* (New York: Museum of Modern Art, 1955)

Spiegel, Lynn, *Welcome to the Dreamhouse: Popular Media and Postwar Suburbs* (London / Durham, NC: Duke University Press, 2001)

Steiner, Nancy Hunter, *A Closer Look at Ariel: A Memory of Sylvia Plath* (New York: Popular Library, 1973)

Stevenson, Adlai, 'A Purpose for Modern Woman', excerpted from a Commencement Address, Smith College, 1955, in *Women's Home Companion* (September 1955)

Stevenson, Anne, *Bitter Fame: A Life of Sylvia Plath* (London: Viking, 1989)

Tarbell, Roberta K., *Hugo Robus (1885–1964)* (Washington, DC: Smithsonian Institute, 1980)

Torgovnik, Marianna, *The War Complex: World War II in Our Time* (Chicago: University of Chicago Press, 2005)

Tuttle, William M., *Daddy's Gone to War: The Second World War in the Lives of American Children* (London/New York: Oxford University Press, 1995)

Wagner, Linda W., 'Plath's "Ladies Home Journal" Syndrome', *Journal of American Culture*, 7(1–2) (1984): pp. 32–7

Wagner-Martin, Linda, *Sylvia Plath: A Life* (London: Abacus, 1990)

Warner, Marina, *From Beast to Blonde: On Fairytales and Their Tellers* (London: Vintage, 1995)

Wille, Diane E., 'The 1990's: Gender Differences in Parenting Roles', *Sex Roles: A Journal of Research* (December 1995), p. 803

Woolf, Virginia, 'Mr Bennet and Mrs Brown' (Richmond: Hogarth Press, 1924)

—— *A Room of One's Own* (Richmond: Hogarth Press, 1929)

—— *The Waves* (London: Hogarth Press, 1931)

NOTES ON CONTRIBUTORS

SALLY BAYLEY teaches Modern and American Literature at Jesus College, Oxford. She has published articles on Sylvia Plath and the Cold War and the influence of D. H. Lawrence on Plath's work. She is editor for a book of interdisciplinary essays, *From Self to Shelf: The Artist under Construction* (Cambridge Scholars Press, 2007) and co-director of the 2007 Sylvia Plath 75th Year Symposium, an interdisciplinary arts and literary event at Oxford. Bayley is a practicing poet.

CHRISTINA BRITZOLAKIS lectures in the Department of English and Comparative Literature at Warwick University. Her book, *Sylvia Plath and the Theatre of Mourning* (Oxford University Press, 1999), situates Plath's poetry in relation to modernism, psychoanalysis, feminism, and Cold War culture. She is currently completing a book on modernism, visuality, and the intersections between local and global spaces in the work of James, Ford, Conrad, Woolf, and Rhys.

KATHLEEN CONNORS is a Visiting Scholar at Indiana University, Bloomington. Her professional field is arts and educational programming, with a focus on youth, Asian, and interdisciplinary initiatives. She is curator for 'Through Children's Eyes: Photographs of Life in India', 'The Sacred Hearth: *Aepan's* Painted Prayers to the Himalayan Deities', and director/curator for 'The Art of Sylvia Plath', an interdisciplinary symposium commemorating Plath's 70th birthday anniversary and 40 years of *Ariel*. Along with co-editor Sally Bayley, she is co-director of the Sylvia Plath 75th Year Symposium held at Oxford in October 2007.

FAN JINGHUA, poet and translator, was formerly an associate professor in Southeast University, Nanjing, P. R. China. He is presently a PhD research scholar in Department of English, National

University of Singapore, doing research on modern and contemporary poetry in English, and the Dream Songs of John Berryman. He is editor of various poetry websites, and has translated most of Plath's *Collected Poems* into Chinese.

SUSAN GUBAR, Distinguished Professor of English at Indiana University, specializes in gender, race, and ethnicity in nineteenth- and twentieth-century British and American literature. Co-authored by Sandra Gilbert, books include *Madwoman in the Attic: The Woman Writer and the Nineteenth Century Literary Imagination* (Yale University Press, 1979), *No Man's Land: The Place of the Woman Writer in Twentieth Century*, in three volumes (Yale University Press, 1994), *Poetry after Auschwitz: Remembering What One Never Knew* (Indiana University Press, 2003). Gilbert and Gubar are currently revising their third edition of *Norton Anthology of Literature by Women* and are writing a new *Norton Reader of Feminist Criticism and Theory*.

LANGDON HAMMER, Chair of the Department of English at Yale University, specializes in modern and contemporary American and British poetry and poetics, biography, the history of authorship, and letters and journals. He is a regular reviewer of poetry for the *New York Times* and poetry editor of *The American Scholar*. His books include *Hart Crane: Complete Poetry and Selected Letters*, editor (New York: Library of America, 2006), and *Hart Crane and Allen Tate: Janus-Faced Modernism* (Princeton: Princeton University Press, 1993). He is currently working on a biography of the poet James Merrill.

DIANE MIDDLEBROOK, formerly a Professor of English at Stanford University, is a professional writer of biographies. She is the author of *Anne Sexton, a Biography* (1991), which was a finalist for the National Book Award, and *Suits Me: The Double Life of Billy Tipton* (1998), a book about an Oklahoma-born female musician who spent fifty years passing as a man. Her latest book is *Her Husband: Hughes and Plath, a Marriage* (2003); in French translation, *Son Mari* won the Prix Du Meilleur Livre Etranger (Essai), best non-fiction book by a foreigner. In 2004 she was elected as a Fellow of the Royal Society of Literature.

ACKNOWLEDGMENTS

I am indebted to Kathleen Connors for her editing of my essay and her expert knowledge of the details of Plath's development as an artist. Her generous sharing of her research and passion for Plath's talent, and her fun with it, have been invaluable both to my own research and the entire book. I am also grateful to Diane Middlebrook for her suggestions on my essay. Many thanks to Karen Kukil for her help and support during my visits to Smith College as well as her provision of expertise on various occasions. The staff of Lilly Library is to be commended for their patient care during my research trip. I am also grateful to Hermione Lee for her generous support of the book. Lastly, many thanks to my body of tremendously talented graduate students who continue to spur me on—in particular, Andrew Hay, William May, Andrew Blades, Alexandra Harris, and Monika Class.

We are both indebted to all the scholars who have joined us in this volume: Christina Britzolakis, Susan Gubar, Langdon Hammer, Fan Jinghua, and Diane Middlebrook. Special thanks also go to Ros Edwards, representing the Plath Estate, who helped with the permissions process, and Frieda Hughes, who endorsed a positive appraisal of Sylvia Plath as interdisciplinary artist. The staff of Oxford University Press, in particular Andrew McNeillie, Jacqueline Baker, Phil Henderson, and Coleen Hatrick, were extremely supportive in handling this project. Director Breon Mitchell, Becky Cape, Michael Taylor, Sue Presnell, and staff at Lilly Library have been particularly helpful in various phases of the book's research and production, as have Director Martin Antonetti and his staff at the Mortimer Rare Book Room. On behalf of all Plath readers, we salute Karen Kukil for bringing *The Unabridged Journals of Sylvia Plath* to life.

Sally Bayley
Oxford

I thank my teachers and administrators at Indiana University who supported my interdisciplinary work on Sylvia Plath. Most notably, Distinguished Professor Susan Gubar provided a stunning introduction to Plath's poetry, and has continued to be a valuable advisor as my research has taken new turns. Professors of English Todd Avery, Catherine Bowman, Alyce Miller, Joan Pong Linton, Helen Sword, and Nicholas Williams have all been immensely encouraging. Betsy Stirratt, Director of the School of Fine Arts Gallery, was largely responsible for my 2002 exhibition of Plath's art and manuscripts, works and research that formed the basis of this volume. Artists Dan Reidy and Dana Sperry, who hung the show, provided historical perspectives on Plath's artwork, as did art historians Kathy Foster and Liese Hilgeman. While helping me sort through the vast folders at Lilly Library, Becky Cape and Katie Peebles offered great insights on some of Plath's paintings and drawings, and Cape's suggestion to include the artwork that became the book cover is greatly appreciated. Sandra Taylor at Lilly Library was very gracious in handling permissions, and Michael McRobbie, current President of Indiana University, gave a major award on behalf of The President's Arts and Humanities Initiative in 2002. Considerable support for this project also came from Chancellor Kenneth Gros Louis, The Hutton Honors College, and Janet James Brady and Mary Morgan of IU Conferences.

The primary mentor for my work on this book has been Diane Middlebrook, whose excellent counsel shaped my essay and my approach to the archives. Anita Helle has been a very supportive of my efforts to bring Plath's visual art and juvenila to the public. Along with *Eye Rhymes* co-editor Sally Bayley, Fan Jinghua has offered unique insights on these topics. Phil Henderson and Colleen Hatrick of Oxford University Press were also helpful in responding to Plath's artwork during the book's production stages, and Eva Nyika, Charles Lander, Jr., and Tony Williams have provided excellent editorial work. Big thanks go to my sisters Ann, Mary, and Nora, my daughter Delia, and friends Karen Cherrington and Christy Seastrom of Bloomington, Leila Hadley Luce of New York, and Jerry and Cathleen Lynch of London for their hospitality, generosity, and support during important periods of my work. For this volume, I am particularly grateful to Aurelia Plath, who carefully saved her daughter's works, and whose love of books created the foundation for her extraordinary education. Dorothy Burns Young, who bestowed a good deal of Plath's artwork to Lilly Library, and all other donors to the two collections are to be commended for their generosity. Our book title is taken from poetry critic Helen Vendler's essay, 'The Intractable Metal', where she identifies Plath's 'eye rhymes'—the visual placement of words across the page found in *Ariel*—as one of her more notable contributions to the world of poetry.

Kathleen Connors
Bloomington, Indiana

Permission acknowledgements

We would like to thank the following parties for permission to quote texts and reproduce visual art and manuscripts:

All works of Sylvia Plath © The Estate of Sylvia Plath.

Fifty-eight works and photos of Sylvia Plath, courtesy Lilly Library at Indiana University.

Ten works and photo of Sylvia Plath, courtesy Smith College Mortimer Rare Book Room, and one work courtesy Smith College Archives.

Giorgio de Chircio Estate permissions for three works, courtesy Artists Rights Society. 'I'll be There...The Glass Dog', 1914 (oil on canvas) and 'Disquieting Muses', 1925 (oil on canvas) from Private Collection/Bridgeman Art Library, with latter from the collection of Peter Willi. 'The Child's Brain', 1914 (oil on canvas), collection and photo of Moderna Museet, Stockholm.

Hugo Robus's 'Three Caryatids without a Portico' 1953–4 (plaster), courtesy Forum Gallery.

Quotations from *Collected Poems* and *The Unabridged Journals of Sylvia Plath*, courtesy Random House publishers.

Quotations from *Letters Home by Sylvia Plath*, courtesy HarperCollins publishers.

Three 1956 and 1959 articles by Sylvia Plath, courtesy *Christian Science Monitor*.

A short version of Chapter 1 by Connors appears as 'Art in the Life of Sylvia Plath: Mining Riches in the Lilly and Smith Archives', chapter 3 of *The Unraveling Archive*, edited by Anita Helle and published by the University of Michigan Press, 2007.

INDEX

(Dates given in brackets for Plath's unpublished works, where known)